"十二五"普通高等教育汽车服务工程专业规划教材

交通运输专业英语

Jiaotong Yunshu Zhuanye Yingyu

杨志发　刘艳莉　主编
陈焕江　李世武　主审

人民交通出版社
China Communications Press

内 容 提 要

本书根据交通运输（汽车运用工程）、汽车服务工程专业课程内容，系统地选编了汽车结构和汽车服务两大类基本知识共6单元21课。其中汽车结构方面包括发动机、底盘、车身和电气系统等，汽车服务工程方面包括车辆维修与检测、车辆改装与回收以及汽车金融服务等。为了方便学生自学，本书每课中均有专业词汇术语表、重难点句参考释译、练习题等，为扩大学生知识面，每单元配备有1~2篇扩展阅读，最后还配备有词汇表和常用缩略词汇表。

本书为"十二五"普通高等教育汽车服务工程专业规划教材，既可作为高等院校交通运输（汽车运用工程）和汽车服务工程专业"专业英语"课程的教材，也可供具有一定英语基础的汽车全生命周期内生产、售后、维修、管理等部门的技术和管理人员参考。

图书在版编目(CIP)数据

交通运输专业英语 / 杨志发，刘艳莉主编. —北京：
人民交通出版社，2014.6
"十二五"普通高等教育汽车服务工程专业规划教材
ISBN 978-7-114-11319-2

Ⅰ.①交… Ⅱ.①杨…②刘… Ⅲ.①交通运输—英语—高等学校—教材 Ⅳ.①H31

中国版本图书馆 CIP 数据核字(2014)第 057169 号

"十二五"普通高等教育汽车服务工程专业规划教材

书　　名：	交通运输专业英语
著 作 者：	杨志发　刘艳莉
责任编辑：	夏　犨　刘　洋
出版发行：	人民交通出版社
地　　址：	(100011)北京市朝阳区安定门外外馆斜街3号
网　　址：	http://www.ccpress.com.cn
销售电话：	(010)59757973
总 经 销：	人民交通出版社发行部
经　　销：	各地新华书店
印　　刷：	北京市密东印刷有限公司
开　　本：	787×1092　1/16
印　　张：	11
字　　数：	270 千
版　　次：	2014 年 6 月　第 1 版
印　　次：	2014 年 6 月　第 1 次印刷
书　　号：	ISBN 978-7-114-11319-2
定　　价：	25.00 元

(有印刷、装订质量问题的图书由本社负责调换)

前　言

随着我国汽车和交通运输业的快速发展,国际上先进技术和理念越来越多地融入我国交通运输和汽车服务行业的发展中,因而广大消费者对交通运输和汽车服务行业也提出了越来越高的要求。为了满足这种需求,广大交通运输和汽车服务从业人员需要了解更多国际上该行业的技术及产品的发展状况,因此,也对从业人员的专业英语水平提出了更高的要求。

为了适应这种新形势发展的需要,给广大交通运输和汽车服务专业的学生和从业人员提供更加专业和符合该专业发展形势的专业外语学习材料,在人民交通出版社主持下,根据高等院校交通运输和汽车服务专业学生培养目标和要求,在参阅大量国内外交通运输、汽车服务专业文献基础上,我们组织编写了《交通运输专业英语》,使学生对能从专业英语的角度对专业基本知识有更加系统的了解。

本书共分成两部分6个单元21课教学内容。第一部分共3个单元,涵盖汽车构造基础知识(包括汽车发动机总体构造、燃油系统、点火系统、冷却系统、润滑系统、气体供给系统)、汽车底盘基础知识(包括动力传动系统、自动变速器、转向系统、制动系统、悬架和轮胎系统)以及车身和电器系统(包括车身、汽车电气系统等);第二部分共3个单元,涵盖车辆维护和检测基础知识(包括汽车维修和检测技术、OBD技术、车载传感技术)、车辆改装和回收基础知识(包括汽车改装、澳大利亚汽车改装法规、车辆回收)以及汽车金融服务基础知识(包括汽车租赁、汽车贷款)。每课以一个主题或一个专业知识为对象,主要包含4方面基本内容:1)专业知识;2)专业词汇和术语表;3)重难点句参考释译;4)课后练习题。为了扩大读者的知识面,在每单元后面附有1~2篇扩展阅读材料,主要是每单元知识点中较前沿的内容和知识。

书末附有单词表和专业缩略词汇表,以方便使用者查阅。

本书既可以作为高等院校交通运输、汽车服务工程专业英语教材,也可以作为高等教育自学考试、成人教育等交通运输和汽车服务相关专业本、专科学生的专业英语教材,还可以作为行业从业人员自学参考用书。

本书由吉林大学杨志发副教授、刘艳莉讲师主编,长安大学陈焕江教授、吉林大学李世武教授主审。编写过程中孙文财讲师、王琳虹讲师、金立生教授、徐艺博士、郭梦竹硕士和于晓东硕士在资料收集、材料组织、文字排版等方面做了大量的工作。具体分工如下:

杨志发撰写 Part Ⅰ Introduction,Part Ⅱ Introduction,Unit 1, Unit 3, Unit 5, Unit 6, Abbreviation;

刘艳莉撰写 Unit 2, Unit 4,Glossary;

孙文财参与了 Extension 的撰写,王琳虹参与了 Glossary 的撰写,金立生参与了 Introduction 的撰写。

本书编写过程中,参考了大量的国内外书籍、教材、资料以及相关网站,部分内容引自其中,在此对其原作者表示衷心的感谢!

由于编者水平有限,书中难免存在一些错误和缺点,恳请广大读者、各位专家不吝指教,以使本书更加完善。

编　者
2014 年 3 月于长春

目录 Mulu

Part I Introduction: Structure of Automobile ············· 1

Unit 1 Engine ············· 4
  Lesson 1 Engine Construction ············· 4
  Lesson 2 Engine Fuel System ············· 10
  Lesson 3 Engine Ignition System ············· 18
  Lesson 4 Engine Cooling System ············· 22
  Lesson 5 Lubrication System ············· 26
  Lesson 6 Automobile Engine Intakes ············· 31
  Extension 1: Formula One Engine ············· 35
  Extension 2: Engine Types of Hybrid Vehicles ············· 38

Unit 2 Chassis ············· 42
  Lesson 1 Drivetrain ············· 42
  Lesson 2 Automatic Transmission ············· 49
  Lesson 3 Steering System ············· 56
  Lesson 4 The Brakes ············· 62
  Lesson 5 Suspension and Tire ············· 66
  Extension 1: Types of Suspension ············· 71
  Extension 2: Frame ············· 76

Unit 3 Body and Electrical System ············· 79
  Lesson 1 Body ············· 79
  Lesson 2 The Electrical System ············· 85
  Extension: Headlamp ············· 90

Part II Introduction: Motor Vehicle and Society ············· 94

Unit 4 Vehicle Maintenance and Testing ············· 99
  Lesson 1 Vehicle Maintenance Inspection ············· 99
  Lesson 2 OBD Technology ············· 104
  Lesson 3 Vehicle Sensors ············· 109
  Extension 1: Road Test ············· 115
  Extension 2: Rig Test ············· 116

Unit 5 Vehicle Modification and Recycling ············· 119

Lesson 1	Car Tuning	119
Lesson 2	National Code of Practice for Light Vehicle Construction and Modification (NCOP, Australia)	124
Lesson 3	Vehicle Recycling	131
Extension: Adapting Motor Vehicles for People with Disabilities		134
Unit 6 Automobile Financial Service		139
Lesson 1	Car Leasing	139
Lesson 2	Car Loan	142
Extension: Proposed Suggestion about Car Rental Industry		145
Glossary		147
Abbreviations		163
References		167

Part I Introduction: Structure of Automobile

The automobile is one of the most fascinating devices that we can own. Automobile is also one of the most pervasive devices.

An automobile contains dozens of different technologies. Everything from engine to tires is its own special universe of design and engineering. But any automobile is made up of four basic sections: engine, chassis, body and electrical system (Fig. 0-1).

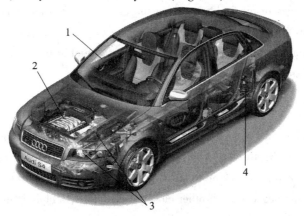

Fig. 0-1 Structure of Automobile
1-Body; 2-Engine; 3-Electrical System; 4-Chassis

Engine

The automobile engine is an internal combustion engine which converts the heat energy of fuel into mechanical energy to make automobile move. In the internal combustion engine, combustible mixture is compressed and then burned inside the engine cylinders. The burning of air-fuel mixture produces high pressure which forces piston to move downward. The movement is transmitted to the crankshaft by the connecting rod. Then the crankshaft is made to rotate. The rotary motion is carried through the power train to the wheels so that they run and the automobile moves.

As the source of power, the engine requires a fuel system to supply with fuel or the mixture of air and fuel. It plays a vital role in the power-producing process. Suppose the engine is a gasoline engine, the fuel system pumps liquid gasoline from a tank into the carburetor where the gasoline can be mixed with air. The mixture is delivered to the cylinder where it is burned. If the engine is EFI engine, fuel is delivered from the tank to the injector by means of an electric fuel pump. The fuel injectors, which directly controls fuel metering to the intake manifold, is pulsed by ECU. ECU determines the air/fuel ratio according to engine condition.

Engine also needs a cooling system, because the combustion of the air-fuel mixture in the cylinder creates a very high temperature (as high as 2000K to 2700K). The cooling system takes heat away from engine by either circulating liquid coolant (water mixed with antifreeze) between the engine and a radiator, or passing air through the radiator. Today, liquid-cooled engines are common. It cools off as it goes through the radiator. Thus, the coolant continually takes heat away from the engine, where it could do damage and delivers it to the radiator.

Engine also includes a lubricating system. The purpose of lubricating system is to supply all moving parts inside the engine with lubricating oil; the oil keeps the moving parts from wearing excessively.

The fourth is a starting system and its purpose is to change electrical power into mechanical energy to push the crankshaft around. By means of this, the engine can be started.

The way to produce heat energy is different between gasoline and diesel engines; there is only an ignition system in gasoline engine. The ignition system provides high-voltage electric sparks that set fire to the charges of air-fuel mixture in the engine combustion chambers. However, the heat energy for igniting the charges is created within the diesel engine by compressing pure air to a degree that will initiate combustion and then injecting the fuel at the right time in relation to the movement of the crankshaft.

Chassis

Chassis which is considered as a support frame for an automobile body is used to assemble all automobile spare parts on it. In fact, when power from engine continues to be transmitted to chassis, it begins with power train, goes on to steering, wheel suspension, brakes and tires. These individual components interact with each other closely. Therefore, a chassis itself can be divided into the following systems.

Driving system connects the transmission with the driving axle. In effect, the driving system works by transmitting engine power to the driving wheels. The driving system consists of the clutch, transmission, universal joint, driving axle, etc.

Steering system is used to control driving direction of an automobile. It is composed of the steering wheel, steering column, worm gear sector, steering drop arm and worm.

Brake system is a balanced set of mechanical and hydraulic devices used to retard the motion of the vehicle by means of friction. It consists of the drum or disc brake assembly, brake lever assembly, etc.

Body

The automobile body which is regarded as the framework is seated on the chassis. Its function is obvious for occupants to provide comfort, protection and shelter. The automobile body is generally divided into four sections: the front, the upper or top, rear and the underbody. These sections are further divided into small units, such as hood, fenders, roof panel, doors, instrument panel, bumpers and luggage compartment.

Electrical System

The electrical system is considered an auto electric power source supplies lighting power for the automobile. The electrical system contains battery, lights, generator, engine ignition, lighting circuit, and various switches that control their use.

With the rapid development of automobile industry, the new models of automobiles are becoming better and better in design and performance. When automobiles are very popular with people, many negative problems corresponding to the facts have to be considered by scientists, such as energy crisis, air pollution and traffic jam. So scientists and automobile manufacturers are doing their best to improve fuel economy, control exhaust emissions; the governments are taking active measures to resolve traffic problems at the same time.

Unit 1 Engine

Lesson 1
Engine Construction

Engine block (Fig. 1-1) forms the main framework, or foundation, of the engine. The block is cast mainly from gray iron or iron alloyed with other metals such as nickel or chromium. However, some blocks have been made from aluminum. In any case, the block itself has many components cast into it or assembled onto it.

Cylinders are cast into the block. The cylinders are circular, tubelike openings in the block, which act as guides for the pistons as they move up and down. In aluminum blocks, the manufacturer usually installs cast-iron or steel cylinder sleeves (liners) because these metals can withstand the wear caused by the moving pistons better than aluminum can. Water jackets are also cast into the block. The water jackets are open spaces between the inner and outer surfaces of the block and cylinders through which the coolant flows. Finally, the block has cast-in bores for both the camshaft and crankshaft.

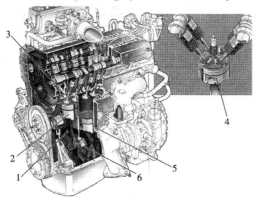

Fig. 1-1 Engine Construction
1- Connecting rod; 2- Piston; 3- Cylinder head; 4- Piston ring; 5- Piston clearance; 6- Crankshaft

Many parts also attach by fastening devices to the average engine block. These items include water pump, oil pan, timing gear or chain cover, flywheel or clutch housing, ignition distributor, oil and fuel pump, and cylinder head. Ignition distributor usually attaches to the block via a C-shaped clamp and a cap screw. Oil pump usually mounts to the upper crankcase area of the block.

1.1 Cylinder Head

Cylinder head (Fig. 1-2) is bolted to a very flat surface above the cylinder portion of the block. The manufacturer casts the head in one piece from iron, from iron alloyed with other metals, or from aluminum alloy. Aluminum has the advantage of combining lightness with rather high heat conductivity. This means simply that an aluminum head tends to operate cooler, other factors being equal.

Depending on the style of engine, the cylinder head serves many functions. For example, in all engine types the head forms an upper cover for the cylinders; therefore, the head forms the upper portion of the combustion chamber. All modern heads provide an access point into the combustion chamber for the spark plug.

The final major components attached to the head are the manifolds: one intake and one or more exhaust.

Fig. 1-2 Cylinder head

1.2 Pistons

The engine manufacturer fits a piston into each cylinder of the engine. Piston (Fig. 1-3) is a movable part or plug that receives the pressure from the burning air/fuel mixture and converts this pressure into reciprocating (up-and-down) motion. In other words, a piston will move within the cylinder due to the force exerted on it by the pressure of the ignited air/fuel mixture.

Manufacturers make most engine pistons from aluminum, which is less than half the weight of iron. Iron pistons were common in early automotive engines. However, aluminum expands faster than iron with increasing temperatures; since the block is iron, in most cases, the manufacturer must provide special provisions in the piston to maintain the proper piston-to-cylinder wall clearance at engine-operating temperature.

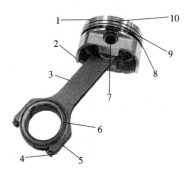

Fig. 1-3 The Piston
1- Piston crown; 2- Piston skirt; 3- Connecting rod shaft; 4- Connecting rod bolt; 5- Connecting rod cap; 6- Bearing; 7- Wrist pin; 8- Oil control ring; 9- Second compression ring; 10- Top compression ring

1.2.1 Piston Clearance

Piston clearance is the distance between the outer circumference of the piston and the cylinder wall itself. This clearance varies somewhat with different engine designs, but it is usually in the neighborhood of 0.001 to 0.004 inch. In operation, oil fills this clearance so that the piston moves on films of lubricating oil.

If this clearance is too small, for whatever reason, several problems can develop. For instance, the engine will lose power due to excessive friction. Also severe wear and possible seizure of the piston to the cylinder wall can occur in an engine with tight pistons. Of course, piston seizure will result in complete engine failure.

On the other hand, excessively large clearance can result in piston slap-a sudden tilting of the piston in the cylinder as the piston stars down on the power strokes. The piston itself actually shifts from one side of the cylinder to the other, with sufficient force to produce a distinct noise, the piston slap.

1.2.2 Piston Rings

Some operating clearance must exist between the piston and the cylinder wall; however, some form of seal is necessary between the piston and the cylinder wall to prevent blowby. Blowby describes the escape of unburned and burned gases from the combustion chamber, past the piston, and into the crankcase. The manufacturer cannot fit a piston to a cylinder close enough to prevent blowby. Consequently, pistons have machined grooves, which accommodate piston rings (Fig. 1-4) used to provide the necessary seal to eliminate blowby and to control oil consumption.

Every automotive-type pistons have two kinds of rings: compression rings and an oil control ring. The compression rings, which fit into the upper two ring grooves, primarily seal against the loss of air/fuel mixture as the piston compresses it and also the combustion pressure as the mixture burns.

The oil control ring usually fits into the lower ring groove. Its function is to prevent excessive amounts of oil from working up into the combustion chamber. When an engine is operating, a great deal of lubricating oil deposits on the cylinder walls due to throw-off of oil from the connecting-rod bearings.

Fig. 1-4 Piston rings

1.3 Connecting Rods

As mentioned earlier, the piston moves up and down in the cylinder, in a reciprocating motion. In order to rotate the drive wheels, a connecting rod (Fig. 1-5) and crankshaft must change reciprocating motion to rotary. The connecting rod itself attaches at one end to the piston and on the other end to the crankpin section of the crankshaft.

1.4 Crankshaft

Fig. 1-5 Connecting rod

Crankshaft (Fig. 1-6) is the main rotating member, or shaft, of the engine. Its function, along with the connecting rod, is to change the reciprocating motion of the piston to rotary. In addition, the crankshaft is responsible for driving the camshaft through timing gears or a timing chain and sprockets, plus operating the accessories via a system of belts and pulleys. Lastly, the crankshaft carries the total torque-turning or twisting effort-produced by the engine and delivers it to the flywheel. From the flywheel the torque then passes either to the friction clutch assembly or to the torque converter.

In order to perform these functions, the crankshaft must possess considerable mechanical strength, but it also must have a design that permits it to operate in balance. To provide the crankshaft with the required strength to take the downward thrusts of the pistons without excessive distortion, manufacturers cast or forge the crankshaft in one piece from heat-treated alloy steel.

Designed into the one-piece crankshaft are areas for main bearing journals, crankpins, counter-

Fig. 1-6 The Crankshaft

weights, flywheel flange, and driving hub. The main bearing journals are places on the shaft that permit the shaft to turn in the main bearings, supported in the lower section of the block. The crankpin is a part of the crankshaft that is offset from the centerline of the shaft; it is at the crankpins that the connecting rods attach. The counterweights are located on the crankshaft opposite to each of the offset crankpins. These weights provide the crankshaft with balance by eliminating the undue vibration, resulting from the weight of the offset crankpins. The flywheel flange is the area at the rear and of the crankshaft, where the flywheel attaches; and the driving hub is the extended section, at the front end of the crankshaft, where the vibration damper mounts.

1.5 Flywheel

Flywheel (Fig. 1-7) is a comparatively heavy wheel, bolted to the flange on the rear end of the crankshaft. Its function is to keep the engine running smoothly between power strokes. In all engines, even those with overlapping power strokes, there are times when more power is available to the crankshaft than at other times. This tendency makes the crankshaft speed up and then slows down.

Fig. 1-7 The Flywheel

However, the flywheel combats this tendency. Its inertia tends to keep the flywheel rotating at a constant speed. In other words, the flywheel absorbs energy as the crankshaft tries to accelerate and returns energy back as it attempts to slow down.

The flywheel also has several other functions. For example, the flywheel has gear teeth around its outer circumference. These teeth mesh with teeth located on the starting motor drive pinion in order to crank the engine over. In addition, the rear surface of the flywheel serves as the driving member of the clutch assembly on vehicles so equipped.

1.6 Vibration Damper

Manufacturers usually install a combination vibration damper and fan-pulley assembly onto the drive end of the crankshaft. This damping device controls torsional vibrations. When a piston moves down on its power stroke, it thrusts through the connecting rod against the crankpin with a force that may exceed 3 tons. This force tends to twist or drive the crankpin ahead of the rest of the crankshaft. Then, in a moment, the termination of the power stroke relieves the force on the crankpin. The pin now tends to untwist or snap back into its original relationship with the rest of the crankshaft. This twist-untwist tendency repeated with every power stroke can set up an oscillating motion in the crankshaft, known commonly as torsional vibration. If not controlled, these oscillations can build up so much that a crankshaft may actually break at certain speeds.

A typical vibration damper consists basically of two parts—a damper flywheels and a pulley-bonded to one another by a rubber insert.

Technical Words and Terms

1. cylinder   n. 汽缸
2. crankshaft   n. 曲轴
3. flywheel   n. 飞轮
4. piston   n. 活塞
5. framework   n. 架构,框架,结构
6. foundation   n. 基础,根本
7. nickel   n. [化]镍
8. aluminum   n. [化]铝
9. cast   n. 铸件;v. 浇铸
10. sleeve   n. 套管,轴套,衬套,缸套
11. coolant   n. 冷冻剂,冷却液,散热剂
12. bore   n. 枪膛,孔;v. 钻孔
13. camshaft   n. 凸轮轴
14. accommodate   vt. 供给,容纳
15. attach   vt. 系上,贴上,使依附
16. crankcase   n. 曲轴箱
17. chain   n. 链(条)
18. clamp   n. 夹子,夹具,夹钳;vt. 夹住
19. bolt   n. 螺栓;v. 用螺栓紧固
20. reciprocating   adj. 往复的
21. circumference   n. 圆周,周围
22. seizure   n. 卡死,卡住,咬住
23. slap   vt. 拍,拍击;n. 拍
24. tilt   v. (使)倾斜,翘起
25. blowby   n. 曲轴箱窜气
26. sprocket   n. 链轮齿
27. crankpin   n. 曲柄销
28. flange   n. 边缘,轮缘,凸缘
29. inertia   n. 惯性,惯量
30. untwist   n. 拆开,解开
31. cylinder head   n. 汽缸盖
32. connecting rod   n. 连杆
33. oil control ring   n. 油环
34. piston clearance   n. 活塞间隙

Notes

1. The engine block forms the main framework, or foundation, of the engine.
发动机汽缸体是发动机的主要框架或基础。

2. The water jackets are open spaces between the inner and outer surfaces of the block and cylinders through which the coolant flows.

汽缸体和汽缸的内、外表面之间具有一个连通的空隙,冷却液在此空间内循环流动,此即为水套。

3. The piston is a movable part or plug that receives the pressure from the burning air/fuel mixture and converts this pressure into reciprocating (up-and-down) motion.

活塞是运动部件,可燃混合气燃烧时对活塞产生强大的压力,使活塞上下往复运动。

4. Piston clearance is the distance between the outer circumference of the piston and the cylinder wall itself.

活塞间隙是指活塞外表面与汽缸壁之间的间隙。

5. Consequently, pistons have machined grooves, which accommodate piston rings used to provide the necessary seal to eliminate blowby and to control oil consumption.

因此,在活塞上加工出多个环槽,环槽中安装活塞环,实现活塞与汽缸壁间密封,防止发动机窜气,减少润滑油消耗。

6. The connecting rod itself attaches at one end to the piston and on the other end to the crankpin section of the crankshaft.

连杆的一端与活塞相连,另一端与曲柄销相连。

7. In order to perform these functions, the crankshaft must possess considerable mechanical strength, but it also must have a design that permits it to operate in balance.

要实现这些功能,曲轴必须具有足够的机械强度,同时在设计上要求曲轴运转平稳。

8. In addition, the rear surface of the flywheel serves as the driving member of the clutch assembly on vehicles so equipped.

另外,在安装了离合器的车辆上,飞轮后端也是离合器总成的主动件。

9. This twist-untwist tendency repeated with every power stroke can set up an oscillating motion in the crankshaft, known commonly as torsional vibration.

多汽缸做功行程对曲轴产生的重复扭曲和反向扭曲形成了曲轴扭转摆动,即为常说的曲轴扭转振动。

Exercises

Questions for discussion

1. What's the main framework of an engine?
2. What are the two types of piston rings? What are their functions?
3. What's the purpose of the connecting rod?
4. What is the function of the flywheel?

Fill in the blank according to the text

1. In aluminum blocks, the _____ usually installs cast-iron or steel cylinder sleeves (liners) because these metals can withstand the wear caused by the moving pistons better than _____ can.

2. For instance, the engine will lose power due to _____ _____.

3. Blowby describes the escape of unburned and burned gases from the _____ _____,

past the _____, and into the _____.

4. Automotive-type pistons have two kinds of rings: _____ and _____ control.

5. Its function, along with the connecting rod, is to change the _____ _____ of the piston to rotary.

6. Lastly, the crankshaft carries the total torque-turning or twisting effort-produced by the engine and delivers it to the _____.

Lesson 2
Engine Fuel System

The function of fuel system is to store and supply fuel to the cylinder chamber where it can be mixed with air, vaporized, and burned to produce energy. Different components are used in a fuel system (Fig. 1-8).

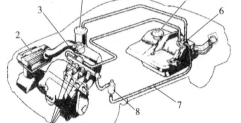

Fig. 1-8 Engine Fuel System
1-Fuel injectors; 2-Air cleaner; 3-Fuel pressure regulator; 4-Evaporative emission control canister; 5-Fuel gauge sending unit; 6-Fuel pump; 7-Fuel line; 8-Fuel filter

2.1 Fuel Tank

Fuel tank is used to store the fuel needed by the engine. It is usually located at the rear of the vehicle and is attached to the vehicle frame with metal traps. In order to strengthen the tank as well as to prevent surging of fuel when the vehicle rounds a curve, rapidly starts or suddenly stops, baffle plates are attached to the inside of the tank.

The fuel cap on the fuel tank is used to keep the fuel from splashing out, release the vacuum created by the fuel removing, and prevent vapors from escaping directly into the atmosphere.

2.2 Fuel Line

Fuel lines are metallic tubes or synthetic rubber hoses. They carry the fuel from the tank to the fuel pump, from the pump to the carburetor or a fuel injector, return excess fuel to the tank, and carry fuel vapors.

2.3 Fuel Pump

Fuel pump draws the fuel from the tank through fuel lines and delivers it through a fuel filter to either a carburetor or a fuel injector, then delivers it to the cylinder chamber for combustion.

There are two types of gasoline engine pumps: mechanical fuel pumps and electric fuel pumps. All fuel injected automobiles today use electric fuel pumps, while most carbureted automobiles use mechanical fuel pumps.

The mechanical fuel pump is driven by the camshaft. There is a cam or an eccentric lobe on the camshaft. As the camshaft turns, the lobe lifts a lever up and down, causing a pumping action. Fuel is drawn from the tank by a vacuum and sent to the carburetor.

An electric fuel pump is quite efficient. It fills the carburetor merely by turning on the key. Another feature is that the electric pump is adaptable to most locations. The electric pump uses an electromagnet (a magnet produced by electricity flowing through a coil) to operate a metal bellows that alternately forms a vacuum and then pressure. Some electric pumps use an electromagnet to work with a regular diaphragm. Other models drive either a vane or an impeller type pump with a small electric motor.

Fuel systems that have electric fuel pumps and fuel injectors may use a fuel pressure regulator to keep the fuel pressure constant. In a multipoint fuel injection system, the fuel pressure regulator has an inlet connection from the fuel rail and an outlet which lets fuel return to tank. A control diaphragm and a pressure spring determine the exposed opening of the outlet and the amount of fuel that can return. So the strength of the pressure spring determines the fuel pressure in the fuel rail, and keeps it at a fixed value.

2.4 Fuel Filter

The job of fuel filter (Fig. 1-9) used on gasoline engines is to remove dirt, rust, water, and other contamination from the gasoline before it can reach the carburetor or the injection system. It can protect not only the float-valve mechanism of the carburetor, but also its fuel-metering devices and internal passages.

Several different types of fuel filters are used, and some systems may contain two or more. Filters can be located either between the fuel pump and carburetor or in the fuel lines. The

Fig. 1-9 Fuel filter

useful life of the filters is limited. If fuel filters are not cleaned or replaced according to the manufacturer's recommendations, they will become clogged and restrict fuel flow.

Many diesel engines used in automotive applications have only one filter, which is called the primary filter. On some engines, a secondary filter is adopted and combined with the primary one to build into a single filter.

2.5 Fuel Supply System for Gasoline Engine and Diesel Engine

The main task of the gasoline fuel supply system is to make up a combustion mixture of considerable concentration and to convey it into the cylinder according to the requirements for different work conditions.

Because of higher viscosity and worse volatile property, diesel cannot be atomized to uniform mist like that of gasoline in the carburetor. Therefore, the structure and operation principle of diesel engine is quite different from gasoline engine. Operation differences of the diesel engine from the gasoline engine may be described as follows: In the intake stroke air (not mixture) is drawn into the cylinder only; in the compression stroke air is compressed to a higher ratio to obtain higher temperature; and in the working stroke diesel is sprayed into the cylinder by high pressure to form misty particles that can be ignited by the hot air.

2.6 The TSI Engine Fuel System (The Volkswagen 2.0 Liter Chain-Driven TSI Engine, Fig. 1-10)

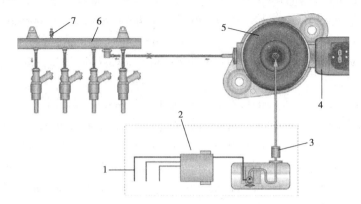

Fig. 1-10 Engine Fuel System of the Volkswagen 2.0 Liter Chain-Driven TSI Engine
1-PWM signal from engine control module; 2-Fuel pump (FP) control module J538; 3-Fuel filter; 4-Fuel pressure sensor G247; 5-High-pressure fuel pump; 6-rail; 7-Fuel pressure regulator valve N276

The fuel system is an advanced version of the system used on earlier TSI engines. All parts which are in direct contact with fuel are designed in such a way that the engine can run on any available fuel grade. Special materials are used to ensure the fuel system meets all requirements relating to corrosion protection.

The high-pressure system is supplied with fuel by a returnless, demand controlled pre-supply system. Fuel is delivered at a variable pressure between 50.7 psi (3.5 bar) and 87.1 psi (6.0 bar). No low pressure sensor is used in this system. The correct fuel pressure is determined by mapped settings of the engine control module and subsequently set by Fuel Pressure Regulator Valve N276.

Fig. 1-11 Location of Fuel Pressure Sensor
1-Camshaft; 2-Four-lobed cam; 3-Cam follower; 4-Fuel high-pressure pump; 5-Fuel pressure regulating valve N276; 6-Rail; 7-From fuel tank; 8-Fuel pressure sensor G247; 9-Fuel injector

2.6.1 Fuel Rail

The fuel delivery rate of the high-pressure pump has been reduced through the use of a four-lobe cam. A quicker pressure build-up is thus possible. This build-up benefits both cold start and hot start situations.

2.6.2 Fuel Pressure Sensor G247

The fuel pressure sensor (Fig. 1-11) is mounted in the fuel rail and is designed for measuring pressures up to 2900 psi (200 bar).

2.6.3 High-Pressure Pump

The demand controlled high-pressure pump by Bosch is driven by a four lobed cam on the end of the intake camshaft. The pump piston is driven by the camshaft and a cam follower. This reduces friction as well as the chain forces. The results are smoother engine operation and higher fuel economy.

The use of the four lobe cam has allowed a reduced piston stroke compared to earlier versions of the 2.0L TSI engine. Due to the shorter stroke, the individual delivery rates are lower. This, in turn, results in reduced pressure fluctuations. The metering precision of the injectors is also improved, as there is now one feed stroke per injection. The advantage of this is that oxygen sensor control and fuel efficiency are improved.

The high-pressure pump produces a maximum pressure of 2175.5 psi (150 bar). The fuel pressure requested by the engine control module is adjusted by Fuel Pressure Regulator Valve N276. The pressure is regulated between 725.1 psi (50 bar) and 2175.5 psi (150 bar) depending on engine requirements. The high-pressure pump now has its own pressure limiting valve. This valve opens at approximately 2900 psi (200 bar) and admits pressure into the pump chamber. Previously, pressure was discharged into the low-pressure circuit. Excessively high-pressures can build up in overrun or when the engine heat soaks after shut-off.

The pressure pulsations in the low-pressure circuit are reduced by a damping element integrated in the pump.

2.6.4 High-Pressure Regulation

Fuel pressure and fuel quantity are regulated by Fuel Pressure Regulator Valve N276 (Fig. 1-12). The signal from Fuel Pressure Sensor G247 is used by the engine control module as a parameter. This sensor is located in the fuel rail.

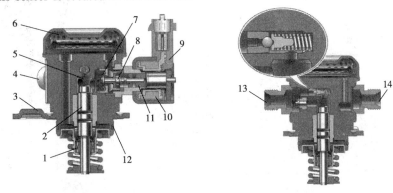

Fig. 1-12 High-Pressure Regulation

1-Seal; 2-Piston; 3-Flange; 4-Outlet; 5-Delivery chamber; 6-Low pressure damper; 7-Inlet valve; 8-Needle; 9-Fuel pressure regulator valve N276; 10-Coil; 11-Amature; 12-Ring; 13-Connection to rail; 14-Connection to low pressure

Power demand has been reduced significantly through a newly designed fuel pressure regulating valve and associated control concept.

At the start of delivery, Fuel Pressure Regulating Valve N276 is activated only very briefly. The intake valve closes, fuel pressure builds up, and fuel delivery immediately begins.

2.6.5 Control Concept

The Fig. 1-13 shows the high-pressure regulation function of the high-pressure pump. The complete delivery cycle for a cam is shown here.

This cycle takes place four times during a single revolution of the camshaft. The bottom diagram shows the movement of the pump piston and the activation of Fuel Pressure Regulator N276.

The operating point of the N276 changes depending on when it is activated by the engine

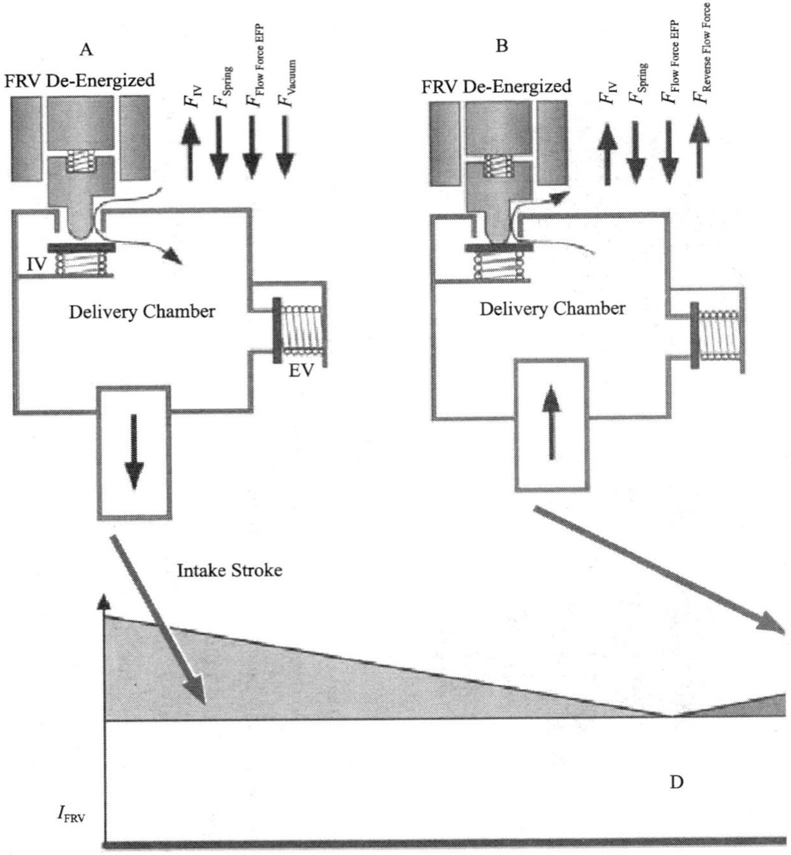

A
- Pump piston intake stroke, fuel flows into pump chamber
- N276 de-energizes
- Intake Valve(IV) opens because spring force is less than flow force of transfer fuel pump—vacuum is present inside pump
- Exhaust Valve(EV) closes

B
- Pump piston feed stroke, fuel flows back to inlet
- N276 de-energizes
- IV opens due to upward motion of pump piston, fuel moves from pump chamber into inlet
- EV closes

Legend
FRV Fuel Pressure Regulator Valve N276
I   Current
F   Force
IV   Intake valve
EFP Electric fuel pump
EV   Exhaust valve

Fig. 1-13 Control Concept (Not activated)

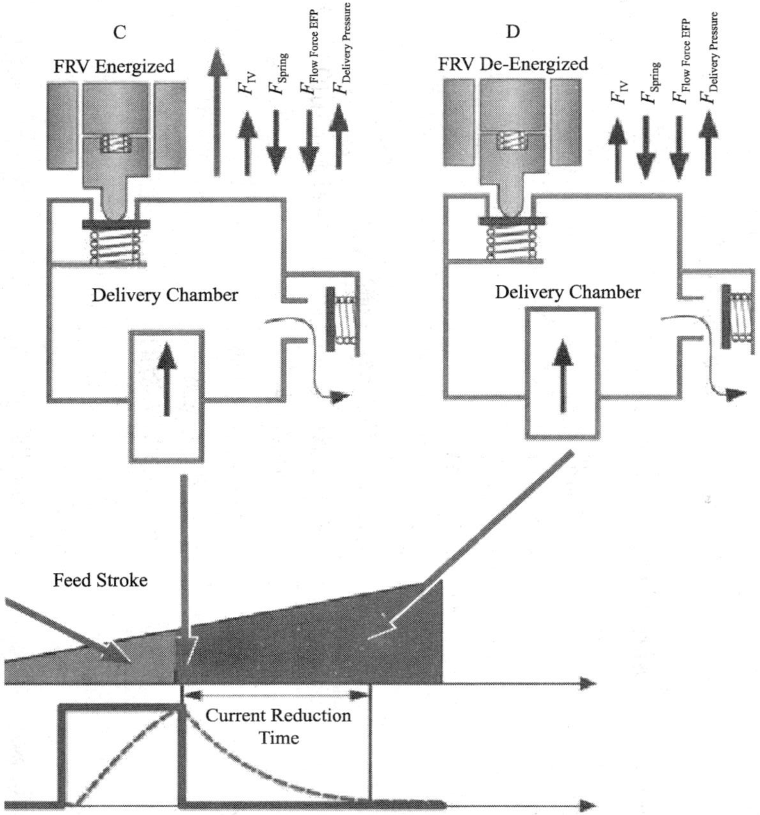

C
- Pump piston feed stroke, fuel flows to rail
- N276 receives short pulse of electrical current from engine control module
- IV closes. Due to upward motion of pump piston, pressure builds up immediately inside pump
- EV opens

D
- Pump piston feed stroke, fuel flows to rail until intake stroke begins
- N276 de-energizes
- IV closes
- EV opens

Legend
FRV   Fuel Pressure Regulator Valve N276
I Current
F Force
IV   Intake valve
EFP   Electric fuel pump
EV   Exhaust valve

Fig. 1-14 Control Concept (Activated)

control module (Fig. 1-14). The ON time remains the same.

The earlier N276 is activated, the more actively the delivery stroke can be used and hence the more fuel can be delivered.

2.6.6 Injector

Each fuel injector has six individual fuel openings (Fig. 1-15), providing better mixture preparation. This also helps prevent "wetting" the intake valves and the combustion chamber surfaces during injection cycles. The angle of cone of the jet is 50°. These modifications have resulted in reduced HC emissions, particulate matter formation, and oil thinning.

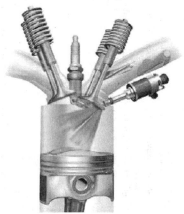

Fig. 1-15　Single Port Injector(left) and Multi Port Injector(right)

Technical Words and Terms

1. carburetor　　　　　　n. 化油器
2. injector　　　　　　　n. 喷油器
3. filter　　　　　　　　n. 滤清器
4. sensor　　　　　　　　n. 传感器
5. viscosity　　　　　　　n. 黏度
6. vaporize　　　　　　　vt. & vi. (使)蒸发,(使)汽化
7. trap　　　　　　　　　n. 圈套,(对付人的)计谋,(练习射击用的)抛靶器,(捕捉动物的)夹子
8. surging　　　　　　　v. 浪涌,冲击,波动
9. splash　　　　　　　　v. 溅,泼,使飞溅
10. synthetic　　　　　　adj. 合成的,人造的
11. hose　　　　　　　　n. 软管
12. cam　　　　　　　　n. 凸轮
13. eccentric　　　　　　adj. 离心的
14. lobe　　　　　　　　n. 凸轮凸台,凸角
15. adaptability　　　　　n. 适应性,改编
16. electromagnet　　　　n. 电磁体(铁)
17. bellows　　　　　　　n. 波纹管,真空膜盒

18. diaphragm	*n.*	膜片,薄膜,振动膜
19. vane	*n.*	叶片,叶轮
20. impeller	*n.*	(驱动)叶轮,驱动涡轮
21. atomize	*v.*	把……喷成雾状,使雾化
22. considerable concentration		一定浓度的可燃混合气
23. fuel rail		燃油分配管
24. pressure regulator		燃油压力调节器
25. volatile property		挥发性

Notes

1. In order to strengthen the tank as well as to prevent surging of fuel when the vehicle rounds a curve, rapidly starts or suddenly stops, baffle plates are attached to the inside of the tank.

为了提高油箱强度,并在车辆急转弯、快速起动或急减速时防止燃油出现较大的波动,一般在油箱内部加装挡油板。

2. Fuel is drawn from the tank by a vacuum and sent to the carburetor.

局部真空度将燃油从油箱吸入化油器。

3. The electric pump uses an electromagnet (a magnet produced by electricity flowing through a coil) to operate a metal bellows that alternately forms a vacuum and then pressure.

电动燃油泵利用电磁铁(电流流经线圈形成的磁体)吸引金属波纹管,交替地产生真空和压力。

Exercises

Questions for discussion

1. What is the function of the fuel system?
2. What are the major parts of the fuel pump?
3. What are the differences between gasoline engines and diesel engines?
4. What are the major parts of the TSI engine fuel system?

Fill in the blank according to the text

1. Metallic tubes or _____ _____ hoses used are called fuel lines.
2. There are two types of gasoline engine pumps: _____ fuel pumps and _____ fuel pumps.
3. The job of the fuel _____ used on gasoline engines is to remove dirt, rust, water, and other contamination from the gasoline before it can reach the _____ or the injection system.
4. The mechanical fuel pump is driven by the _____.
5. Some electric pumps use a/an _____ to work a regular diaphragm.
6. Fuel systems that have electric fuel pumps and fuel injectors may use a/an _____ _____ _____ to keep the fuel pressure constant.
7. The main task of the gasoline fuel supply system is to make up a _____ _____ of considerable concentration.
8. Because of higher _____ and worse _____ _____, diesel cannot be atomized to a uniform mist like that of gasoline in the carburetor.

Lesson 3
Engine Ignition System

Nowadays, there are three types of ignition systems. The mechanical (conventional) ignition system, used prior to 1975, was mechanical and electrical and used no electronics. The electronic ignition system became popular when better control and improved reliability became important with the advent of emission controls. Finally, the distributorless ignition system became available in the mid 1980s. This system was always computer controlled and contained no moving parts, so reliability was greatly improved.

3.1 Mechanical (Conventional) Ignition System

The ignition system (Fig. 1-16) on an internal combustion engine provides the spark to the correct cylinder at the correct time to ignite the combustible air-fuel mixture in the combustion chamber. Conventional systems consist of the battery, ignition coil, distributor, condenser, ignition switch, spark plug, resistor and the necessary low and high tension wiring.

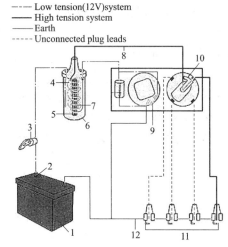

Fig. 1-16 Mechanical (Conventional) Ignition System

1-Battery; 2-Battery terminal; 3-Ingnition switch; 4-Primary winding; 5-Soft iron core; 6-Coil; 7-Secondary winding; 8-High-tension lead; 9-Contact-breaker; 10-Distributor; 11-Spark plugs; 12-Earth

The battery is the heart of the total electrical system. In regard to the primary circuit, its function is to supply voltage and current flow to the primary windings of the ignition coil, in order to produce the electromagnetic force.

The ignition distributor is a pulse transformer designed to set up the primary voltage (received from the battery and generator) of 12V to approximately 20,000 V required to jump the spark plug gap in the combustion chamber. It is composed of a primary winding, secondary winding and core of soft iron.

The ignition distributor is the nerve center of the mechanical ignition system. It opens and closes the primary ignition circuit, and also distributes high tension current to the proper spark plug at the correct time.

The distributor cap transfers the high voltage from the distributor rotor to spark plug wires.

A distributor rotor is a conductor designed to rotate and distribute the high tension current to the towers of the distributor cap. The distributor rotor is provided with some sorts of spring connection to the center tower or terminal of the distributor cap.

The purpose of the ignition condenser is to reduce arcing at the breaker points, and prolong their life.

The spark (Fig. 1-17) plug provides the gap in the combustion chamber across which the high tension electric spark jumps to the combustible charge.

In most 12V system, an ignition resistor is connected in series with the primary circuit of the ignition coil during normal operation. However, during the starting period, the resistor is cut out of the circuit so that full voltage is applied to the coil. This insures a strong spark during the starting period, and in that way quicker starting is provided.

The purpose of the ignition switch is to connect or disconnect the ignition system from the battery, so the engine can be started and stopped as desired. With the ignition switch ON, and the ignition distributor contacts closed, current will flow from the battery, through the primary winding of the ignition coil, to the distributor contact (breaker) points, to the ground connection and back to the battery.

The current flowing through the primary winding of the ignition coil produces a magnetic field in the coil. When the distributor contact points open (break), the magnetic field collapses and the movement of the magnetic field induces current in the secondary winding of the coil. Since there are many more turns of wire in the secondary winding than those in the primary winding, the voltage is increased up to 20,000V.

The distributor then directs this high voltage to the proper spark plug, where it jumps the gap. The heat of this spark ignites the air-fuel mixture in the combustion chamber. The burning fuel expands and forces the piston down. Downward motion of the piston, in turn, rotates the crankshaft.

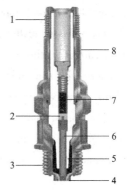

Fig. 1-17 The Spark Plug
1-Plated threads prevent seizing; 2- Fired glass seal provides; 3- Plated threads prevent seizing; 4- Nickel alloy electrodes provide excellent resistance to spark and heat erosion; 5- Aluminum oxide insulator has excellent thermal properties to resist cracking; 6- Copper core assures efficient heat transfer and maximum electrical conductivity; 7-Silicon carbide resistor prevents wear from voltage drain for prolonged plug life; 8- Two layers of corrosion protection

The ignition system must be timed accurately so that the spark occurs in the combustion chamber at the correct instant. Incorrect ignition timing results in loss of efficiency and power.

A mechanism is provided to automatically advance and retard the spark as conditions require. On automotive engines, two methods are usually employed to actuate that mechanism, centrifugal advance components and vacuum advance units. The corresponding devices are centrifugal advance components and vacuum advance units.

3.2 Electronic Ignition System

Electronic ignition systems are now being used with many automobile engines because they provide superior ignition and engine performance and at the same time require considerably less service and maintenance than conventional ignition systems.

The purpose of the electronic ignition system is to create a spark at each spark plug electrode gap at the right instant. In electronic ignition system, the points and condenser are replaced by electronics. There are several methods used to replace the points and condenser in order to trigger the coil to fire. One method uses a metal wheel with teeth, usually one for each cylinder, which is called an armature or reluctor. A magnetic pickup coil senses and sends a signal to the control module when a tooth passes to fire the coil.

The purpose of the control module is to open and close the primary ignition circuit. The induced voltage in the pickup coil decreases when the reluctor tip moves a very short distance out of alignment with the pickup coil. When this occurs, the control module closes the primary circuit and the primary current flow resumes.

The control module must keep the primary circuit turning on long enough to allow the magnetic field to build up in the ignition coil. This "on time" for the primary circuit is referred to as dwell time. In most electronic ignition systems, the dwell time is determined electronically by the control module.

The advantage of the electronic ignition system is that the control module can handle much higher primary voltage than the mechanical points. Voltage can even be stepped up before sending it to the coil, so the coil can create a much hotter spark, on the order of 50,000 volts instead of 20,000 volts that is common with the mechanical system.

The higher voltage that the system provided allows the use of a much wider gap on the spark plug for a longer, fatter spark. This larger spark also allows a leaner mixture for better fuel economy and still ensures a smooth running engine.

Fig. 1-18 The Distributor
(Chrysler 95-00 T5T57171)

In the later systems, the inside of the distributor (Fig. 1-18) is empty and all triggering is performed by a sensor called crankshaft position sensor or camshaft position sensor. In these systems, the job of the distributor is solely to distribute the spark to the correct cylinder through the distributor cap and rotor. The computer handles the timing and any timing advance necessary for the smooth running of the engine.

3.3 Distributorless Ignition System

The distributorless ignition system, completely controlled by the on-board computer, is a completely solid state electronic system with no moving parts. In place of the distributor, there are multiple coils that each serves one or two spark plugs.

In systems with single-spark ignition coils, each cylinder has its own ignition coil with driver output stage, installed either directly above the spark plug or separately. This system, suitable for engines with any number of cylinders, provides the greatest latitude for adjustment, as there is only one spark per cycle. All these advantages mean that the single-spark ignition coil is being increasingly used and is taking over from the dual-spark ignition coil in spite of costing more.

In systems with dual-spark ignition coils, one ignition coil is required for every two cylinders. The crankshaft can be used for synchronization. The high-voltage end of each ignition coil is connected to the spark plugs for two cylinders whose operating cycles are 360° out of phase with each other.

As there is an additional spark during the exhaust stroke, it is important to ensure that residual mixture or fresh mixture is not ignited. Furthermore, the dual-spark system is only suited for use with even numbers of cylinders. Owing to its cost advantage relative to the single-spark unit, the dual-spark ignition system is the most common distributorless ignition in use today.

Technical Words and Terms

1. electronic   *a.* 电子的
2. condenser   *n.* 电容器
3. resistor   *n.* 电阻器
4. voltage   *n.* 电压
5. pulse   *n.* 脉冲,脉搏,电流之突然增加或减弱
6. transformer   *n.* 变压器
7. terminal   *n.* 接线头,接线柱
8. arcing   *n.* 电压
9. turn   *n.* 一圈,(线圈的)匝数
10. ground   *n.* 接地,搭铁,路面
11. trigger   *v.* 触发
12. armature   *n.* 电枢
13. reluctor   *n.* 磁阻轮,变磁阻转子
14. module   *n.* 组件,模块,电子控制总成
15. resume   *v.* 恢复,重新开始,再继续
16. in series   串联,连续的,逐次的
17. primary winding   初级线圈,初级绕组
18. breaker point   断电器触点
19. ignition timing   点火正时
20. vacuum advance   真空式点火提前
21. pickup coil   传感线圈
22. control module(CM) (电子)控制组件,控制模块
23. dwell time(DT)   延迟时间,延长时间,停歇时间
24. lean mixture   稀混合气
25. on-board computer   车载电脑
26. high tension wiring 高压电线,高压电路
27. with the advent of 随着……的出现
28. distributor cap   分电器盖

Notes

1. The distributor is provided with some sorts of spring connection to the center tower or terminal of the distributor cap.

分电器通过特定的弹簧装置连接到配电器的中央触头或分电器盖上。

2. With the ignition switch ON, and the ignition distributor contacts closed, current will flow from the battery, through the primary winding of the ignition coil, to the distributor contact

(breaker) points, to the ground connection and back to the battery.

当点火开关打开,并且断电器白金触点闭合时,电流会从蓄电池经过点火线圈初级绕组,到断电器的白金触点,再通过蓄电池负极搭铁形成闭路。

3. The control module can handle much higher primary voltage than the mechanical points.

电子控制点火系统可以比机械式点火系统提供更高一些的初级电压。

Exercises

Questions for discussion

1. How many types of engine ignition systems nowadays and what are the differences among them?
2. How does the mechanical (Conventional) ignition system work?
3. What are the advantages of electronic ignition system?
4. How to keep the single-spark ignition coil being increasingly used?

Fill in the blank according to the text

1. The ignition _____ is the nerve center of the mechanical ignition system.
2. On automotive engines, two methods are usually employed to actuate that _____ _____ advance components and _____ advance units.
3. In place of the distributor, there are _____ coils that each serves one or two spark plugs.
4. The _____ system is only suited for use with even numbers of cylinders.

Lesson 4
Engine Cooling System

During the working stroke, temperature will rise up to 2000℃ in the cylinder. It may cause parts in direct contact with cylinder block, cylinder head, piston and valve to expand and jam, or make troubles such as abnormal burning and lubricant dilution. The main task of the cooling system is to bring the heat from the high temperature parts to outside atmosphere and to maintain normal working temperature for the engine.

Actually, there are two types of cooling systems used on motor vehicles: water-cooling systems and air-cooling systems. But for the most part, automobiles and trucks use water-cooling systems.

Fig. 1-19 shows a cooling system which is circulated by engine power. Under the action of water pump which driven by engine crankshaft through V-belt, water circulates as the arrows show in the figure.

4.1 Water-Cooling System

A water-cooling system means that water is used as a cooling agent to circulate through the engine to absorb the heat and carry it to the radiator for disposal. Engine is cooled mainly through heat transfer and heat dissipation. The heat generated by the mixture burned in engine must be transferred from cylinder to the water in water jacket. The outside of the water jacket dissipates some of the heat to the air surrounding it, but most of the heat is carried by the cooling water to the radiator for dissipation.

4.1.1 Coolant

The cooling water used in cooling system is called coolant. Pure water is no longer employed as coolant; today's coolant is a mixture of water (drinking quality), antifreeze (generally ethylene glycol), and various corrosion inhibitors selected for the specific application. An antifreeze concentration of 30% ~ 50% raises the coolant mixture's boiling point to allow operating temperatures of up to 120℃ at a pressure of 1.4 bar in passenger automobiles.

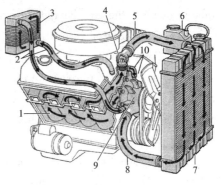

Fig. 1-19 Engine Cooling System
1-Cooling jackets; 2-Heater hoses; 3-Heater core; 4-Thermostat; 5-Upper radiator hose; 6-Coolant-recovery system; 7-Down-flow radiator; 8-Lower radiator hose; 9-Water pump; 10-Bypass hose

4.1.2 Coolant Flow

Engine coolant is forced from the water pump into the engine block. The coolant flows around the outside of the cylinder to cool the cylinder walls. Coolant continues to flow from the engine block through passages in the head gaskets into the cylinder head. The coolant flow through the cylinder head provides cooling for the valves, combustion chambers, and spark plugs. After flowing through the cylinder head, the coolant flows through the thermostat housing and top radiator hose to the inlet tank. As the coolant flows through the radiator, heat is transferred to the air flowing through the radiator. Coolant returns from the outlet tank and lower hose to the water pump.

When the coolant is cold, the thermostat is closed and the coolant flows through the intake manifold and heater core. Under this condition there is no coolant flow through the radiator. Once the engine reaches normal operating temperature, the thermostat opens and the coolant begins to flow through the radiator. When the thermostat is open, the coolant continues to flow through the intake manifold passage and the heater core.

4.1.3 Water Pump

A water pump is used to circulate the coolant. Coolant passages in the engine are connected to the pump. A drive belt from a crankshaft pulley is connected to the water pump. When engine is running, the crankshaft turns the drive belt, and the hot coolant is pumped out of the engine and through a radiator. Water pumps aredesigned by many types, but most of them are the centrifugal type which consists of a rotating fan, or impeller, and seldom are of the positive displacement type that uses gears or plungers.

4.1.4 Radiator

A radiator is designed to dissipate the heat that the coolant has absorbed from the engine. It is constructed to hold a large amount of water in tubes or other passages which provide a large area in contact with the atmosphere. The radiator usually mainly consists of the radiator core and radiator tank. Radiator cores are of two basic types: the fin and tube type (fins are placed around the tube to increase the area for radiating the heat) and the ribbon cellular or honeycomb type.

4.1.5 Radiator Cap

A radiator cap mounted on the top of the radiator is used to control the pressure in the cooling system. It is designed to release pressure if it reaches the specified upper limit that the system was designed to handle. This improves cooling efficiency and prevents evaporation of the coolant. Since evaporation is reduced or eliminated, it is not necessary to add coolant as often.

4.1.6 Thermostat

A thermostat (Fig. 1-20) is needed to control the temperature of the coolant by its work of opening or closing a valve to control the flow of coolant. It is designed to open and close at predetermined temperatures to maintain efficient engine operating temperatures. The closed thermostat helps engine warm up rapidly. As soon as the coolant heats up, the thermostat opens and allows coolant to flow to the radiator.

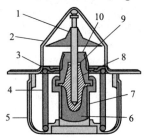

Fig. 1-20 Thermostat
1-Piston; 2-Body; 3-Poppet;
4-Spring; 5-Lower bracket;
6-Pellet material; 7-Cup; 8-Bag;
9-Anti-chafe ring; 10-Guide

4.1.7 Cooling Fan

The belt-driven fan is usually mounted on an extension of the water pump shaft and is driven by a V-belt from a pulley mounted on the front end of the crankshaft. Usually the alternator is also driven by the same belt. The fan blades are curved so that they pull air through the radiator as they rotate.

Many vehicles have cooling fans which are driven by an electric motor. The electrically driven fan only runs when additional cooling is required. Therefore, this type of fan uses less engine power than a belt-driven fan that rotates continuously. Since less engine power is used to drive the cooling fan, fuel economy and performance is improved. Many fuel-efficient front-wheel-driveautomobiles have electric cooling fans.

4.2 Air-Cooling System

The air-cooling system is not commonly used. Air-cooled engines are just found on a few older automobiles and many modern motorcycles.

An air-cooling system means that air is used as a cooling agent to circulate through the engine to carry the heat away from the moving parts. The system consists of a centrifugal fan, a thermostat, a fan drive belt, radiation fins, baffle plates, an air control ring, etc. When the engine is running, forced air is directed over and through the fins to dissipate the heat.

In order to regulate the engine temperature by controlling the volume of the cooling air, a thermostat is installed inside the metal housing which encloses the engine. The thermostat unit is connected to an air control ring. As the engine becomes hotter, the control ring opens wider to admit more air, and closes when the engine is cold. With the ring closed, air circulation is restricted, and a cold engine warms up more rapidly. Rapid warm-up is one of the characteristics of air-cooled engines, since they do not have heated water in cylinder jackets and radiators.

In conclusion, the engine cooling system is actually a temperature regulation system. It is very critical for the operation of the engine.

Technical Words and Terms

1.	agent	*n.* 剂,介质
2.	disposal	*n.* 处理,处置,清除
3.	transfer	*n./v.* 传到,传递
4.	dissipation	*n.* 分散,消散
5.	antifreeze	*n.* 防冻液,防冻剂
6.	pulley	*n.* 滑轮,滑车,带轮
7.	centrifugal	*adj.* 离心的
8.	ribbon	*n.* 带状物,带子
9.	cellular	*a.* 多孔的,蜂窝状的
10.	honeycomb	*n.* 蜂房,蜂窝结构
11.	housing	*n.* 外壳,外罩
12.	enclose	*v.* 封入,装入
13.	thermostat	*n.* 节温器
14.	shutter	*n.* 百叶窗
15.	regulate	*vt.* 调节,调整,校准,控制,管理
16.	operating temperature	工作温度,运转温度
17.	cooling agent	冷却介质
18.	ethylene glycol	乙二醇
19.	heater core	加热器芯子
20.	positive displacement type	变容式,容积式
21.	in contact with	和……接触,和……保持联系
22.	radiator core	散热器芯
23.	warm up	预热
24.	centrifugal fan	离心式风扇
25.	fan drive belt	风扇皮带
26.	baffle plate	隔板,折流板
27.	air control ring	空气量调节圈
28.	water cooling system	水冷系统
29.	V-belt	V 形传送带
30.	water jacket	水套
31.	drain cock	放水龙头
32.	anti-freezing coolant	防冻液,防冻冷却液

Notes

1. The function of the radiator is to bring the heat in the circulating water out to the atmosphere by the help of the cooling fan behind it.

散热器的作用是通过安装在后端的冷却风扇的帮助,将循环冷却液收集来的热量传递到大气中。

2. The outside of the water jacket dissipates some of the heat to the air surrounding it, but most of the heat is carried by the cooling water to the radiator for dissipation.

冷却水套可以将一些热量直接散发到水套周围的空气中,但大部分热量是由冷却液带入散热器中散发出去。

3. Water pumps are of many designs, but most of them are the centrifugal type which consists of a rotating fan, or impeller, and seldom are of the positive displacement type that uses gears or plungers.

水泵的结构设计多种多样,但多数采用一个旋转叶片或叶轮的离心式结构,而极少数采用齿轮或柱塞的变容式结构。

4. A radiator cap mounted on the top of the radiator is used to control the pressure in the cooling system.

安装在散热器顶部的散热器盖可用于调节冷却系统的压力。

Exercises

Questions for discussion

1. How many parts of the engine cooling system?
2. What is the function of the engine cooling system?
3. How does the coolant flow work?
4. What is the advantage of the air-cooling system?

Fill in the blank according to the text

1. A/An _____ concentration of 30% ~ 50% raises the coolant mixture's boiling point to allow operating temperatures of up to 120℃ at a pressure of 1.4 bar in passenger automobiles.

2. A _____ is designed to dissipate the heat which the coolant has absorbed from the engine.

3. Since _____ is reduced or eliminated, it is not necessary to add coolant as often.

4. The closed _____ helps the engine warm up rapidly.

5. In order to regulate the engine temperature by controlling the volume of the cooling air, a _____ is installed inside the metal housing which encloses the engine.

Lesson 5
Lubrication System

Without the aid of friction, an automobile could not move itself. Excessive friction in the engine, however, would mean rapid destruction. Internal friction cannot be eliminated, but it can be reduced to a considerable degree by the use of lubricating oil so that the automobile can move smoothly with proper friction.

The main task of the lubrication system is to supply the lubricant to the contact surface of the moving parts to reduce friction and abrasion. Moreover, it can remove the abrasive particles, cool the friction surfaces and prevent them from corrosion.

The main lubricant of the lubrication system is oil. Brands of the oil are divided into classes expressed by English alphabets. The expression of the first alphabet "S" refers to oil used in the gasoline engine and "C" refers to diesel engine. Classes A, B, C, D, E, F, G, and H express the performance levels. The level of the latter alphabet is higher than the former. There are six classes SC, SD, SE, SF, SG and SH of local made oil for gasoline engine and five classes CC, CD, CD-II, CE and CF-4 for diesel engine.

Apart from the lubricating oil, the lubrication system also contains other mechanical parts, such as oil pump, oil filter, oil pressure relief valve; also pipes, passages and drillings in various parts of engine through which the oil can flow. A quantity of oil is held in the oil pan. From this, oil is taken by the oil pump and circulated throughout the engine before returning to the oil pan. The oil cooler is also used in the lubrication system (Fig. 1-21).

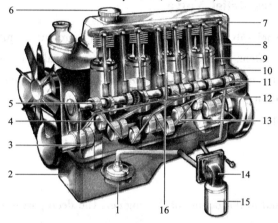

Fig. 1-21   Lubrication System

1-Sump strainer; 2-Oil pan; 3-Big-end bearing; 4-Crankshaft connecting rod bearing; 5-Camshaft bearing; 6-Oil fill port; 7-Valve rocker; 8-Push rod; 9-Cylinder; 10-Tappet; 11-Cam; 12-Feed to the main bearings; 13-Crankshaft drillings; 14-Oil pump forces oil under pressure to filter, main bearings and other parts; 15-Oil filter; 16-Main oil gallery

5.1 Oil Pump

The oil pump induces oil circulation in the engine lubrication system. It is usually bolted to a boss on the lower face of the crankcase or to a crankshaft main bearing cap. Generally, the oil pump is located in the sump of the oil pan.

Oil pumps are of the positive displacement type in several designs. Vanes, plungers, rotors and gears are all used to build up the necessary pressure. The two most widely used are the gear and the rotor types. The pumps of gear and rotor types are always positively driven, usually from the camshaft either by means of gears or cams.

The oil pump in tractor engines is driven from a gear on the nose of the crankshaft; while in automobile engines, it is driven from a gear made integral with the camshaft.

5.2 Oil Filter

Oil filters are used in the lubrication system to filter dirt and solids out of the oil. As these particles of foreign matter are prevented from entering the engine by oil filters, the wear rate of engine parts is reduced. Engines of more recent designs generally use full-flow centrifugal oil filters.

That is, all oil passes through the filter before it reaches the bearings. However, in the event the filter gets clogged, a bypass valve is provided so that oil will continue to reach the bearings.

This full-flow centrifugal oil filter is a reaction-type centrifugal filter which all of the oil delivered by the oil pump is cleaned in the filter rotor. This filter has an oil outlet pipe fitted inside the hollow spindle of the filter rotor and connected to the oil line that distributes the oil to the various parts of the lubrication system.

Some engines use a new, impulse-reaction centrifugal oil filter. In contrast to the reaction-type centrifugal oil filter, this type of oil filter has no jet nozzles, and the oil used to drive the filter rotor does not drain to the oil pan but goes instead to lubricate the working parts of the engine.

5.3 Oil Pressure Relief Valve

The oil pressure relief valve is mainly to act both as a pressure regulator and as a safety device in the lubrication system. As a pressure regulator, the valve prevents the oil pump from building up excessive pressure. When the oil pump is in good condition, the valve will regulate the oil pressure within limits. As a safety device, the valve prevents oil pressure from building up to a dangerous level. The valve can secure the oil circulation through engine parts under proper pressure.

5.4 Oil Pan

The oil pan is bolted to the bottom of the engine. The deep part of the oil pan houses an oil pump and pick-up screen. The pan also collects the oil that runs off engine parts after lubrication. A plug in the bottom of the oil pan is used to drain the oil at required intervals. The oil pan stores and collects the oil. Engines usually have an oil pan that holds 4, 5, or 6 quarts. A pick-up screen in the oil pan is connected by a pipe to the inlet of the oil pump. One end of the pan is lower and forms a reservoir called a sump. The drain plug is placed in the bottom of the sump.

5.5 Oil Cooler

The purpose of the oil cooler is to cool the oil in summer time. It is a one-piece unit consisting of a series of steel tubes of a flattened oval section and two tanks: a top tank and a bottom tank. To enlarge the cooling surface area, a spiral of thin steel ribbon is wound around each cooler tube. The oil coolers of some engines have their tubes passing through a large number of flat cooling fins, and their tanks are divided into several compartments by partitions. Welded to the tanks are the inlet and outlet oil pipe connections and mounting lugs. The oil cooler is mounted in front of the cooling system radiator. In air-cooled engines, the oil cooler takes the form of a single tube repeatedly bent in and out and carrying a ribbon spiral wound around it. With the radiator shutter or blind fully open, the oil flowing through the cooler tubes that are exposed to the flow of cooling air on the outside gets colder by 10 ~ 12℃.

5.6 Lubrication Ways

Engines are lubricated in three ways: pump pressure, splashing, or a combination of both. In the pressure system, the oil is fed to the majority of engine parts under the pump pressure, especially to the main bearings and connecting rod bearings.

In the splash system, there are dippers on the lower parts of the connecting rod bearing caps; these dippers enter oil trays in the oil pan with each crankshaft revolution. The dippers splash the oil to the upper parts of the engine. The oil is thrown up as the oil sprays, which provides adequate lubrication to valve mechanisms, cylinder walls, piston rings and bearings.

In modern engine designs, these two methods are often combined. Pressure is developed by the oil pump, which delivers the oil to the filter for cleaning before it is sent to the camshaft and valve train components at the top of the engine. Other components are lubricated by splashing the oil and by a network of passages.

5.7 Ventilation

As the engine is working, the gasoline vapor or burnt gas may be leaked to the crankcase and spoil the oil. Therefore, ventilation is required to drive the vapor and gas outside from the crankcase. The way of ventilation is to connect a pipe from the crankcase to the intake path of the carburetor and remove the vapor and gas by the help of vacuum suction during the intake stroke.

Technical Words and Terms

1. destruction	*n.*	毁坏,破坏
2. lubricate	*v.*	润滑,加润滑油
3. pan	*n.*	盘,槽
4. induce	*v.*	引起,诱发,感应
5. sump	*n.*	油底壳,贮槽
6. rotor	*n.*	轮子,涡轮
7. particle	*n.*	微粒
8. regulator	*n.*	调节器
9. screen	*n.*	滤网
10. partition	*n.*	隔板,隔开
11. weld	*v.*	焊接,熔接
12. lubricating oil		润滑油
13. oil pump		油泵
14. oil filter		机油滤清器
15. oil pressure relief valve		机油减压阀
16. oil cooler		润滑油冷却器
17. main bearing cap		主轴承盖
18. positive displacement type		容积式
19. build up		增大,集结
20. foreign matter		杂质,异物
21. rate of wear		磨损率,磨损度

22. full-flow type　　　　　　　　　　　全流式
23. bypass valve　　　　　　　　　　　　分流阀,旁通阀
24. reaction-type centrifugal filter　　　反馈式离心过滤器
25. outlet pipe　　　　　　　　　　　　排气管
26. impulse-reaction centrifugal filter　冲击-反击式离心过滤器
27. jet nozzle　　　　　　　　　　　　　喷油嘴
28. pick-up screen　　　　　　　　　　集滤器
29. at required intervals　　　　　　　在规定时间
30. mounting lug　　　　　　　　　　　安装用吊耳
31. be fed to　　　　　　　　　　　　　向……提供……

Notes

1. As these particles of foreign matter are prevented from entering the engine by oil filters, the rate of wear of engine parts is reduced.

由于机油滤清器可以阻止外来的杂质微粒进入发动机内部,因此,可以降低发动机部件的磨损率。

2. …in the event the filter gets clogged, a bypass valve is provided so that oil will continue to reach the bearings…

如果机油滤清器被阻塞,此时将会打开一个旁通阀保证机油继续到达各个轴承。

3. Engines are lubricated in three ways:pump pressure, splashing, or a combination of both.

发动机一般采用3种润滑方式:压力润滑、飞溅润滑和复合润滑。

Exercises

Questions for discussion

1. How many parts of the lubrication system and what is the main function of it?
2. How does the oil filter work?
3. What will be happened without the oil cooler?
4. How many lubrication ways are there of the engine and how do they work?

Fill in the blank according to the text

1. The _____ pump is to induce oil circulation in the engine lubrication system.

2. This full-flow _____ oil filter is a reaction-type centrifugal filter with which all of the oil delivered by the oil pump is cleaned in the filter rotor.

3. The oil pressure relief valve is mainly to act both as a _____ _____ and as a _____ in the lubrication system.

4. The purpose of the oil _____ is to cool the oil in summer time.

5. Engines are lubricated in three ways: _____ pressure, _____, or a combination of both.

6. The oil is thrown up as the oil sprays, which provides adequate lubrication to _____ _____, _____ _____, _____ _____ and _____.

Lesson 6
Automobile Engine Intakes

Early automobile intake systems were simple air inlets connected directly to carburetors. The first air filter was implemented on the 1915 Packard Twin Six.

A modern automobile air intake system has three main parts, an air filter, mass flow sensor, and throttle body. Some modern intake systems can be highly complex, and often include specially-designed intake manifolds to optimally distribute air and air/fuel mixture to each cylinder. Many automobiles today now include a silencer to minimize the noise entering the cabin. Silencers impede air flow and create turbulence which reduces total power, so performance enthusiasts often remove them.

All the above is usually accomplished by flow testing on a flow bench in the port design stage. Automobiles with turbochargers or superchargers which provide pressurized air to the engine usually have highly-refined intake systems to improve performance dramatically.

Productionautomobiles have specific-length air intakes to cause the air to vibrate and buffet at a specific frequency to assist air flow into the combustion chamber. Aftermarket companies for automobiles have introduced larger throttle bodies and air filters to decrease restriction of flow at the cost of changing the harmonics of the air intake for a small net increase in power or torque.

Porsche in the 1980s designed an intake system for their automobiles that changed the length of the intake system by alternating between a longer and shorter set of tubing using a butterfly valve, creating a small amount of positive pressure which increased overall performance of the engine. Audi began to use a similar system in some automobiles in the 1990s. Alfa Romeo used variable-length intakes in their 2.0 Twin Spark engines powering the model 156.

The TSI Engine Air Intake System
(The Volkswagen 2.0 Liter Chain-Driven TSI Engine)

6.1 Intake Manifold Module

The body of the intake manifold module (Fig. 1-22) is made of polyamide and consists of two shells which are plastic-welded together.

The intake manifold flaps are trough shaped. Through this shape and their arrangement in the intake port, the intake airflow is improved when the flaps are open. An improvement in tumble capacity is also achieved when closing the flaps.

The intake manifold flaps are adjusted by a vacuum motor. The motor uses a two stage process.

Feedback about the flap position is provided by Intake Manifold Runner Position Sensor G336. When the engine is not running, the intake manifold flaps are closed.

Blow-by gases and vapor from the charcoal canister vent directly into the airflow downstream of the throttle valve assembly.

6.2 Air Supply

The air supply system is shown in Fig. 1-23.

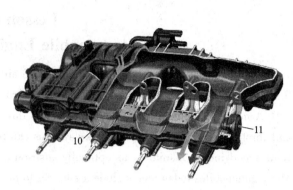

Fig. 1-22 Intake Manifold Module

1-Throttle valve control module;2-Intake air temperature (IAT) sensor G42;3-Evaporative (EVAP) emission canister purge regulator valve N80;4-Vacuum motor for intake manifold flap changeover;5-Fuel port high-pressure pump;6-Fuel port high pressure fuel rail;7-Double check valve for EVAP system;8- High pressure fuel rail;9-Fuel pressure sensor G247;10-Intake manifold flaps;11-Intake manifold runner position sensor G332

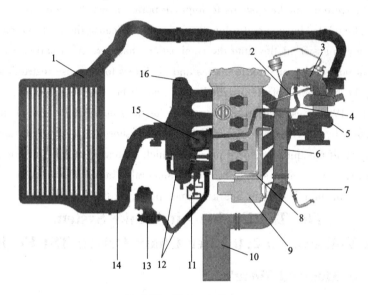

Fig. 1-23 Air Supply System

1-Charge air cooler;2-Charcoal canister line;3-Air intake;4-Vent hose;5-Turbocharger;6-Intake tube;7-Vacuum line;8-Positive crankcase ventilation (PCV) line;9- Vacuum pump;10- Air filter;11- Intake manifold runner control (IMRC) valve N316; 12-Vent hose;13-Oil separator;14-Pressure hose;15-Pressure regulating valve;16-Intake manifold

6.3 Evaporative Emission System (Fig. 1-24)

Venting of fuel vapors from the charcoal canister while the engine is running involves using two different paths.

When boost pressure from the turbocharger is present, fuel vapors cannot directly flow into the intake manifold. In this case, the vapors are directed to the intake side of the turbocharger.

When boost pressure is not present, the vapors are drawn in through the intake manifold downstream of the throttle body. A double check valve in the evaporative system accomplishes this task.

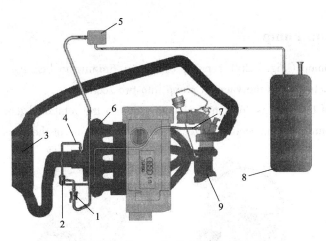

Fig. 1-24 Evaporative Emission System

1-Evaporative (EVAP) emission canister purge regulator valve N80;2-Double valve check;3-Charge air cooler;4-Inflow into intake manifold (no charge pressure);5-Charcoal canister;6-Intake manifold;7-Inflow into intake manifold (charge pressure present);8-Fuel tank;9-Exhaust gas turbocharger

6.4 Vacuum Supply (Fig. 1-25)

The required vacuum for the brake booster and other vacuum driven components of the engine is produced by a mechanically driven vacuum pump.

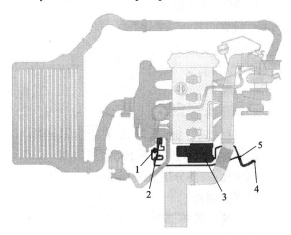

Fig. 1-25 Vacuum Supply

1-Vaccum motor;2-Intake manifold runner control (IMRC) valve N316;3-Vacuum pump on the exhaust camshaft-mechanically driven;4-To break servo;5-Check valve with integrated T-piece

The pump is a swivel vane pump driven by the exhaust camshaft and is installed behind the high-pressure fuel pump.

The vacuum pump is capable of providing a sufficient vacuum for all vacuum components under any operating condition.

For this reason, it is not necessary to use an additional vacuum reservoir. The pump is rated to deliver a continuous absolute pressure of 0.73 psi (50 mbar).

Oil for lubricating the pump and to enhance the sealing of the pump vanes is provided through a special port in the cylinder head.

6.5 Vacuum Pump

The vacuum pump (Fig. 1-26) consists of a rotor running in bearings and a moving vane made of plastic which divides the vacuum pump into two sections.

The position of the vane is constantly changing due to the rotational movement of the rotor. As a result, the volume of one section increases while the volume of the other section decreases.

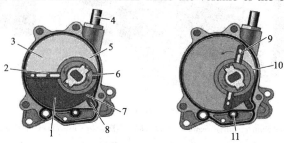

Fig. 1-26 Vacuum Pumps

1-Pressure end;2-Vane;3-Intake end;4-Air inflow from vacuum system;5-Induced air;6-Rotor;7-Compressed air;8-Air outflow to cylinder head (shuttle valve);9-Vane;10-Rotor;11-Oil way

Technical Words and Terms

1. intake   v. 进气,空气摄入
2. manifold   n. 歧管
3. impede   v. 阻碍;妨碍;阻止
4. turbulence   n. 扰流,湍流
5. turbocharger   n. 涡轮增压器
6. supercharger   n. 增压器
7. valve   n. 气门,阀,[解剖]瓣膜;真空管,活门
8. torque   n. 转矩,[力]扭矩,项圈,金属领圈
9. TSI (Turbo FSI)   双增压-燃油分层直喷
10. air filter   空气滤清器
11. mass flow sensor   质量流量传感器
12. throttle body   节气门体
13. boost pressure   增压压力

Notes

1. Some modern intake systems can be highly complex, and often include specially-designed intake manifolds to optimally distribute air and air/fuel mixture to each cylinder.

一些现代进气系统的结构非常复杂,经常出现某种特别设计的进气歧管,它们能使空气和燃油混合气更均匀地进入到每一个汽缸。

2. Oil for lubricating the pump and to enhance the sealing of the pump vanes is provided through a special port in the cylinder head.

用于润滑各个泵体的机油和提高叶片密封效果的机油通过汽缸盖内部的特殊通道

提供。

3. The vacuum pump consists of a rotor running in bearings and a moving vane made of plastic which divides the vacuum pump into two sections.

真空泵由一个安装在轴承上转动的转子和一个塑料回转叶片组成,后者可以将真空泵内部分为两部分。

Exercises

Questions for discussion

1. How many parts of a modern automobile air intake system and what is the function of each part?

2. How to keep a high air pressure in the chamber and keep the gas highly efficient mixed?

3. What is the advantage of Porsche's design?

Fill in the blank according to the text

1. Early automobile intake systems were simple air inlets connected directly to _____.

2. The body of the intake manifold module is made of _____ and consists of two shells which are plastic-welded together.

3. Venting of fuel _____ from the _____ canister while the engine is running involves using two different paths.

4. The _____ pump consists of a rotor running in bearings and a moving vane made of plastic which divides the vacuum pump into two sections.

Extension 1: Formula One Engine

Formula One (Fig. 1-27) currently uses four-stroke V8, naturally aspirated reciprocating engines. They typically produce 224 kilowatts (300 bhp, 304 PS) per liter of displacement, far higher than most naturally aspirated internal combustion engines.

Fig. 1-27　F1 Motor

The power a Formula One engine produces is generated by operating at a very high rotational speed, up to 18,000 revolutions per minute (RPM). This contrasts with road car engines of a similar size which operate safely at typically less than 7,000 rpm. The basic configuration of a naturally aspirated Formula One engine has not been greatly modified since the 1967 Cosworth

DFV and the mean effective pressure (MEP) has stayed at around 14 bar. Until the mid-1980s Formula One engines were limited to around 12,000 rpm due to the traditional metal valve springs used inside the engine to close the valves. The speed required to operate the engine valves at a higher RPM is much greater than the metal valve springs can achieve and they were replaced by pneumatic valve springs introduced by Renault. Since the 1990s, all Formula One engine manufacturers now use pneumatic valve springs with the pressurized air allowing engines to reach speeds of nearly 20,000 rpm.

The bore is the diameter of the cylinder in the engine block, and the stroke is the distance the piston travels from top dead-centre (TDC) to bottom dead-centre (BDC) inside the cylinder. To operate at high engine speeds the stroke must be relatively short to prevent catastrophic failures, usually connecting rod failures as they are under very large stresses at these speeds. Having a short stroke means that a relatively large bore is required to make the 2.4 liter displacement. This results in a less efficient combustion stroke, especially at lower RPM. The stroke of a Formula One engine is approximately 39.7 mm (1.56 in), less than half as long as the bore is wide (98.0 mm) producing an over-square configuration.

In addition to the use of pneumatic valve springs, the Formula One engine's high RPM output has been made possible due to advances in metallurgy and design allowing lighter pistons and connecting rods to withstand the accelerations necessary to attain such high speeds, also by narrowing the connecting rod ends allowing for narrower main bearings. This allows for higher RPM with less bearing-damaging heat build-up. For each stroke, the piston goes from a null speed, to almost two times the mean speed, (approx. 40 m/s) then back to zero. This will occur 4 times for each of the 4 strokes in the cycle. Maximum piston acceleration occurs at top dead center and is in the region of 95,000 m/s^2, about 10,000 times standard gravity or 10,000 g.

Formula One engines have come through a variety of regulations, manufacturers and configurations through the years.

In recent years, the engines had to be 90° V8 of 2.4 liters maximum capacity with a 98 mm maximum circular bore, which imply a 39.7 mm minimum stroke. They had to have two circular inlet and exhaust valves per cylinder, be normally aspirated and have a 95 kg (209 lb) minimum weight. The previous year's engines with a rev-limiter were permitted for 2006 and 2007 for teams who unable to acquire a V8 engine, with Scuderia Toro Rosso using a Cosworth V10 (Fig. 1-28), after Red Bull's takeover of the former Minardi team did not include the new engines.

Fig. 1-28 3L V10 F1 Engine

Pre-cooling air before it enters the cylinders, injection of any substance other than air and fuel into the cylinders, variable-geometry intake and exhaust systems, variable valve timing were forbidden. Each cylinder could have only one fuel injector and a single plug spark ignition. Separate starting devices were used to start engines in the pits and on the grid. The crankcase and cylinder block had to be made of cast or wrought aluminum alloys. The crankshaft and camshafts had to be made from an iron alloy, pistons from an aluminum alloy and valves from alloys based on iron, nickel, cobalt or titanium. These restrictions were in place to reduce development costs on the engines.

The reduction in capacity was designed to give a power reduction of around 20% from the three liter engines, to reduce the increasing speeds of Formula One cars. However in many cases, performance of the car improved. In 2006 Toyota F1 announced an approximate 740 hp (552 kW) output at 19000 rpm for its new RVX-06 engine, but real figures are of course difficult to obtain.

The engine specification was frozen in 2007 to keep development costs down. The engines which were used in the 2006 Japanese Grand Prix were used for the 2007 and 2008 seasons and they were limited to 19,000 rpm. In 2009 the limit was reduced to 18,000 rpm with each driver allowed to use a maximum of 8 engines over the season. Any driver needing an additional engine is penalized 10 places on the starting grid for the first race the engine is used. This increases the importance of reliability, although the effect is only seen towards the end of the season. Certain design changes intended to improve engine reliability may be carried out with permission from the FIA. This has led to some engine manufacturers, notably Ferrari and Mercedes, exploiting this ability by making design changes which not only improve reliability, but also boost engine power output as a side effect. As the Mercedes engine was proven to be the strongest, re-equalizations of engines were allowed by the FIA to allow other manufacturers to match the power.

2009 saw the exit of Honda from Formula 1. The team was acquired by Ross Brawn, creating Brawn GP and the BGP 001. With the absence of the Honda engine, Brawn GP retrofitted the Mercedes engine to the BGP 001 chassis, which resulted in a very successful season: the newly branded team won both the Constructors' Championship and the Drivers' Championship from better-known and established contenders Ferrari, McLaren-Mercedes, and Renault.

Cosworth, absented since the 2006 season, returned in 2010. New teams Lotus Racing, HRT, and Virgin Racing, along with the established Williams, used this engine. The season also saw the withdrawal of the BMW and Toyota engines, as the car companies withdrew from Formula One due to the recession.

The FIA has announced the intention to change the 2.4-litre V8 engines to 1.6 liter V6 turbo engines including energy recovery systems and containing fuel flow restrictions, in order to make Formula One more environmentally aware and to attract more commercial partners for 2014. The engines would also be limited to 15,000 rpm. In addition to the current suppliers, a new company, Propulsion Universelle et Recuperation d'Energie (PURE), has been founded to produce the 2014-specification engines, in the ex Toyota F1 base in Cologne. The new formula is set to reintroduce turbocharged engines, which last appeared in 1988, have their efficiency improved by turbo-compounding and introduce more energy recovery systems – with power to be harvested from the brakes and exhaust gases. The original proposal for four-cylinder turbocharged engines was not welcomed by the racing teams, in particular Ferrari. Adrian Newey stated during the 2011 European Grand Prix that the change to a V6 enables teams to carry the engine as a stressed member, whereas an inline 4 would have required a space frame. A compromise was reached to adopt V6 turbocharged engines instead.

Extension 2: Engine Types of Hybrid Vehicles

Hybrid electric-petroleum vehicles

When the term hybrid vehicle is used, it most often refers to hybrid electric vehicle. These encompass such vehicles as the Saturn Vue, Toyota Prius, Toyota Camry Hybrid, Ford Escape Hybrid, Toyota Highlander Hybrid, Honda Insight, Honda Civic Hybrid, Lexus RX 400h and 450h and others. A petroleum-electric hybrid most commonly uses internal combustion engines (generally gasoline or diesel engines, powered by a variety of fuels) and electric batteries to power the vehicle. There are many types of petroleum-electric hybrid drivetrains, from Full hybrid to Mild hybrid, which offer varying advantages and disadvantages.

Henri Pieper in 1899 developed the first petro-electric hybrid automobile in the world. In 1900, Ferdinand Porsche developed a series-hybrid using two motor-in-wheel-hub arrangements with a combustion generator set providing the electric power, setting two speed records (Fig. 1-29). While liquid fuel/electric hybrids date back to the late 19th century, the braking regenerative hybrid was invented by David Arthurs, an electrical engineer from Springdale, Arkansas in 1978 ~ 1979. His home-converted Opel GT was reported to return as much as 75MPG with plans still sold to this original design, and the "Mother Earth News" modified version on their website.

Fig. 1-29 Porsche 911 GT3 R-Hybrid
1-Power electronics; 2-Portal shaft with two electric motors; 3- High-voltage cable;
4- Electrical flywheel battery; 5- Power electronics

The plug-in-electric-vehicle (PEV) is becoming more and more common. It has the range needed in locations where there are wide gaps with no services. The batteries can be plugged in to house (mains) electricity for charging, as well being charged while the engine is running.

Continuously outboard recharged electric vehicle (COREV)

Given suitable infrastructure, permissions and vehicles, BEVs can be recharged while the user drives. The BEV establishes contact with an electrified rail and the plate or overhead wires on the highway via an attached conducting wheel or other similar mechanism. The BEV's batteries are recharged by this process—on the highway—and can then be used normally on other roads until the battery is discharged. Some of battery-electric locomotives used for maintenance trains on the London Underground are capable of this mode of operation. Power is picked up from the electrified rails where possible, switching to battery power where the electricity supply is disconnected.

This provides the advantage, in principle, of virtually unrestricted highway range as long as you stay where you have BEV infrastructure access. Since many destinations are within 100 km of a major highway, this may reduce the need for expensive battery systems. Unfortunately private use of the existing electrical system is nearly universally prohibited.

The technology for such electrical infrastructure is old and, outside of some cities, is not widely distributed. Updating the required electrical and infrastructure costs can be funded, in principle, by toll revenue, gasoline or other taxes.

Hybrid fuel (dual mode)

In addition to vehicles that use two or more different devices for propulsion, some also consider vehicles that use distinct energy sources or input types ("fuels") using the same engine to be hybrids, although to avoid confusion with hybrids as described above and to use correctly the terms, these are perhaps more correctly described as dual mode vehicles:

Some electric trolley buses can switch between an on board diesel engine and overhead electrical power depending on conditions. In principle, this could be combined with a battery subsystem to create a true plug-in hybrid trolleybus, although as of 2006, no such design seems to have been announced.

Flexible-fuel vehicles can use a mixture of input fuels mixed in one tank—typically gasoline and ethanol, or methanol, or biobutanol.

Bi-fuel vehicle: liquefied petroleum gas and natural gas are very different from gasoline or diesel and cannot be used in the same tanks, so it would be impossible to build an (LPG or NG) flexible fuel system. Instead vehicles are built with two, parallel, fuel systems feeding one engine. While the duplicated tanks cost space in some applications, the increased range and flexibility where (LPG or NG) infrastructure is incomplete may be a significant incentive to purchase.

Some vehicles have been modified to use another fuel source if it is available, such as cars modified to run on autogas (LPG) and diesels modified to run on waste vegetable oil that has not been processed into biodiesel.

Fluid power hybrid

Hydraulic and pneumatic hybrid vehicles use an engine to charge a pressure accumulator to drive the wheels via hydraulic or pneumatic (i.e. compressed air) drive units. In most cases the engine is detached from the drivetrain merely only tocharge the energy accumulator and the transmission is seamless.

Petro-air hybrid

A French company, MDI, has designed and has running models of a petro-air hybrid engine car. The system does not use air motors to drive the vehicle, being directly driven by a hybrid engine. The engine uses a mixture of compressed air and gasoline injected into the cylinders. A key aspect of the hybrid engine is the "active chamber", which is a compartment heating air via fuel doubling the energy output. Auto giant Tata Motors of India has assessed the design passing phase 1, the "proof of the technical concept" towards full production for the Indian market. Tata has moved onto phase 2, "completing detailed development of the compressed air engine into specific vehicle and stationary applications".

Petro-hydraulic hybrid

Petro-hydraulic configurations have been common in trains and heavy vehicles for decades. The auto industry recently focused on this hybrid configuration as it now shows promise for introduction into smaller vehicles.

In petro-hydraulic hybrids, the energy recovery rate is high and therefore the system is more efficient than battery charged hybrids using the current battery technology, demonstrating a 60% ~70% increase in energy economy in U.S. Environmental Protection Agency (EPA) testing. The charging engine needs only to be sized for average usage with acceleration bursts using the stored energy in the hydraulic accumulator, which is charged when in low energy demanding vehicle operation. The charging engine runs at optimum speed and load for efficiency and longevity. Under tests undertaken by the U.S. Environmental Protection Agency (EPA), a hydraulic hybrid Ford Expedition returned 32 miles per US gallon (7.4 L/100 km; 38 mpg-imp) city, and 22 miles per US gallon (11 L/100 km; 26 mpg-imp) highway. UPS currently has two trucks in service with this technology.

Although petro-hybrid technology has been known for decades, and used in trains and very large construction vehicles, heavy costs of the equipment precluded the systems from lighter trucks and cars. In the modern sense an experiment proved the viability of small petro-hybrid road vehicles in 1978. A group of students at Minneapolis, Minnesota's Hennepin Vocational Technical Center, converted a Volkswagen Beetle car to run as a petro-hydraulic hybrid using off-the shelf components. A car rated at 32mpg was returning 75mpg with the 60HP engine replaced by 16HP engine. The experimental car reached 70 mph.

In the 1990s, a team of engineers working at EPA's National Vehicle and Fuel Emissions Laboratory succeeded in developing a revolutionary type of petro-hydraulic hybrid powertrain that would propel a typical American sedan car. The test car achieved over 80 mpg on combined EPA city/highway driving cycles. Acceleration was 0 ~ 60 mph in 8 seconds, using a 1.9 liter diesel engine. No lightweight materials were used. The EPA estimated that produced in high volumes the hydraulic components would add only $700 to the base cost of the vehicle.

While the petro-hydraulic system has faster and more efficient charge/discharge cycling and is cheaper than petro-electric hybrids, the accumulator size dictates total energy storage capacity and may require more space than a battery set.

Research is underway in large corporations and small companies. Focus has now switched to smaller vehicles. The system components were expensive which precluded installation in smaller trucks and cars. A drawback was that the power driving motors were not efficient enough at part load. A British company has made a breakthrough by introducing an electronically controlled hydraulic motor/pump, the digital displacement motor/pump, that is highly efficient at all speed ranges and loads making small applications of petro-hydraulic hybrids feasible. The company converted a BMW car as a test bed to prove viability. The BMW 530i gave double the mpg in city driving compared to the standard car. This test was using the standard 3,000cc engine. Petro-hydraulic hybrids using well sized accumulators entail downsizing an engine to average power usage, not peak power usage. Peak power is provided by the energy stored in the accumulator. A smaller more efficient constant speed engine reduces weight and liberates space for a larger accumulator.

Current vehicle bodies are designed around the mechanicals of existing engine/transmission setups. It is restrictive and far from ideal to install petro-hydraulic mechanicals into existing bodies not designed for hydraulic setups. One research project's goal is to create a blank paper design new car, to maximize the packaging of petro-hydraulic hybrid components in the vehicle. One design has claimed to return 130mpg in tests by using a large hydraulic accumulator which is also the structural chassis of the car. The small hydraulic driving motors are incorporated within the wheel hubs driving the wheels and reversing to claw-back kinetic braking energy. The hub motors eliminates the need for friction brakes, mechanical transmissions, drive shafts and U joints, reducing costs and weight. Hydrostatic drive with no friction brakes are used in industrial vehicles. The aim is 170mpg in average driving conditions. Energy created by shock absorbers and kinetic braking energy that normally would be wasted assists in charging the accumulator. A small fossil fuelled piston engine sized for average power use charges the accumulator. The accumulator is sized at running the car for 15 minutes when fully charged. The aim is a fully charged accumulator with an energy storage potential of 670 HP, which will produce a 0 ~ 60 mph acceleration speed of less than 5 seconds using four wheel drive.

In January 2011 industry giant Chrysler announced a partnership with EPA to design and develop an experimental petro-hydraulic hybrid powertrain suitable for use in large passenger cars.

Unit 2 Chassis

Lesson 1
Drivetrain

In order to transmit the power of the engine to the road wheels of an automobile, a drivetrain is normally equipped. Although the details of the drivetrain vary widely in different types of automobiles, the general principle are the same in all cases.

1.1 Clutch

The clutch (Fig. 2-1) is a device to engage and disengage power from the engine, allowing the vehicle to stop and start.

The major parts of the clutch include the flywheel, clutch disc, cover assembly, pressure plate, release bearing, and clutch linkage. Other parts which make up the clutch assembly are the transmission input shaft and the clutch housing.

The pressure plate (or "driving member") is bolted to the engine flywheel and the clutch plate (or "driven member") is located between the flywheel and the pressure plate. The clutch plate is splined to the shaft extending from the transmission or "gear box" to the flywheel, commonly called a clutch shaft or input shaft.

When the clutch and the pressure plate are locked together by friction, the clutch shaft rotates with the engine crankshaft. Power is transferred from the engine to the transmission, where it is routed through different gear ratios to obtain the best speed and power to start and keep the automobile moving.

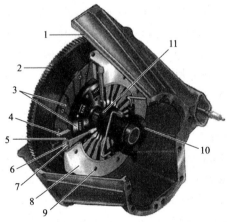

Fig. 2-1 Diaphragm Spring Clutch
1-Clutch housing; 2-Flywheel; 3-Cluch disk; 4-Pressure plate; 5-Wire support ring (in); 6-Diaphragm spring; 7-Wire support ring (out); 8-Clutch cover; 9-Clinch bolt; 10-Clutch working cylinder assembly; 11-Release sleeve and release bearing assembly

1.1.1 Flywheel

The flywheel provides a base for the starter ring gear, and also forms the foundation on which the other clutch parts are attached. The surface of the flywheel that mates with the clutchdisc is machined smoothly. For the clutch to work property, the flywheel must be perpendicular to the crankshaft with very little allowable runout.

1.1.2 Clutch Disc

The clutch disc (or driven disc) contains a circular metal plate attached to a reinforced splined hub. Normally the hub is mounted on coil springs to provide cushion engagements. The splined hub is free to slide lengthwise along the splined of the transmission input shaft. When engaged, the clutch disc drives the input shaft through these splines. The clutch disc operates in conjunction with a pressure plate or a clutch cover. In its operating position in the engine transmission linkup, the clutch disc is sandwiched between the machined face of the flywheel and the clutch pressure plate.

1.1.3 Cover Assembly

The clutch cover assembly contains the pressure plate, springs, and other parts according to the design of the clutch. The cover is bolted to the flywheel and rotates with it at the speed of the crankshaft.

The clutch cover assembly smooth on the side facing the engine and driven disc (or discs) and is itself driven by pins or lugs on the clutch cover. The plate is free to slide back and forth on the pinstripe or lugs, and when spring pressure is applied to the plate, it meshes with the driven friction plates sandwiched between it and the flywheel. If the clutch has two driven discs, an intermediate, or center plate will separate the discs. The plate is machined smooth on both sides since it is pressed between two friction surfaces.

Between the cover and the pressure plate are springs. Depending on the design of the clutch, any number of coil springs might be used to force the plate against the driven discs, or the clutch might utilize a single diaphragm spring.

1.1.4 Clutch Linkage

Engagement and disengagement of the clutch assembly are controlled by a foot pedal and linkage that must be properly adjusted and relatively easy to apply. The clutch linkage connects the clutch pedal to the clutch fork. The clutch fork and linkage provide the means of converting the up-and-down movement of the clutch pedal into the back-and-forth movement of the clutch release bearing assembly. The clutch release bearing, in most cases, is a ball bearing assembly with a machined face on one side that is designed to contact the pressure plate diaphragm release fingers during disengagement. Most clutches on heavy-duty automobiles are controlled by a mechanical linkage between the clutch pedal and the release bearing. Some automobiles have hydraulic clutch controls.

The transmission, pressure plate, flywheel, clutch disc, flywheel housing, and crankshaft must be properly aligned to prevent slippage, vibration, and noise.

1.1.5 Double Clutch

A double clutch is a driving procedure primarily used for automobile with an unsynchronized manual transmission. The double clutching technique involves the following steps:

(1) The throttle (accelerator) is released, and the clutch pedal is pressed, and the gearbox is shifted into neutral.

(2) The clutch pedal is then released, and the driver matches the engine RPM to the gear RPM either using the throttle (accelerator) (when changing down) or waiting for RPM to decrease (when changing up) until they are at a level suitable for shifting into the next gear.

(3) At the moment when the revs between the engine and gear are closely matches, the driver then instantly presses the clutch again to shift into the next gear. The whole maneuver can, with practice, take no more than a fraction of a second, and the result is a very smooth gear change.

The purpose of the double-clutch technique is to aid in matching the rotational speed of the input shaft being driven by engine to the rotational speed of the gear you wish to select (directly connected to rotating wheels). When the speedster is matched, the gear will engage smoothly and no clutch is required. If the speeds are not matched, the dog teeth on the collar will "crash" or grate as they attempt to fit into the holes on the desired gear. A modern synchromesh gearbox accomplishes this synchronization more efficiently. However, when the engine speed is significantly different from the transmission speed, the desired gear can often not be engaged even in a fully synchronized gearbox. An example is trying to shift into a gear near the top of 2nd, or intentionally from reverse to a forward gear while still moving at speed.

Double clutching, although time consuming, eases gear selection when an extended delay or variance exists between engine and transmission speeds.

1.2 Gearbox (transmission)

A higher torque is required to drive a heavily-loaded truck up a hill than required to drive an empty truck on a flatroad. The engine will provide the necessary torque within a limited speed rang. The provision of a gearbox (or transmission) allows for optimum utilization of the engine torque in driving the truck. In addition, the direction of the road wheels can be changed without the need for stopping the engine and restarting it in the reverse direction.

The gearbox contains a number of gearwheels. If gearwheels of different size rotate in mesh with each other, the shaft of the larger wheel will rotate more slowly than that of the smaller wheel. If the smaller wheel is the one driving the assembly, the speed will therefore be reduced at the larger wheel. As a result the torque at the larger wheel will be greater by a corresponding amount. A gearbox normally consists of an input shaft, a countershaft (layshaft) and an output shaft known as the main shaft. The engine torque is applied at the input shaft of the gearbox and is transmitted to the countershaft by means of a smaller gearwheel on the input shaft and a larger gearwheel on the countershaft. The torque at the countershaft will thus be higher than the engine torque. Several gearwheels of different sizes are mounted on the countershaft and these can be combined with corresponding gearwheels on the output shaft. By this means, different increase in the torque supplied by the engine can be selected. As an example, five stages can be selected in a five-speed gearbox. When the input and output shafts are coupled together, the torque of the engine will be transmitted through the gearbox without change. The required gear ratio is selected by means of the gear lever, which moves a sliding sleeve on the output shaft so that the appropriate gearwheels will mesh with the corresponding gearwheels on the countershaft.

To reverse the vehicle, the direction of rotation must be reversed and this is achieved by engaging an intermediate gearwheel located between the countershaft and the output shaft.

1.3 Propeller Shaft

The main task of the propeller shaft is to transmit power between two shafts at different positions and angles, for example the output shaft of the gearbox and the input shaft of the drive axle. There are propeller shafts installed between gearbox, transfer case and drive axles. The gearbox is fixed on the frame and the drive axle follows the deformation of the leaf spring to move up and down. In this case bothof the transmitting angle and the length of the propeller shaft are changing.

Universal joint (U-joint) is used to solve the problem of angle change. The left one in Fig. 2-2 is the most popular Cardan type (cross type) U-joint. The cross or spider consists of two shafts perpendicular to each other. One shaft connects to the driving fork and other connects to the driven fork. There are four needle bearings on the four ends of two shafts. This structure permits the axis of the driving fork to lie at an angle to the axis of the driven fork. During the process of the plane where the cross lies on is swinging fore and aft. In this case the instant angular velocity of the driving fork is not equal to that of the driven fork, and therefore this type of universal joint is called the U-joint of inconstant angular velocity.

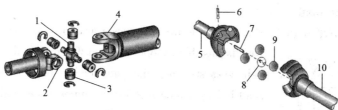

Fig. 2-2 Cardan Type U-joint and Weiss Type U-joint (constant angular velocity)
1-Cross;2,10-Driving fork;3-Needle bearing;4,5-Driven fork;6-Locking pin;7-Dowel pin;
8-Central steel ball;9-Power transmitting balls

To solve the problem of inconstancy two U-joints of cross type are used.

As the power transmits from the output shaft of the gearbox to the propeller shaft through the first U-joint, the instant angular velocity of the latter is not the same as the former. As the power transmits through the second U-joint, because of the principal of reverse symmetry the instant angular velocity of the input shaft of the drive axle is not equal to that of the propeller shaft but equal to that of the output shaft of the gearbox.

The right one in Fig. 2-2 is Weiss type U-joint. It is a type of constant velocity U-joint. In this joint the driving fork has the same shape as the driven fork, and power transmits through four steel balls. A central steel ball is provided to hold all the parts in position. No matter what angle is between the driving fork and the driven fork, the plane of four balls is in the half angle position. Therefore, the angular velocity of the driving fork is equal to that of the driven fork all the time.

For the FF cars, the drive shaft has to transmit power to the frontwheels at different steering angles. Having better performance than Weiss type U-joint, Rzeppa type (ball and cage type) U-joint is widely used in most of the FF cars. The structure has six steel balls and a retainer (cage) between the driving part (inner race) and the outer part (housing with outer race). Two Rzeppa joints are for one drive shaft and totally four for a FF car.

A spline structure is used in the propeller shaft to solve the problem of length change. The spline structure is the coupling of two parts, the spline shaft and spline sleeve. They are somewhat like the coupling of an inner gear with long teeth and an outer gear with long teeth. As power transmits through a spline structure, the spline shaft and spline sleeve can slide from each other to change the length of the propeller shaft.

1.4 Drive Axle

A drive axle includes final drive, differential, axle shafts and axle housing.

1.4.1 Final Drive

The engine speed is too high and the engine torque is too small to connect the roadwheels directly. There must be a set of gears called final drive to reduce the engine speed and increase the engine torque. The power transmitting direction from the gearbox to the drive axle is longitudinal, but after the final drive the transmitting direction becomes lateral. A pair of bevel gears is used to change the transmitting direction. For the lateral arranged engine, the final drive is equipped with a pair of spur gears and it is not necessary to change the transmitting direction.

1.4.2 Differential

The task of a differential (Fig. 2-3) is to transmit power and to make the left and right road wheels possible to operate at different speeds. When the motor vehicle is steering, the path for the outer wheel on the curved road is longer than that for the inner wheel and the speed of the outer wheel is greater than the inner wheel.

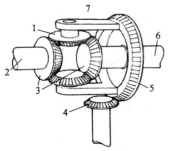

Fig. 2-3 Bevel Gear Differential
1-Planetary gear; 2-Output shaft; 3-Sun gear; 4- Gear; 5- Differential side gear; 6-Output shaft; 7-Cage

A planetary gear system is widely used in most of the differentials and it includes left side gear, planetary pinions, pinion shaft, differential housing and right side gear. Power goes from the final drive pinion to the drive ring gear. The differential housing is mounted on the ring gear and therefore turns together with it. Then the power transmits to the pinion shaft, the planetary pinions and to the left and right side gears. When the motor vehicle is going along a straight road, the planetary pinions turn together with the differential housing (orbit motion) and do not rotate on the planetary shaft (rotary motion), thus the speed of the left side gear is equal to the speed of the right side gear. When the motor vehicle is going along a curved road, the planetary pinions not only do orbit motion, but also rotary motion, thus make the left side gear and the right side gear possible to turn at different speed.

The main feature of a common planetary differential is equal distribution of the torque to left and right road wheels at any time. For example, if the torque transmitted to the final drive ring gear is 100 N · m. If one wheel is on slippery surface (for example icy road), traction force on this side is limited by rather small adhesive force. In this case, traction force onthe other side is also as small as this side and the motor vehicle may not develop enough traction to overcome all the resistances. Therefore, a phenomenon can be seen quite often that one wheel on slippery surface may spin quite fast and the other wheel even on good road surface is too weak as the former to drive the motor vehicle.

In order to overcome such shortcoming of the common planetary differential, a special structure of anti-skid differential (ASD) is used to lock one axle shaft with the differential housing together or to increase friction between the left and the right parts, that is, to change the situation of equal distribution of torque for the common planetary differential.

1.4.3 Axle Shaft

The task of an axle shaft is to transmit the power from the differential to the roadwheels. The inner end connects with the differential side gear by spline and the outer end connects with the wheel hub. As mentioned above the axle shaft for a FF car is also called the drive shaft and is provided with U-joints.

1.4.4 Axle Housing

The task of the axle housing is to hold the parts (final drive, differential, axle shaft etc) in correct positions. Besides, an integrated axle housing (equipped with dependent suspension) is able to support the weight of the motor vehicle.

Technical Words and Terms

1. drivetrain		*n.* 动力传动系
2. clutch		*n.* 离合器,控制;*vi.* 攫,企图抓住;*vt.* 抓住
3. engage		*vi.* 从事,啮合;*vt.* 吸引,占据;预定
4. pressure plate		压盘
5. driving member		主动件
driven member		从动件
6. spline		*n.* 花键,齿条;*vt.* 开键槽;用花键连接
7. perpendicular		*adj.* 垂直的,正交的;*n.* 垂线,垂直位置
8. runout		*n.* 径向振摆,偏转
9. cushion		*n.* 垫子;*vt.* 给……安上垫子
10. lengthwise		*adv.* 纵向地;*adj.* 纵向的
11. in conjunction with		连同,共同,与……协力;
12. sandwich		*vt.* 夹入,挤进;*n.* 三明治
13. intermediate		*adj.* 中间的;*vi.* 起媒介作用
14. linkage		*n.* 联动装置,连接,接合
15. align		*vi.* 排列,排成一行,定位;*vt.* 使结盟
16. synchronize		*vt.* (使)同步,(使)同时发生,(使)同速
17. maneuver		*n.* 调动,演习;*vt.* 演习,调遣
18. friction		*n.* 摩擦,摩擦力
19. grate		*vi.* 发出摩擦声;*vt.* 摩擦
20. propeller shaft		传动轴
21. universal joint		万向节
22. inconstant angular velocity		等角速度;
23. symmetry		*n.* 对称(性),匀称
24. weiss type U-joint		球叉式万向节
25. drive axle		驱动桥,传动轴
26. final drive		主减速器
27. differential		*adj.* 微分的,差别的;*n.* 微分,差别,差速器
28. axle shaft		半轴

29. bevel gear	锥齿轮	
30. spur gear	圆柱齿轮	
31. planetary	*adj.* 行星的	
32. pinion	*n.* 小齿轮；翅膀，鸟翼；*vt.* 绑住，束缚	
33. axle housing	桥壳	

Notes

1. The clutch disc operates in conjunction with a pressure plate or a clutch cover.

离合器盘连同离合器压盘或离合器外壳一起工作。

2. Engagement and disengagement of the clutch assembly are controlled by a foot pedal and linkage that must be property adjusted and relatively easy to apply.

离合器总成的接合与分离由驾驶员通过脚踏板及联动装置控制，脚踏板及联动装置必须进行适当的调整，以便于驾驶员控制。

3. To reverse the vehicle, the direction of rotation…located between the countershaft and the output shaft.

要使汽车向后行驶，则发动机输出轴必须反向转动，可以通过啮合位于中间轴和输出轴之间的惰性齿轮来实现。

4. The main feature of a common planetary differential is equal distribution of the torque to left and right road wheels at any time.

普通行星差速器的主要特点是在任何时候都将发动机转矩平均分配到左右车轮上。

Exercises

Questions for discussion

1. What's the function of the clutch?
2. Please name the major parts that make up the clutch.
3. What role does the flywheel play in the clutch?
4. What's the function of the pressure plate?
5. What are the engagement and disengagement of the clutch assembly controlled by?
6. What's the function of the final drive and the differential?

Fill in the blank according to the text

1. When the clutch and pressure plate are locked together by _____, the clutch shaft rotates with the _____.

2. The _____ and _____ provide the means of converting the _____ movement of the clutch pedal into the _____ movement of the clutch release bearing assembly.

3. The purpose of the double-clutch technique is to aid in matching the rotational speed of _____ being driven by engine to the rotational speed of _____ you wish to select (directly connected to rotating wheels).

4. _____ is used to solve the problem of angle change.

5. There must be a set of gears called _____ to reduce the _____ and increase the _____.

Lesson 2
Automatic Transmission

The modern automatic transmission (Fig. 2-4) is by far, the most complicated mechanical component in today's automobile. Automatic transmission contains mechanical systems, hydraulic systems, electrical systems and computer controls, all working together in perfect harmony which goes virtually unnoticed until there is a problem. This article will help you understand the concepts behind what goes on inside these technological marvels and what goes into repairing them when they fail.

The transmission is a device that is connected to the back of the engine and sends the power from the engine to the drive wheels. An automobile engine runs at its best at a certain RPM (Revolution per Minute) range and it is the transmission's job to make sure that the power is delivered to the wheels while keeping the engine within that range.

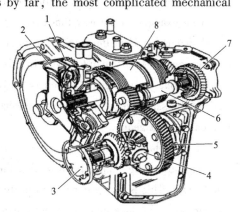

Fig. 2-4 Automatic Transmission of Bora
1- Torque converter; 2- One-way clutch; 3- Flange plate; 4- Differential; 5- Final drive; 6- Idler shaft; 7- Idle gear; 8- Planetary gear sets

It does this through various gear combinations. In first gear, the engine turns much faster in relation to the drive wheels, while in high gear the engine is loafing even though the car may be going in excess of 70 MPH(Mile per Hour). In addition to various forward gears, a transmission also has a neutral position which disconnects the engine from the drive wheel, and reverse, which causes the drive wheels to turn in the opposite direction allowing you to back up. Finally, there is the park position. In this position, a latch mechanism is inserted into a slot in the output shaft to lock the drive wheels and keep them from turning, thereby preventing the vehicle from rolling.

2.1 Transmission Components

The modern automatic transmission consists of many components and systems that are designed to work together in a symphony of clever mechanical, hydraulic and electrical technology that has evolved over the years into what many mechanically inclined individuals consider to be an art form. We try to use simple and generic explanations where possible to describe these systems, but due to the complexity of some of these components, you may have to use some mental gymnastics to visualize their operation.

The main components that make up an automatic transmission include:

2.1.1 Planetary Gear Sets

Automatic transmission contains many gears in various combinations. In a manual transmission, gears slide along shafts as you move the shift lever from one position to another, engaging various sized gears as required in order to provide the correct gear ratio. In an automatic transmission, however, the gears are never physically moved and are always engaged to the same gears. This is accomplished through the use of planetary gear sets.

The basic planetary gear set consists of a sun gear, a ring gear and two or more planet gears, all remaining in constant mesh. The planet gears are connected to each other through a common carrier which allows the gears to spin on shafts called "pinions" which are attached to the carrier.

One example of the way that this system can be used is by connecting the ring gear to the input shaft coming from the engine, connecting the planet carrier to the output shaft, and locking the sun gear so that it can't move. In this scenario, when we turn the ring gear, the planets will "walk" along the sun gear (which is held stationary) causing the planet carrier to turn the output shaft in the same direction as the input shaft but at a slower speed causing gear reduction (similar to a car in first gear).

If we unlock the sun gear and lock any two elements together, this will cause all three elements to turn at the same speed so that the output shaft will turn at the same rate of speed as the input shaft. This is like a car that is in third or high gear. Another way that we can use a planetary gear set is by locking the planet carrier from moving, then applying power to the ring gear which will cause the sun gear to turn in the opposite direction giving use reverse gear. Many more combinations are possible using two or more planetary sets connected in various waysides to provide the different forward speedster and reverse that are found in modern automatic transmissions.

Some of the clever gear arrangements found in four and now, five-speed automatics are complex enough to make a technically astute lay person's head spin trying to understand the flow of power through the transmission as it shifts from first gear through top gear as the vehicle accelerates to highway speed. In newer vehicles, the vehicle's computer monitors and controls these shifts so that they are almost imperceptible.

2.1.2 Clutch Packs

A clutch pack consists of alternating disks that fit inside a clutch drum. Half of the disks are steel and have splines that fit into grooves on the inside of the drum. The other half have a friction material bonded to their surface and have splines on the inside edge that fit grooves on the outer surface of the adjoining hub. There is a piston inside the drum that is activated by oil pressure at the appropriate time to squeeze the clutch pack together so that the two components become locked and turn as one.

2.1.3 One-way Clutch

A one-way clutch is a device that will allow a component such as ring gear to turn freely in one direction but not in the other. This effect is just that of a bicycle, where the pedals will turn the wheel when pedaling forward, but will spin free when pedaling backward.

A common place where a one-way clutch is used is in first gear when the shifter is in the drive positing. When you begin to accelerate from a stop, the transmission starts out in first gear. But have you ever noticed what happens if you release the gas while it is still in first gear? The vehicle continues to coast as if you were in neutral. Now, shift into Low gear instead of Drive. When you let the gas in this case go of, you will feel the engine slow you down just like a standard shift car. The reason for this is that in Drive, a one-way clutch is used whereas in low, a clutch pack or a band is used.

2.1.4 Bands

A band is a steel strap with friction material bonded to the inside surface. One end of the band is anchored against the transmission case while the other end is connected to a servo. At the appropriate time hydraulic oil is sent to the servo under pressure to tighten the band around the drum to stop other from turning.

2.1.5 Torque Converter

On automatic transmission, the torque converter takes the place of the clutch found on standard shift vehicles. It is that to allow the engine to continue running when the vehicle comes to a stop. The principal of a torque converter is like taking a fan that is plugged into the wall and blowing air into another fan which is unplugged. If you grab the blade on the unplugged fan, you are able to hold it from turning but as soon as you let go, it will begin to speed up until it comes close to the speed of the powered fan. The difference with a torque converter is that instead of using air, it uses oil or transmission fluid to be more precise.

A torque converter is a large doughnut shaped device that is mounted between the engine and the transmission. It consists of three elements of the torque converter that work together to transmit power to the transmission. The three elements of the torque converter are the Pump, the Turbine, and the Stator. The pump is mounted directly to the converter housing which in turn is bolted directly to the engine's crankshaft and turns at engine speed. The turbine is inside the housing and is connected directly to the input shaft of the transmission providing power to move the vehicle. The stator is mounted to a one-way clutch so that it can spin freely in one direction but not in the other. Each of the three elements fins has mounted in them to precisely direct the flow of oil through the converter.

With the engine running, transmission fluid is pulled into the pump section which starts it turning, the fluid continues in a circular motion back towards the center of the turbine where it centers the stator. If the turbine is moving considerably slower than the pump, the fluid will make contact with the front of the stator fins which push the stator into the one way clutch and prevent it from tuning. With the stator stopped, the fluid is directed by the stator fins to re-enter the pump at a 'helping' angle providing a torque increase. As the speed of the turbine catches up with the pump, the fluid starts hitting the stator blades on the backside causing the stator to turn in the same direction as the pump and turbine. As the speed increase, all three elements begin to turn at approximately the same speed.

In order to improve fuel economy, torque converters have been equipped with a lockup clutch, which locksmith the turbine to the pump as the vehicle speed reaches approximately 45 ~ 50MPH. This lockup is controlled by computer and usually won't engage unless the transmission is in 3rd or 4th gear.

2.1.6 Hydraulic System

The hydraulic system is a complex maze of passages and tubes that sends transmission fluid under pressure to all parts of the transmission and torque converter. Transmission fluid serves a number of purposes including: shift control, general lubrication and transmission cooling. Unlike the engine, which uses oil primarily for lubrication, every aspect of a transmission's functions is dependent on a constant supply of fluid under pressure. This is like the human circulatory system where even a few minutes of operation when there is a lack of pressure can be harmful or even fatal to the life of the transmission. In order to keep the transmission at normal operation temperature, a portion of the fluid is sent through one of two steel tubes to a special chamber that is submerged in anti-freeze in the radiator. Fluid passing through this chamber is cooled and then returned to the transmission through the other steel tube. A typical transmission has an average of ten quarts of fluid between the transmission, torque converter, and cooler tank. In fact, most of the components of a transmission are constantly submerged in fluid including the clutch packs and bands. The friction surfaces on these parts are designed to operate properly only when they are submerged in oil.

2.1.7 Oil Pump

The transmission oil pump (not to be confused with the pump element inside the torque converter) is responsible for producing all the oil that is required in the transmission. The oil pump is mounted to the front of the transmission case and is directly connected to a flange on the torque converter housing. Since the torque converter housing is directly connected to the engine crankshaft, the pump will produce pressure whenever the engine is running as long as there is sufficient amount of transmission fluid available. The oil enters the pump through a filter that is located at the bottom of the transmission oil pan and travels up a pickup tube directly to the oil pump. The oil is then sent, under pressure to the pressure regulator, the valve body and the rest of the components, as required.

2.1.8 Valve Body

The valve body is the brain of the automatic transmission. It contains a maze of channels and passages that direct hydraulic fluid to the numerous valves which then activate the appropriate clutch pack of band servo to smoothly shift to the appropriate gear for each driving situation. Each of the many valves in the valve body has a specific purpose and is named for that function. For example the;2-3 shift valve activates the 2nd gear to 3rd gear up-shift of the;3-2 shift timing valve which determines when a down-shift or up-shift should occur. The most important valve, and one that you have direct control over is the manual valve. The manual valve is directly connected to the gear shift handle and covers (or uncovers) various passages depending on what position the gear shift is placed in. When you place the gear shift in Drive, for instance, the manual valve directs fluid to the clutch pack that activates 1st gear. It also sets up to monitor vehicle speed and throttle position that it can determine the optimal time and the force for the 1-2 shift. On computer controlled transmissions, you will also have electrical solenoids that are mounted in the valve body to direct fluid to the appropriate clutch packs or bands under computer control to more precisely control shift points.

2.1.9 Computer Controls(Fig. 2-5)

The computer uses sensors on the engine and transmission to detect such things as throttle position, vehicle speed, engine speed, engine load, stop light switch position, etc. to control exact shift points as well as how soft or firm the shift should be. Some computerized transmissions even learn your driving style and constantly adapt to it so that every shift is timed precisely when you would need it.

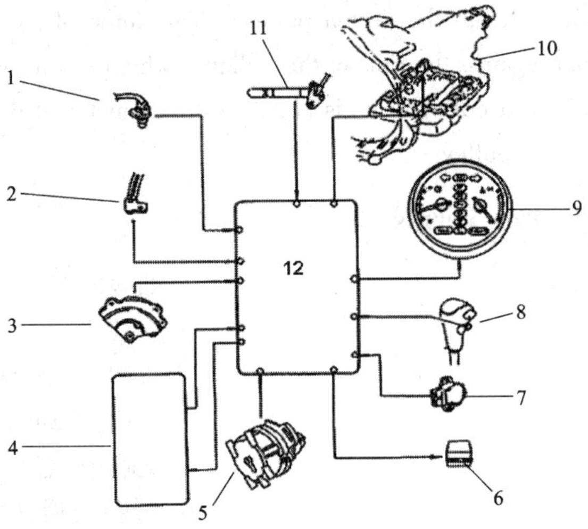

Fig. 2-5 Automatic Transmission Electric Control System

1-Vehicle speed sensor; 2-The hydraulic oil temperature sensor; 3-Gear select sensor; 4-Engine electronic control sensor (EE-CU); 5-Engine speed sensor; 6-Fault detection socket; 7-Throttle position sensor; 8-Mode switch; 9-Gear indicator; 10-Solenoid valve; 11-Input shaft speed sensor; 12-Electronic control unit (ECU)

Because of computer controls, coming out with the ability to take manual control of the transmission as though it were a stick shift, allowing the driver to select gears manually. This is accomplished on some cars by passing the shift lever through a special gate, then tapping it in one direction or the other in order to up-shift or down-shift at will. The computer monitors this activity to make sure that the driver does not select gear that could over speed the engine and damage it.

Another advantage of these "smart" transmissions is that they have a self diagnostic mode which can detect a problem early and warn you with an indicator light on the dash. A technician can then plug test equipment in and retrieve a list of trouble codes that will help pinpoint where the problem is.

2.2 Continuously Variable Transmission (CVT)

The continuously variable transmission (CVT) is a type of automatic transmission that can change the gear ratio (gears are not generally involved) to any arbitrary setting within the limits. The CVT can respond instantly to throttle pressure, giving smooth and rapid acceleration. Its advantage over conventional fixed-ratio transmission lies in the potential for enhancing performance and fuel economy while reducing exhaust emissions. The continuously variable transmission can operate mechanically (belt or friction-roller), hydraulic or electrically. Here, we give a brief introduction to the continuously variable mechanical transmission.

The major elements in the continuously variable mechanical transmission for passenger cars are: engagement mechanism for starting off, primary and secondary disks with axially adjustable taper-disk sections and power transfer via steel bands, electronic / hydraulic transmission control, reversing mode, and final drive unit with differential.

Instead of using gears, rotary motion can be transmitted from one shaft pulley to another by an endless flexible metal belt. It is the force of friction that compels the driving pulley to drive the belt and likewise the belt to rotate the driven pulleys. This force of friction is derived from the contact pressure of the belt against the rims of the pulleys, which in turn is imposed by initial belt tension. The velocity ratio of a pulley drive is equal to the diameter of the driving pulley divided by the diameter of the driven pulley.

Technical Words and Terms

1. automatic transmission 自动变速器
2. hydraulic system 液压系统
3. harmony *n.* 协调,和谐,融洽
4. latch *n.* 挂钩,止动销; *vi.* 占有,抓住
5. symphony *n.* 交响乐,谐声,和声
6. evolve *vt.* (使)发展,(使)进化
7. incline *vt.* 使倾向于,使倾斜; *n.* 倾斜,斜面
8. gear set 齿轮组
9. sun gear 太阳轮
10. ring gear 齿圈
11. planet gear 行星齿轮
12. spin *vi.* 旋转; *vt.* 使旋转; *n.* 旋转,疾驰
13. scenario *n.* 方案,情况,场景
14. astute *adj.* 机敏的,狡猾的,诡计多端的
15. imperceptible *adj.* 感觉不到的,极细微的
16. pack *n.* 包装,组合件; *vt.* 包装,压紧
17. groove *n.* 凹槽,槽; *vt.* 开槽于
18. bond *n.* 结合,债券; *vt.* 使接合
19. adjoining *adj.* 邻接的,相邻的; *v.* 邻接
20. squeeze *vi.* 压榨; *vt.* 挤,握紧挤榨; *n.* 压榨
21. band *n.* 带,乐队,松紧带镶边
22. anchor *vi.* 抛锚; *vt.* 抛锚,使固定; *n.* 锚
23. servo *n.* 伺服,伺服机构
24. tighten *vt.* 变紧,使变紧; *vi.* 绷紧,拉紧
25. plug *vt.* 插入,塞住; *n.* 插头,塞子
26. unplug *vt.* 拔去(塞子,插头等)
27. torque converter 变矩器
28. doughnut 油炸圈饼,圆环图,【美俚】汽车轮胎
29. turbine *n.* 涡轮(机)
30. stator *n.* 固定片,定子
31. fin *n.* 鳍,翅片
32. maze *n.* 迷宫,迷惑; *vt.* 迷失,使混乱
33. passage *n.* 通路,走廊,一段(文章)

34. circulatory		*adj.* 循环的
35. submerge		*vi.* 淹没,潜入水中;*vt.* 淹没,沉浸
36. quart		*n.* 夸脱(容量单位)
37. up-shift		换入高挡
38. down-shift		换入低挡
39. diagnostic		*adj.* 诊断的,特征的;*n.* 诊断法
40. pinpoint		*vt.* 查明,确认;*adj.* 详尽的,精确的;*n.* 针尖,精确位置
41. gear ratio		速比
42. continuously variable mechanical transmission		机械式无级变速器
43. multi-plate clutch		多盘离合器
44. throttle		*n.* 节气阀,风门 *vt.* 压制,使……节流;*vi.* 节流
45. final drive unit		最终传动装置,主(轮边)减速器
46. metal belt		金属带
47. velocity ratio		传动比

Notes

1. The modern automatic transmission consists of…consider to be an art form.

自动变速器包括许多部件和机构,它们在一个智能化的机-电-液系统中协调工作,经过许多年的发展,以至于现在许多热衷于机械的人认为该系统已经发展成为一件艺术品。

2. One example of the way that this system can be…and locking the sun gear so that it can't move.

该系统工作的一种方式就是使齿圈与变速器输入轴接合,行星齿轮支架与输出轴接合,同时锁止太阳齿轮使之不能转动。

3. The other half have a friction material bonded to their surface and have splines on the inside edge that fit groves on the outer surface of the adjoining hub.

另外一半的表面上附着一层摩擦材料,并在内边缘用花键与相邻轴套外表面上的键槽相连接。

4. The difference with a torque converter is that instead of using air, it uses oil or transmission fluid to be more precise.

变矩器的不同在于,它不是采用空气而是采用机油或变速器油使之控制得更为精确。

5. As the speed of the turbine catches up with the pump, the fluid starts hitting the stator blades on the backside causing the stator to turn in the same direction as the pump and turbine.

涡轮的转速追赶泵轮的过程中,油液开始冲击导轮叶片的后端,使得导轮与泵轮和涡轮按相同的方向转动。

6. This is like the human circulatory system where even a few minutes of operation when there is a lack of pressure can be harmful or even fatal to the life of the transmission.

就像人体的循环系统那样,在运转中即使只是几分钟的压力不足也可能是有害的,甚至会对变速器寿命造成致命的影响。

7. Since the torque converter housing is directly connected to the engine crankshaft, the pump will produce pressure whenever the engine is running as long as there is sufficient amount of transmission fluid available.

由于变矩器壳直接与发动机曲轴相连接,只要发动机运转并有充足的变速器油,油泵就会产生压力。

8. The oil is then sent, under pressure to the pressure regulator, the valve body and the rest of the components, as required.

油液将在压力的作用下按照其各自的需要输送到压力调节器、阀体和其余部件。

9. It contains a maze of channels and passages that direct hydraulic fluid to the numerous valves which then activate the appropriate clutch pack of band servo to smoothly shift to the appropriate gear for each driving situation.

自动变速器就像一个由通道和通路构成的迷宫,这些通道可以把油液输送到多个阀门处,以此触发相应的制动带伺服机构的离合器组件,以便在各种运行工况下实现挡位的平稳转换。

Exercises

Questions for discussion

1. What are the main components of the automatic transmission?
2. What are the three elements of a planetary gear set?
3. Please describe the principal of the torque converter.
4. Please describe the function of the transmission fluid.
5. What are the major elements in the continuously variable mechanical transmission?

Fill in the blank according to the text

1. Automatic transmission contain _____, _____, electrical systems and _____, all working together in perfect harmony which goes virtually unnoticed until there is a problem.
2. A band is a _____ with _____ bonded to the inside surface.
3. In order to improve fuel economy, torque converters have been equipped with a _____, which locksmith the _____ to the pump.
4. The CVT can respond instantly to _____ pressure, giving smooth and rapid acceleration.
5. Instead of using gears, rotary motion can be transmitted from one _____ to another by an endless flexible _____.

Lesson 3
Steering System

3.1 Steering System

The function of the steering system is guiding the vehicle where the driver wants it to go. The steering system must deliver precise directional control. In a manual steering system, the driver's effort to turn the steering wheel is the primary force that causes the front wheels to swivel to the left or right on the steering knuckles. In a power steering system, power-assisted units are added so that the driver's effort is reduced.

Fig. 2-6 shows the structural components of a typical steering system equipped with a steering gear of re-circulating ball type. For this type there are some balls between the threads of the screw and the nut, there are some balls re-circulating from the end to the front of the threads through a guide tube. As the driver turns the steering wheel (for example left turn), this action is transmitted through the steering shaft, U-joints and steering drive shaft to the steering screw. As the steering screw turns, the steering nut slides along its axis. Some teeth are at the bottom of the steering nut and mesh with the teeth on the sector shaft. A pitman arm connects to the outer end of the sector shaft and transmits the action to the drag link and then to the knuckle arm. The action of the knuckle arm turns the steering knuckle around the king pin mounted on the axle beam. Motion of the left steering knuckle transmits to the right steering knuckle through the left steering arm, the tie rod and the right steering arm. The left and right road wheels are installed on the left and right knuckles respectively and turn together with them.

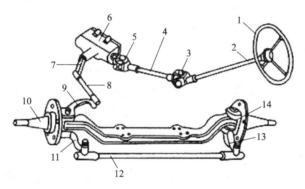

Fig. 2-6 Manual Steering System

1-Steering wheel; 2-Steering shaft; 3,5-U-Joints; 4-Steering drive shaft; 6-Steering gear; 7-Pitman arm; 8-Drag link; 9-Knuckle arm; 10-Left steering knuckle; 11-Left steering arm; 12-Tie rod; 13-Right steering arm; 14-Right steering knuckle

When the motor vehicle is steering, the inner wheel on the curved road turns greater than the outer wheel. If the inner steering knuckle is linked to the outer steering knuckle by a parallelogram linkage, they will turn at the same angle. Obviously, a parallelogram does not meet the requirement of the angular difference between the inner knuckle and the outer knuckle. Therefore the linkage must be a trapezoid, that is, the length of the tie rod is shorter than the distance between the left and right king pins.

Most of the modern cars use a steering gear of rack and pinion type. This type of steering gear is advantageous by its simple structure, light weight and good road sensation. Because independent suspension is quite common in modern cars, the tie rods should be divided into two parts. The length of the tie rods is equal to the length of the control arms and the tie rod is parallel to the control arm on each side. When the motor vehicle is steering, the steering wheel makes the pinion rotate. The rotation of the pinion drives the rack and the tie rods and to move laterally, and then turns the left and right steering arms and the knuckles.

3.2 Power Steering System

Power steering system (or power assisted system) is widely used in modern cars, heavy trucks and other typeset of motor vehicles. A power hydraulic pump driven by the engine is used to force high pressure oil to a power assisted cylinder through a control valve. The operation of the control valve and the flow of the power oil should keep pace with steering angle and steering force of the steering wheel.

In the power-assisted rack and pinion steering gear, hydraulic fluid pressure from the power steering pump is used to reduce steering effort. A rack piston is integral with the rack and located in a sealed chamber in the steering gear housing. Hydraulic fluid lines are connected to each end of the chamber, and rack seals are positioned in the housing at the ends of the chamber. A seal is also located on the rack piston.

When a right turn is made, fluid is pumped into the right side of the fluid chamber, and fluid flows out of the left end of the chamber. Thus hydraulic pressure is exerted on the right side of the rack piston which assists the pinion gear in moving the rack to the left.

When a left turn is completed, fluid is pumped into the left side of the fluid chamber and exhausted from the right chamber area. This hydraulic pressure on the left side of the rack piston helps the pinion to move the rack to the right.

Since the steering gear is mounted behind the front wheels, rack movement to the left is necessary for a right turn, while rack movement to the right causes a left turn.

Fluid direction is controlled by a rotary valve attached to the pinion assembly. A rotary valve body contains an inner spool valve that is mounted over the torsion bar on the pinion assembly.

When the front wheels are in the straight-ahead position, fluid flows from the pump through the high-pressure hose to the center rotary valve body passage. Fluid is then routed through the valve body to the low-pressure return hose and the pump reservoir.

In the recirculating-ball power steering gear, the ball nut and pitman shaft sector are similar in both manual and power recirculating-ball steering gears. In the power steering gear, a torsion bar is connected between the steering shaft and the worm shaft. Since the front wheels resting on the road surface resist turning, the parts attached to the worm shaft also resist turning. This turning resistance causes torsion bar deflection when the wheels are turned. The extent of deflection is limited to a predetermined amount.

When the car is driven with the front wheels straight-ahead, oil flows from the power steering pump through the spool valve and the rotary valve body.

When the driver makes a left turn, deflection of the torsion bar moves the valve spool inside the rotary valve body so that oil flow is directed through the rotary valve to the upper side of the recirculating-ball piston. This hydraulic pressure on the piston assists the driver in turning the wheels to the left.

During a right turn, hydraulic pressure applied to the lower end of the recirculating-ball piston helps the driver to turn the wheels.

When a turn is being made and a front wheel strikes a bump which drives the wheel in the direction opposite to the turning direction, the recirculating-ball piston tends to move against the hydraulic pressure and force oil back out the pressure inlet port. This action would tend to create "kickback" on the steering wheel, but a poppet valve in the pressure inlet fitting closes and prevents kickback.

In the straight-ahead steering gear position, oil pressure is equal on both sides of the recirculating-ball piston. The oil acts as a cushion which prevents road shocks from reaching the steering wheel.

Many recirculating-ball power steering gears have a variable ratio which provides faster steering with fewer steering wheel turns.

3.3 Wheel Alignment

Wheel alignment is to position the wheels so that they roll reasonably on the road surface without scuffing and slipping under all operation conditions. Wheel alignment is essential to handling stability, safety, fuel economy and tire life.

In a modern motor vehicle the wheels are not really perpendicular to the road surfaces but at proper angles. Five angles or parameters are needed for correct wheel alignment: caster, camber, steering axis inclination, toe and tracking. These parameters of wheel alignment can be checked on a test rig called four-wheel aligner.

Caster is the forward or rearward tilt angle γ of the steering axis or kingpin axis on the side view of the motor vehicle. As shown in Fig. 2-7, suppose the wheel deviates to the right by interference, the reaction force y of the ground to the wheel is opposite the centrifugal force. Because of the angle γ, the force y has an arm l to the steering axis. The force y and the arm l form a return moment to correct the deviation of the wheel.

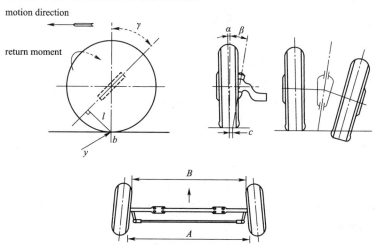

Fig. 2-7 Wheel Alignment

Camber is the inward or outward tilt angle α of the wheel on the front view of the motor vehicle. The reasons for camber are: to let the wheel perpendicular to the road crown and to load the inner bearing of the wheel on the knuckle spindle.

Steering axis inclination is the inward tilt angle β of the steeling axis on the front view of the motor vehicle. Steering axis inclination can reduce the arm c on the ground thus reduce the resistant moment and make the steering easier. Suppose the wheel turns 180 degrees. It seems that the wheel presses into the road. Actually the road is too hard to press down, in other words, the turning of the wheel lifts the motor vehicle up to a higher position. In this case, the gravity of the motor vehicle would force the motor vehicle to return down to the original lower position. Therefore, steeling axis inclination aids directional stability by forcing the wheel in return to the original straight ahead position.

Toe is the difference between the distance B measured from the front of the left wheel to the front of the right wheel and the distance A measured from the rear of the left wheel to the rear of the right wheel. Toe-in means that B is shorter than A; and toe-out means that B is longer than A. For a rear wheel drive motor vehicle, resistant force tend to make the front wheels toe-out, therefore the toe setting should be toe-in ($B < A$); whereas for a front wheel drive motor vehicle, traction forces tend to make the front wheels toe-in, therefore the toe setting should be toe-out ($B > A$). Incorrect toe is much concerned with bent or damaged steering parts.

Tracking means the rear wheels should run along the tracks of the front wheels. A new motor vehicle does not have tracking problem. Because of collision or damage of the parts of the frame, body, axle housing, suspension or wheel, inharmonious motion of the wheels may happen and lead to poor handling, excess fuel consumption and tire wear.

Technical Words and Terms

1. re-circulating ball type   循环球式
2. thread   *n.* 螺纹,线; *vt.* 穿过; *vi.* 通过,穿透过
3. steering screw   转向螺杆
4. steering nut   转向螺母
5. sector shaft   齿扇轴
6. pitman arm   摇臂
7. drag link   直拉杆
8. knuckle   *n.* 关节; *vi.* 开始认真工作
9. king pin   主销
10. axle beam   前桥梁
11. tie rod   横拉杆
12. parallelogram   *n.* 平行四边形
13. trapezoid   *n.* 梯形,不规则四边形; *adj.* 四边形的
14. rack and pinion type   齿轮齿条式
15. integral   *adj.* 整体的,完整的; *n.* 部分,积分,完整
16. incorporate   *vt.* 把……合并,列入,包含; *vi.* 合并,混合
17. deflection   *n.* 偏转,变形,变位,弯曲
18. kickback   *n.* 转向盘反冲,急速回摆,逆转,回跳
19. wheel alignment   车轮定位
20. scuffing   *n.* 变形,刮痕,擦伤; *v.* 使磨损

21. slipping	*n.* 滑动;*adj.* 逐渐松弛的;*v.* 滑动	
22. caster	*n.* 转向轴线后倾,后倾角	
23. camber	*n.* 车轮外倾,弧形;*vt.* 外倾角,使拱起	
24. steering axis inclination	转向轴线内倾	
25. toe	*n.* 前束	
26. tracking	*n.* 随辙,追踪;*v.* 跟踪	
27. return moment	回正力矩	
28. road crown	道路(横断面)的鼓形;	
29. toe-in	正前束	
30. toe-out	后束	

Notes

1. The power steering system adds a hydraulic pump, a fluid reservoir, hoses, lines, and a power assist unit either mounted on, or integral with a steering wheel gear assembly.

动力转向系统增加了一个液压泵、一个油缸、油管和一个动力辅助单元,该单元或者直接安装在转向齿轮总成上,或者与转向齿轮总成集成一体。

2. The reasons for camber are: to let the wheel perpendicular to the road crown and to load the inner bearing of the wheel on the knuckle spindle.

车轮外倾的原因包括:使车轮能够垂直于鼓形的道路,以使得车辆装载质量直接由转向节枢轴上车轮内侧的轴承承载。

3. Because of collision or damage of the parts of the frame, body, axle housing, suspension or wheel, inharmonious motion of the wheels may happen and lead to poor handling, excess fuel consumption and tire wear.

由于行驶系统的各部件(车架、车身、后桥壳、悬架或车轮)的碰撞或损坏,车轮的运动可能变得不协调,从而导致车辆操纵性能变差、油耗增加和轮胎磨损加剧。

Exercises

Questions for discussion

1. What's the function of the steering system?
2. Please list the main components of the steering system.
3. What's the purpose of the power steering?
4. Please list the main parameters of the wheel alignment.
5. What are the reasons for camber?

Fill in the blank according to the text

1. Motion of the left steering knuckle transmits to the _____ through the left steering arm, the _____ and the _____.

2. When a right turn is made, fluid is pumped into the right side of the _____, and fluid flows out of the left end of the chamber.

3. Wheel alignment is essential to _____, safety, _____ and _____.

4. _____ aids directional stability by forcing the wheel in return to the original straight a-

head position.

5. _____ can reduce the arm c on the ground thus reduce the resistant moment and make the steering easier.

Lesson 4
The Brakes

The brakes function is absorbing in the energy of friction possessed by the moving car. By doing so, they convert the energy into heat.

There are two types of brakes, the drum brake and the disc brake. Either or both types may be fitted. But where both types are used, it is usual for the disc brakes to be fitted to the front wheels. In both drum and disc brakes, a hydraulic system applies the brakes. The hydraulic system connects the brake pedal to the brake at each wheel.

4.1 Drum Brakes

The drum brake consists of a pair of semicircular brake shoes mounted on a fixed back plate and situated inside a drum. This drum is fixed to the road wheel and rotates with it. One end of each shoe is on a pivot and a spring holds the other end in contact with the piston of a hydraulic cylinder. In front brakes it is usual to use two hydraulic cylinders in order to equalize the pressure exerted by the shoes, as shown in Fig. 2-8. Each shoe is faced with material, known as brake lining, which produces high frictional resistance.

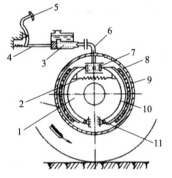

Fig. 2-8 Drum Brake
1-Brake base plate;2-Return spring; 3-Master cylinder; 4- Push rod; 5-Brake pedal;6-Oil tube;7-Brake cylinder;8- Brake drum; 9- Friction lining;10- Brake shoe;11-Pivots

The hydraulic system comprises a master cylinder and the slave cylinders which are the cylinders on the road wheels. The slave cylinders are connected to the master cylinder by tubing and the whole system is filled with hydraulic fluid. A piston in the master cylinder is connected to the brake pedal, so that when the driver depresses the pedal, the fluid is forced out to each slave cylinder and operates their pistons. The fluid pushes the pistons out of their cylinders. They, in turn, push against the inner ends of the brake shoes and force them against the brake drums in each wheel. We say that the brakes are on. This friction of the shoes against the drums, which are fixed to the road wheels, slows down or stops the car. As the brake pedal is allowed to come up, the hydraulic fluid returns to its original position, the piston retract, and a spring attached to each brake shoe returns it also to its original position. Free of the brake drum. Now we say that the brakes are off.

The brakes may also be operated by mechanical linkage from the foot pedal and handbrake lever. Common practice is to operate both front and rear brakes hydraulically with a secondary mechanical system operating the rear brakes only from the hand lever. One of the great advantages of hydraulic operation is that the system is self-balancing, which means that the same pressure is automatically produced at all four brakes, whereas mechanical linkages have to be very carefully adjusted for balance. Of course, if more pressure is put on one of the brakes than on the others there is a danger that the car will skid.

The mechanical linkage on the rear brakes is a system of rod sand cables connecting the handbrake lever to the brake-shoe mechanism, which work entirely independently.

Drum brakes are prone to a reduction in the braking effort, known as "fade", caused by the overheating of the brake linings and the drum. Fade can affect all or only some of the brakes at a time, but it is not permanent, and full efficiency returns as soon as the brakes have cooled down. However, fading is unlikely to occur except after the brakes have been used repeatedly in slowing the car from a high speed or after braking continuously down a steep hill. Descending such a hill, it would have been preferable to use engine braking by changing down into a lower gear. Drum brakes can be made less prone to fade by improving the cooling arrangements, by arranging for more air to be deflected over them, for example.

4.2 Disc Brakes

The disc brake (Fig. 2-9) consists of a steel disc with friction pads operated by slave hydraulic cylinders. The steel disc is attached to the road wheel and rotates with it. Part of this steel disc is enclosed in caliper. This caliper contains two friction pads, one on each side of the disc, and two hydraulic cylinders, one outside each pad. The pads are normally held apart by a spring, but when the driver depresses the brake pedal, pistons from the hydraulic cylinders force the pads against the sides of the disc. Because the disc is not enclosed all the way round, the heat generated when the brakes are applied is dissipated much more quickly than it is from brake shoes which are entirely enclosed inside a drum. This means that disc brakes are less prone to fade than drum brakes.

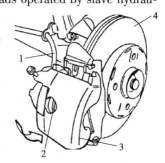

Fig. 2-9　Disc Brake
1-Brake pipe; 2-Friction linings;
3-Caliper body; 4-Disc

4.3 Anti-lock Brake System (ABS)

The function of an anti-lock, or anti-skid braking system is to prevent the wheels from locking under hard braking. Maximum braking force is obtained just before the wheels lock and skid. Such anti-skid systems are useful on slippery surfaces, such as ice and snow, where the wheels may lock easily. Locked wheels are dangerous because the car needs a much longer distance to stop. Locked wheels also can cause the driver to lose control.

The system uses a sensor that knows when one wheel (or a pair of wheels) is skidding (Fig. 2-10). The sensor sends a signal to a computer, which signals a modulator valve. The modulator connects into the hydraulic system and can momentarily release the brake pressure and prevent the wheels from locking (The pressure release is so last that a driver is seldom aware of it). Pressure is then reapplied until the sensor again senses that the wheel is about to lock up. Thus, this systems keeps the wheels as close to lock up as possible, without actually allowing the wheels to lock up and skid. This is called incipient lock up. Maximum braking occurs at that point.

If any parts of the system should fail to work, the system goes into a "fail-safe" mode. The brakes operate normally, as they would on a car that is not equipped with ABS.

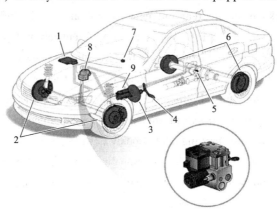

Fig. 2-10 ABS System

1-ABS control module;2-Disc brakes;3-Brake booster;4-Brake pedal;5-ABS differential sensor;6-Drum brakes;
7-Brake warning light;8-ABS pump;9-Master cylinder

Today, ABS is an optional or standard feature that typically is found on expensive luxury cars and sports cars. In the future, ABS may be available for all cars.

4.4 Electronic Brake Force Distribution (EBD)

EBD is a technology that enables the braking force of a vehicle to be increased or applied automatically, depending on road conditions, speed of the vehicle, weight of vehicle, etc.

What EBD does is it electronically monitors, through sensors, the conditions of the road, the feel of pressure on the brake pedal, and vehicle weight, to determine when to apply pressure to the wheel cylinders. The sensors are designed to monitor the movements of the wheels and determine based on weight, which wheels may need the maximum force applied, as per the condition met. Supposedly, this is to provide better and more precise braking under every condition imaginable.

Since the front end has the most weight on a vehicle, the EBD system recognizes this and electronically controls the back brakes so when the driver applies the brakes, the back brakes do not lock up causing a skid.

EBD is a system which can increase the vehicle's ability to stop under any conditions. But this is only effective if the brains of the computer works, along with the sensors that make up the system. If one of those sensors should fail, and you run into a bad situation, you could end up in a precarious predicament.

Technical Words and Terms

1. drum brake   鼓式制动器
2. disc brake   盘式制动器
3. semicircular   *adj.* 半圆的

4. shoe	*n.* 制动片,闸瓦;*vi.* 给……穿上鞋
5. brake shoe	制动蹄
6. situate	*vt.* 设置,定位,使位于;*adj.* 位于……的
7. equalize	*vt.* 使相等,平衡,补偿;*vi.* 成为相等
8. lining	*n.* 衬套,衬垫(带)
9. comprise	*vt.* 包含,包括,由……组成
10. master cylinder	主缸,制动主缸
11. slave cylinder	辅助(汽、油)缸,制动轮缸
12. tubing	*n.* 管道,导管;*v.* 使成管状
13. retract	*vt.* 缩回,缩进
14. handbrake	*n.* 手制动,手闸
15. prone	*adj.* 易于……的,倾斜的,有……倾向的
16. be prone to	易于……
17. deflect	*vt.* 使偏转,偏斜,使转向;*vi.* 转向,偏斜
18. pad	*n.* 衬垫,垫片,基座;*vi.* 填补,走
19. caliper	*n.* 制动钳,卡钳;*vt.* 用卡钳测量
20. dissipate	*vt.* 浪费,使消散;*vi.* 驱散,放荡
21. modulator	*n.* 调节器
22. momentarily	*adj.* 随时的,立刻的
23. incipient	*adj.* 起初的,初始的
24. booster	*n.* 助力器,支持者
25. optional	*adj.* 随意的,任选的,可选择的
26. luxury	*n.* 奢侈(品),享受;*adj.* 奢侈的
27. as per	按照,依据;如同
28. precarious	*adj.* 危险的,不确定的
29. predicament	*n.* 窘况,困境,状态

Notes

1. But where both types are used, it is usual for the disc brakes to be fitted to the front wheels.

在同时使用两种类型制动器的汽车上,通常将盘式制动器安装在前轮。

2. Each shoe is faced with material, known as brake lining, which produces high frictional resistance.

每一个制动蹄上都粘有一层摩擦材料,也就是制动衬片,它可以产生很高的摩擦阻力。

3. A piston in the master cylinder is connected to the brake pedal, so that when the driver depresses the pedal the fluid is forced out to each slave cylinder and operates their pistons.

制动主缸的活塞与制动踏板相连,当驾驶员踩下踏板时,迫使油液加压向外流到每一个制动轮缸中,推动其活塞向外移动。

4. As the brake pedal is allowed to come up, the hydraulic fluid returns to its original position, the piston retract, and a spring attached to each brake shoe returns it also to its original po-

sition.

当制动踏板抬起时,液压油返回原处,活塞复位,安装在每一个制动蹄上的复位弹簧使制动蹄复位。

5. Common practice is to operate both front and rear brakes hydraulically with a secondary mechanical system operating the rear brakes only from the hand lever.

通常惯例是前、后制动器均由液力操纵,同时利用辅助机械系统的手制动手柄操纵后制动器。

6. However, fading is unlikely to occur except after the brakes have been used repeatedly in slowing the car from a high speed or after braking continuously down a steep hill.

然而,在汽车高速行驶过程时反复制动减低车速或者在汽车下陡坡时连续制动的情况下容易出现制动衰退现象,其他情况下一般不易发生。

7. Because the disc is not enclosed all the way round, the heat generated when the brakes are applied is dissipated much more quickly than it is from brake shoes which are entirely enclosed inside a drum.

由于制动盘直接裸露在空气中,制动过程中所产生热消散速度,比完全包围在制动鼓中的制动蹄的热消散速度要快很多。

Exercises

Questions for discussion

1. What's the working principal of the brake?
2. What's the advantage of the hydraulic operation system in brakes?
3. What's the main difference between drum brakes and disc brakes?
4. What's the function of the ABS?
5. What's the advantage of the vehicle with EBD?

Fill in the blank according to the text

1. Each shoe is faced with material, known as _____, which produces high _____.
2. Drum brakes are prone to a _____ in the braking effort, known as _____, caused by the overheating of the _____ and the drum.
3. The disc brake consists of a _____ with friction pads operated by slave _____.
4. EBD is a technology that enables the braking force of a vehicle to be increased or applied automatically, depending on _____, _____, and _____.

Lesson 5
Suspension and Tire

5.1 Suspension

A suspension is a system which locates between the frame (or integrated body) and the axle (or the wheel) to connect them and to transmit forces. Types of suspension may differ from each other, but all of them may consist of three components including elastic element, shock absorber and guiding mechanism.

The function of an elastic element is to cushion the road shock. Two types of elastic element are quite common: leaf spring and coil spring. Leaf spring is formed by a group of elastic steel pieces of different length (Fig. 2-11). The front and rear ends of the upper two pieces are rolled up to form spring eyes. The central part of the leaf spring is clamped on the axle housing by two U-bolts. A central bolt is used to hold the pieces in position and the spring clips are used to keep the pieces close together. From the principal of mechanics, it is clear to see that the bending moment is largest at the central part of the leaf spring which is the thickest and both ends are the thinnest.

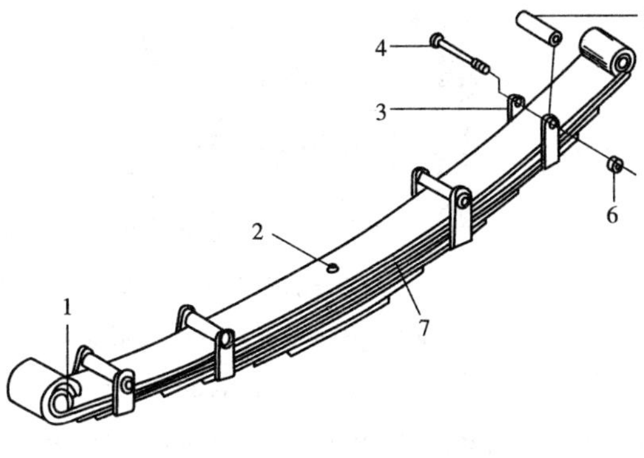

Fig. 2-11 Leaf Spring
1-Spring eye; 2-Central bolt; 3-Clip; 4-Clip bolt; 5-Sleeve; 6-Nut; 7-Elastic pieces

A coil spring is made of a long elastic steel bar. Compared with the leaf spring, the coil spring has the advantage of light weight and little space and is widely used in modern cars.

A torsion bar is an elastic steel bar, its one end is fixed on the frame and the other end is mounted on the control arm. The road wheel is installed on the other end of the control arm. As the road wheel jounces and rebounds, the torsion bar twists over and over again.

An air spring is a hollow chamber filled with compressed air. Compression and expansion of the air play the role of elastic action.

Jounce and rebound of the road wheel causes reciprocal vibration of the elastic element. In order to improve comfort, shock absorber should be incorporated in the suspension system. The shape of a shock absorber is like a telescopic container filled with oil. The shock absorber compresses and extends just like elastic element does. This time oil in the absorber is forced to flow through the small holes reciprocally to cause resistance and to damp the vibration. Damping resistance of the shock absorber is small during the compression stroke to avoid a hard jounce to the occupants, and is large during the extension stroke to reduce vibration.

A guiding mechanism is a linkage to transmit forces and to guide the up and down motion of the wheel along a certain trajectory. There are various types of guiding mechanism, and some timer the suspension system are named after the guiding mechanism such as, single control arm type, double wishbone type, longitudinal swing arm type, strut type etc. In the McPherson suspension system, the guiding mechanism includes a strut and a lower control arm on each side. Either strut consists of a shock absorber and a coil spring.

Suspension systems include two main categories, dependent suspension system and independent suspension system. In the dependent suspension there is a rigid axle to connect the left and right wheel together, and the motion of one wheel would affect the motion of the other wheel. On the left in Fig. 2-12, the upward motion of one wheel would make the other wheel together with the axle incline, and the body inclines too. In the independent suspension each wheel is connected to the frame through an independent linkage. On the right in Fig. 2-12, the motion wheel would not affect the other wheel and therefore structure can improve the quality of ride and comfort and also increase adhesion between tire and road.

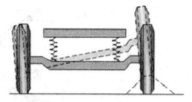 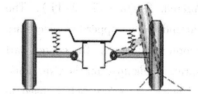

Fig. 2-12 Dependent Suspension and Independent Suspension

The suspension system of some modern cars is equipped with an intelligent system controlled by electronic device. The intelligent system is able to adjust the stiffness of the elastic element and the damping resistance of the shock absorber to remove shock and vibration effectively. Moreover, the system is able to adjust the body height from the ground too. When the car drives on the rough road or even makeshift a sharp steer, the occupants would not feel uncomfortable because the body is able to keep leveling.

5.2 Wheel and Tire

The task of wheel and tire is to support the weight of the motor vehicle, to cushion the road shock, to transmit forces such as traction force and braking force by adhesion to the road, and to increase crossing performance by the special tire pattern.

The rim is the round part of the wheel to install the tire. The hub is the central part of the wheel to install the wheel on the axle. The spoke is the part of the wheel to connect the rim and the hub. They can be made by sheet steel stampings or by pressure casting of aluminum alloy. The wheel made of aluminum alloy can reduce one third of the weight and moment of inertia compared to sheet steel stamping.

Fig. 2-13 Structure of Common Bias Ply Tire
1-Thread (crown); 2-Side wall; 3-Bead core flipper;
4-Ply layer; 5-Rims; 6-Cushion layer

Fig. 2-13 is the structure of a common bias ply tire. The outside is the rubber layer including thread or crown, shoulder and side wall. Some groves are cut on the tread to improve tire performance, they are called pattern. The cord is the important part of the tire to withstand load and is made of several piles of fabric strings including nylon strings or steel wires. Direction of the strings in a common bias ply tire inclines at an angle with the central line of the tread. The strings on one ply inclines to the left and the other to the right. The number of piles is even number and the left and the right inclining piles overlap one another. There is a cushion layer between the tread and the cord to strengthen the periphery of the tire and to prevent the cord from separation with the tread. All the above components are called tire carcass. The rubber tube is a closed space to be filled with air and a bleed valve is needed. There is a protector between the tube and the rim.

Radial tubeless tire is widely used in most of the modern cars, light trucks and buses. Direction of the cord strings in a radial tire is radial, that is, perpendicular to the central line of the tread (Fig. 2-14). The appearance of the tubeless tire is similar to the tube-type tire. On the inner wall of the tubeless tire a sealing layer of rubber is incorporated. Radial tire has many advantages such as light weight, small moment of inertia, low rolling resistance, high duty, low cost, low probability of leakage and burst etc. therefore radial tire is much better than bias ply tire.

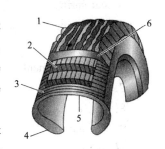

Fig. 2-14 Radial Tire
1-Thread; 2-Belted layer; 3- Cord;
4- Beam; 5- Radial section;
6-Tire shoulder

Nomination of a tire is used to express its specifications. There are two common kinds of nominations. The first kind is the nomination of common low pressure tires, for example 9.00-20. As shown in Fig. 2-15, the figure 9.00 is the nominal profile width (in.) of tire B and the figure 20 is the nominal diameter (in.) of rim d. The second kind is the nomination of radial tire, for example 185/70SR14. The figure 185 is nominal profile width (mm) of tire B; the figure 70 (percentage) is nominal height-width ratio of tire profile H/B; the alphabet S is speed level code (Tab. 2-1), the alphabet R refers to radial structure and the figure 14 is nominal diameter (in.) of rim d.

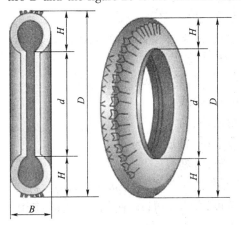

Fig. 2-15 Expression of Tire Nomination

Low profile is the trend of tire development, i.e. the height-width ratio becomes smaller and smaller. The smaller the ratio is, the better the handling stability will be. For example, the height-width ratio was nearly 100% fifty years ago, 80% thirty years ago and is 70% ~60% nowadays.

The Speed Level Code   Tab. 2-1

Code	Maximum speed (km/h)	Code	Maximum speed (km/h)
J	100	R	170
K	110	S	180
L	120	T	190
M	130	U	200
N	140	H	210
P	150	V	240
Q	160	X	>240

Technical Words and Terms

1. elastic   *adj.* 有弹性的；灵活的；易伸缩的；*n.* 松紧带，橡皮圈

2. shock absorber   减振器

3.	leaf spring	钢板弹簧
4.	coil spring	螺旋弹簧
5.	spring eye	弹簧孔
6.	bending moment	弯矩
7.	torsion bar	扭杆
8.	jounce	$n.$ 震动,颠簸;$vt.$ 使震动,使颠簸;$vi.$ 震动
9.	rebound	$n.$ 回弹,篮板球;$vt.$ 使回弹;$vi.$ 回升
10.	twist	$n.$ 扭曲,拧,扭伤;$vt.$ 捻,扭伤;$vi.$ 扭动
11.	damping resistance	阻尼力
12.	single control arm type	单摆臂式
13.	double wishbone type	双横臂式
14.	longitudinal swing arm type	纵摆臂式
15.	strut type	滑柱式
16.	McPherson type	麦弗逊式悬架
17.	stiffness	$n.$ 刚度,僵硬,坚硬,顽固
18.	pattern	$n.$ 模式,图案,样品;$vt.$ 模仿,以图案装饰;$vi.$ 形成图案
19.	rim	$n.$ 边,边缘,轮辋;$v.$ 作……的边
20.	hub	$n.$ 中心,轮毂
21.	spoke	$n.$ 轮辐,制动
22.	alloy	$n.$ 合金;$vt.$ 使成合金
23.	moment	$n.$ 力矩,时刻
24.	bias	$adj.$ 偏斜的;$adv.$ 偏斜地;$n.$ 偏见,偏爱,斜纹
25.	ply	$n.$ 厚度,板层,褶;$vt.$ 使用,不住的使用,折,弯;$vi.$ 辛勤工作
26.	common bias ply tire	普通斜交轮胎
27.	tread of crown	胎冠(胎面)
28.	side wall	胎侧
29.	cord	$n.$ 帘布层,绳索;$vt.$ 用绳子捆绑
30.	even	$adj.$ 偶数的,平坦的,相等的;$adv.$ 甚至;$vt.$ 使平坦,使相等;$vi.$ 变平
31.	overlap	$n.$ 重叠,重复;$vt.$ 与……重叠
32.	cushion layer	缓冲层
33.	carcass	$n.$ 尸体,残骸
34.	tire carcass	外胎
35.	rubber tube	橡胶内胎
36.	bleed	$vt.$ 使出血,榨取;$vi.$ 渗出,流血
37.	bleed valve	放气阀,排气门
38.	radial tubeless tire	子午线无内胎轮胎
39.	nominal profile width (in.) of tire	轮胎名义断面宽度

40. nominal height-width ratio of tire profile   轮胎断面名义高宽比

Notes

1. When the car drives on the rough road or even makeshift a sharp steer, the occupants would not feel uncomfortable because the body is able to keep leveling.

当汽车行驶在不平路面或剧烈震动时,由于悬架能够使车身基本保持水平状态,所以乘员不会感到不舒适。

2. The wheel made of aluminum alloy can reduce one third of the weight and moment of inertia compared to sheet steel stamping.

与钢板冲压件相比,铝合金制成的车轮可减少1/3的重量和转动惯量。

3. The number of piles is even number and the left and the right inclining piles overlap one another.

帘布层的数目是偶数并且左倾斜层和右倾斜层交替叠合。

4. Direction of the cord strings in a radial tire is radial, that is, perpendicular to the central line of the tread.

子午线轮胎帘布层帘线的方向是径向,即垂直于胎面中心线方向。

5. Nomination of a tire is used to express its specifications.

轮胎命名用以表达其规格。

Exercises

Questions for discussion

1. What are the main components of the suspension?
2. What's the difference between dependent suspension system and independent suspension system?
3. What's the function of the wheel and tire?
4. Please list the main elements of the radial tire?
5. How to name a tire?

Fill in the blank according to the text

1. A suspension is a system which locates between _____ and the _____ (or the wheel) to connect them and to _____.
2. In order to improve comfort, _____ should be incorporated in the suspension system.
3. Suspension systems include two main categories, _____ system and _____ system.
4. Direction of the _____ in a radial tire is radial, that is, perpendicular to the central line of _____.
5. _____ is the trend of tire development, the _____ becomes smaller and smaller.

Extension 1: Types of Suspension

Suspension Types: Front

The four wheels of a car work together in two independent systems—the two wheels connected by the front axle and the two wheels connected by the rear axle. That means that a car can and usually does have a different type of suspension on the front and back. Much is determined by whether a rigid axle binds the wheels or if the wheels are permitted to move independently. The former arrangement is known as a dependent system, while the latter arrangement is known as an independent system. In the following sections, we'll look at some of the common types of front and back suspensions typically used on mainstream cars.

Dependent Front Suspensions

Dependent front suspensions have a rigid front axle that connects the front wheels. Basically, this looks like a solid bar under the front of the car, kept in place by leaf springs and shock absorbers. Common on trucks, dependent front suspensions haven't been used in mainstream cars for years.

Independent Front Suspensions

In this setup, the front wheels are allowed to move independently. The MacPherson strut, developed by Earle S. MacPherson of General Motors in 1947, is the most widely used front suspension system, especially in cars of European origin.

The MacPherson strut combines a shock absorber and a coil spring into a single unit. This provides a more compact and lighter suspension system that can be used for front-wheel drive vehicles.

Double-Wishbone Suspension

The double-wishbone suspension (Fig. 2-16), also known as an A-arm suspension, is another common type of front independent suspension.

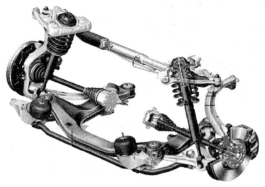

Fig. 2-16 Unequal Length Double-wishbone Suspension on Audi A4

While there are several different possible configurations, this design typically uses two wishbone-shaped arms to locate the wheel. Each wishbone, which has two mounting positions to the frame and one at the wheel, bears a shock absorber and a coil spring to absorb vibrations. Double-wishbone suspensions allow for more control over the camber angle of the wheel, which describes the degree to which the wheels tilt in and out. They also help minimize roll or sway and provide for a more consistent steering feel. Because of these characteristics, the double-wishbone suspension is common on the front wheels of larger cars.

Suspension Types: Rear

Dependent Rear Suspensions

If a solid axle connects the rear wheels of a car, then the suspension is usually quite simple—based either on a leaf spring or a coil spring. In the former design, the leaf springs clamp directly to the drive axle. The ends of the leaf springs attach directly to the frame, and the shock absorber is attached at the clamp that holds the spring to the axle. For many years, American car manufacturers preferred this design because of its simplicity.

The same basic design can be achieved with coil springs replacing the leaves. In this case, the spring and shock absorber can be mounted as a single unit or as separate components. When they're separated, the springs which reduce the amount of space the suspension takes up can be much smaller.

Independent Rear Suspensions

If both the front and back suspensions are independent, then all of the wheels are mounted and sprung individually, resulting in what car advertisements tout as "four-wheel independent suspension." Any suspension that can be used on the front of the car can be used on the rear, and versions of the front independent systems described in the previous section can be found on the rear axles. Of course, in the rear of the car, the steering rack—the assembly that includes the pinion gear wheel and enables the wheels to turn from side to side—is absent. This means that rear independent suspensions can be simplified versions of front ones, although the basic principles remain the same.

Specialized Suspensions:

The Baja Bug

For the most part, this article has focused on the suspensions of mainstream front-wheel-drive and rear-wheel-drive cars—cars that drive on normal roads in normal driving conditions. But what about the suspensions of specialty cars, such as hot rods, racers or extreme off-road vehicles? Although the suspensions of specialty autos obey the same basic principles, they do provide additional benefits unique to the driving conditions they must navigate. What follows is a brief overview of how suspensions are designed for three types of specialty cars—Baja Bugs (Fig. 2-17), Formula One racers and American-style hot rods.

Fig. 2-17 Courtesy Car Domain Baja Bug

The Volkswagen Beetle, or Bug, was destined to become a favorite among off-road enthusiasts. With a low center of gravity and engine placement over the rear axle, the two-wheel-drive Bug handles off-road conditions as well as some four-wheel-drive vehicles. Of course, the VW Bug isn't ready for off-road conditions with its factory equipment. Most Bugs require some modifications, or conversions, to get them ready for racing in harsh conditions like the deserts ofBaja California.

One of the most important modifications takes place in the suspension. The torsion-bar suspension, standard equipment on the front and back of most Bugs between 1936 and 1977, can be raised to make room for heavy-duty, off-road wheels and tires. Longer shock absorbers replace the standard shocks to lift the body higher and to provide for maximum wheel travel. In some cases, Baja Bug converters remove the torsion bars entirely and replace them with multiple coil-over systems, an aftermarket item that combines both the spring and shock absorber in one adjustable unit. The result of these modifications is a vehicle that allows the wheels to travel vertically 20 inches (50 cm) or more at each end. Such a car can easily navigate rough terrain and often appears to "skip" over desert washboard like a stone over water.

Formula One Racers

The Formula One race car (Fig. 2-18) represents the pinnacle of automobile innovation and evolution. Lightweight, composite bodies, powerful V10 engines and advanced aerodynamics have led to faster, safer and more reliable cars.

Fig. 2-18 Formula One Race Car

To elevate driver skill as the key differentiating factor in a race, stringent rules and requirements govern Formula Onerace car design. For example, the rules regulating suspension design say that all Formula One racers must be conventionally sprung, but they don't allow computer-controlled, active suspensions. To accommodate this, the cars feature multi-link suspensions, which use a multi-rod mechanism equivalent to a double-wishbone system.

Recall that a double-wishbone design uses two wishbone-shaped control arms to guide each wheel'sup and down motion. Each arm has three mounting positions—two at the frame and one at the wheel hub—and each joint is hinged to guide the wheel's motion. In all cars, the primary benefit of a double-wishbone suspension is control. The geometry of the arms and the elasticity of the joints give engineers ultimate control over the angle of the wheel and other vehicle dynamics, such as lift, squat and dive. Unlike road cars, however, the shock absorbers and coil springs of a Formula One race car don't mount directly to the control arms. Instead, they are oriented along the length of the car and are controlled remotely through a series of push rods and bell cranks. In such an arrangement, the push rods and bell cranks translate the up and down motions of the wheel to the back-and-forth movement of the spring-and-damper apparatus.

Hot Rods

The classic American hot rod era lasted from 1945 to about 1965. Like Baja Bugs, classic hot rods required significant modification by their owners. Unlike Bugs, however, which are built on Volkswagen chassis, hot rods were built on a variety of old, often historical, car models: Cars manufactured before 1945 were considered ideal fodder for hot rod transformations because their bodies and frames were often in good shape, while their engines and transmissions needed to be replaced completely. For hot rod enthusiasts, this was exactly what they wanted, for it allowed them to install more reliable and powerful engines, such as the flathead Ford V8 or the Chevrolet V8.

One popular hot rod was known as the T-bucket (Fig. 2-19) because it was based on the Ford Model T. The stock Ford suspension on the front of the Model T consisted of a solid I-beam front axle (a dependent suspension), a U-shaped buggy spring (leaf spring) and a wishbone-shaped radius rod with a ball at the rear end that pivoted in a cup attached to the transmission. Ford's engineers built the Model T to ride high with a large amount of suspension movement, an ideal design for the rough, primitive roads of the 1930s. But after World War II, hot rodders began experimenting with larger Cadillac or Lincoln engines, which meant that the wishbone-shaped radius rod was no longer applicable. Instead, they removed the center ball and bolted the ends of the wishbone to the frame rails. This "split wishbone" design lowered the front axle about 1 inch (2.5 cm) and improved vehicle handling.

Fig. 2-19　Courtesy Street Rod Central 1923 T-bucket

Lowering the axle more than an inch required a brand-new design, which was supplied by a company known as Bell Auto. Throughout the 1940s and 1950s, Bell Auto offered dropped tube axles that lowered the car a full 5 inches (13 cm). Tube axles were built from smooth, steel tubing and balanced strength with superb aerodynamics. The steel surface also accepted chrome plating better than the forged I-beam axles, so hot rodders often preferred them for their aesthetic qualities, as well.

Some hot rod enthusiasts, however, argued that the tube axle's rigidity and inability to flex compromised how it handled the stresses of driving. To accommodate this, hot rodders introduced the four-bar suspension, using two mounting points on the axle and two on the frame. At each mounting point, aircraft-style rod ends provided plenty of movement at all angles. And the four-bar system improved how the suspension worked in all sorts of driving conditions.

While there have been enhancements and improvements to both springs and shock absorbers, the basic design of car suspensions has not undergone a significant evolution over the years. But all of that's about to change with the introduction of a brand-new suspension design conceived by Bose—the same Bose known for its innovations in acoustic technologies. Some experts are going so far as to say that the Bose suspension (Fig. 2-20) is the biggest advance in automobile suspensions since the introduction of an all-independent design.

Fig. 2-20　Bose Suspension System

How does it work? The Bose system uses a linear electromagnetic motor (LEM) at each wheel in lieu of a conventional shock-and-spring setup. Amplifiers provide electricity to the motors in such a way that their power is regenerated with each compression of the system. The main benefit of the motors is that they are not limited by the inertia inherent in conventional fluid-based dampers. As a result, an LEM can extend and compress at a much greater speed, virtually eliminating all vibrations in the passenger cabin. The wheel's motion can be so finely controlled that the body of the car remains level regardless of what's happening at the wheel. The LEM can also counteract the body motion of the car while accelerating, braking and cornering, giving the driver a greater sense of control.

Extension 2: Frame

A frame is the main structure of the chassis of a motor vehicle. All other components fasten to it; a term for this design is body-on-frame construction.

In 1920, every motor vehicle other than a few cars based on motorcycles had a frame. Since then, nearly all cars have shifted to unit-body construction, while nearly all trucks and buses still use frames. Fig. 2-21 shows the cross section of a Chevy Silverado HD 2011 frame.

Fig. 2-21 Cross Section of a Chevy Silverado HD 2011 Frame

Construction

There are three main designs for frame rails. Their cross-sections include:

C-shape

By far the most common, the C-rail has been used on nearly every type of vehicle at one time or another. It is made by taking a flat piece of steel (usually ranging in thickness from 1/8 ~ 3/16) and rolling both sides over to form a C-shaped beam running the length of the vehicle.

Boxed

Originally, boxed frames were made by welding two matching c-rails together to form a rectangular tube. Modern techniques, however, use a process similar to making C-rails in that a piece of steel is bent into four sides and then welded where both ends meet.

In the 1960s, the boxed frames of conventional American cars were spot-welded here and there down the seam; when turned into NASCAR "stock car" racers, the box was continuously welded from end to end for extra strength (as was that of the Land-Rover from its first series).

Hat

Hat frames resemble a "U" and may be either right-side-up or inverted with the open area facing down. Not commonly used due to weakness and a propensity to rust, however they can be found in 1936 ~ 1954 Chevrolet cars and some Studebakers.

Abandoned for a while, the hat frame gained popularity again when companies started welding it to the bottom of unibody cars, in effect creating a boxed frame.

Design Features

While appearing at first glance as a simple hunk of metal, frames encounter great amounts of stress and are built accordingly. The first issue addressed is beam height, or the height of the vertical side of a frame. The taller the frame, the better it is able to resist vertical flex when force is applied to the top of the frame. This is the reason semi-trucks have taller frame rails than other vehicles instead of just being thicker.

Another factor considered when engineering a frame is torsional resistance, or the ability to resist twisting. This, and diamonding (one rail moving backwards or forwards in relation to the other rail), are countered by crossmembers. While hat-shaped crossmembers are the norm, these forces are best countered with "K" or "X"-shaped crossmembers (Fig. 2-22).

Fig. 2-22 2007 Toyota Tundra Chassis Showing An X-shaped Crossmember at the Back

As looks, ride quality, and handling became more of an issue with consumers, new shapes were incorporated into frames. The most obvious of these are arches and kick-ups. Instead of running straight over both axles, arched frames sit roughly level with their axles and curve up over the axles and then back down on the other side for bumper placement. Kick-ups do the same thing, but don't curve down on the other side, and are more common on front ends.

On perimeter frames, the areas where the rails connect from front to center and center to rear are weak compared to regular frames, so that section is boxed in, creating what's known as torque boxes.

Another feature seen is tapered rails that narrow vertically and/or horizontally in front of a vehicle's cabin. This is done mainly on trucks to save weight and slightly increase room for the engine since the front of the vehicle doesn't bear as much of a load as the back.

The latest design element is frames that use more than one shape in the same frame rail. For example, the new Toyota Tundra uses a boxed frame in front of the cab, shorter, narrower rails underneath the cab for ride quality, and regular C-rails under the bed.

Types

Ladder Frame

So named for its resemblance to a ladder, the ladder frame is the simplest and oldest of all designs. It consists merely of two symmetrical rails, or beams, and crossmembers connecting them. Originally seen on almost all vehicles, the ladder frame was gradually phased out on cars around the 1940s in favor of perimeter frames and is now seen mainly on trucks.

This design offers good beam resistance because of its continuous rails from front to rear, but poor resistance to torsion or warping if simple, perpendicular crossmembers are used. Also, the vehicle's overall height will be higher due to the floor pan sitting above the frame instead of inside it.

Backbone tube

Instead of a two-dimensional ladder type structure, Backbone chassis is a type of automobile construction chassis that is similar to the body-on-frame design.

Perimeter Frame

Similar to a ladder frame, but the middle sections of the frame rails sit outboard of the front and rear rails just behind the rocker panels/sill panels. This was done to allow for a lower floor pan, and therefore lower overall vehicle in passenger cars. This was the prevalent design for cars in theUnited States, but not in the rest of the world, until the unibody gained popularity and is still used on US full frame cars. It allowed for annual model changes introduced in the 1950s to increase sales, but without costly structural changes.

In addition to a lowered roof, the perimeter frame allows lower seating positions when that is desirable, and offers better safety in the event of a side impact. However, the design lacks stiffness, because the transition areas from front to center and center to rear reduce beam and torsional resistance, hence the use of torque boxes, and soft suspension settings.

Superleggera

An Italian term (meaning "super-light") for sports-car construction using a three-dimensional frame that consists of a cage of narrow tubes that, besides being under the body, run up the fenders and over the radiator, cowl, and roof, and under the rear window; it resembles a geodesic structure. The body, which is not stress-bearing, is attached to the outside of the frame and is often made of aluminum.

Unibody

By far the most common design in use today and sometimes referred to as a sort of frame.

But the distinction still serves a purpose: if a unibody is damaged in an accident, getting bent or warped, in effect its frame is too bad to repair, and the vehicle undrivable. If the body of a body-on-frame vehicle is similarly damaged, it might be torn in places from the frame, which may still be straight, in which case the vehicle is simpler and cheaper to repair.

Sub frame

The sub frame, or stub frame, is a boxed frame section that attaches to a unibody. Seen primarily on the front end of cars, it is also sometimes used in the rear. Both the front and rear are used to attach the suspension to the vehicle and either may contain the engine and transmission.

Unit 3 Body and Electrical System

Lesson 1
Body

Body provides place for the driver's operation and for the passenger and goods. It includes body shell, doors, windows, front end panels, seats, ventilation, heating, air-conditioning devices etc. For trucks and special utility motor vehicles body includes platform or other special equipments also.

1.1 Body shell and front end panels

Body shell is the base to install all the body systems. It usually refers to the structure formed by longitudinal, lateral, vertical support elements and panels welded on them. Most of the bus bodies have evident frame structure, but cars and truck cabs do not. Body shell also includes isolation layers of noise, heat and vibration and coatings of anti-corrosion and sealing.

According to the way of load carrying, body shells can be classified into three kinds:

1.1.1 Separated Body-Frame Structure

The main feature of this kind of body structure is the connection of the body and the frame through flexible mountings such as rubber pads or springs. In this case the frame is the base to support the whole motor vehicle and bears all the loads from the working systems. And the body is not taken into account of sharing the loads of the frame.

1.1.2 Combined Body-Frame Structure

The main feature of this kind of body structure is the connection of the body and the frame through stiff joints such as welded, riveted or bolted connections. In this case the frame is the base to support all the systems and bears most part of the loads from the working systems. The body is taken into account of helping the frame and sharing a part of the loads.

1.1.3 Integrated or Monocoque Body Structure

This kind of body structure has no frame. In this case the body is the base to install all the systems and bears all the loads from them.

In order to get rid of the rather heavy frame, almost all the cars and most of the buses choose the integrated body structure. Because the cab occupies only a small part of the whole length of the truck, it is impossible to use integrated body structure. For those motor vehicles without a complete body framework (such as convertibles) it is difficult to choose integrated body structure. Some of the local made buses always use the combined body-frame structure because the chassis (together with the frame) and the body are made by different manufacturers and it is easier to weld them together.

Fig. 3-1 is a typical integrated body shell of a family car. After careful consideration the structural parts are grouped together by flanged edge or lap welding in a particular order. At last the body shell is made up by rear floor assembly, left and right side panel assembly, front floor and cowl assembly and roof assembly to form a perfect space structure.

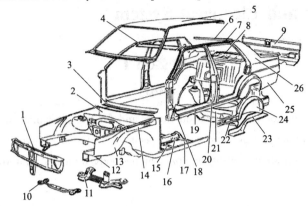

Fig. 3-1 Typical Integrated Body Shell of a Family Car

1-Radiator support;2-Dash board (fire wall);3-Cowl upper panel;4-Front windshield frame upper brace;5-Roof;6-Rear windshield upper brace;7-Toof rail;8-Package tray panel;9-Rear end panel;10-Front cross member;11-Sub-frame;12-Front side rail;13-Front fender apron;14-Fender apron reinforced brace;15-Front seat cross member;16-Floor tunnel;17-Front floor;18-Front pillar (A-pillar);19-Rocker panel (side sill);20-Center pillar (B-pillar);21-Rear floor;22-Rear floor cross member;23-Rear side rail;24-Rear wheel house panel;25-Rear fender (quarter panel);26-Rear pillar (C-pillar)

  The body shell of separate body-frame structure is similar to that of the integrated-body structure. Their differences are: the former is weaker; panel thickness and structural section size are smaller. Besides, the latter has a front and structure welded by left and right front side rails, left and right front fender aprons and radiator support, but the former has not.

  Almost all the truck cabs belong to the separate body-frame structure and are connected to the frame through three or four elastic mountings. The structural sections, the formation of panels and the manufacturing process of the cab are much similar to those of the car body but are simpler than those of the latter.

  Most of the buses look like the shape of regular square boxes. Therefore have a complete body framework. On the early days of the history, the bus body was formed by the special body manufacturer and installed on a readymade chassis frame, therefore belonged to the separate body-frame structure. The advantage of this kind of structure is the possibility of installing different bus bodies on a given chassis frame. Because the body is not used to share the loads of the frame, heavy weight must be the remarkable disadvantage. Many modern buses belong to the integrated body structure. The structure has a truss underbody instead of a thick and heavy frame. All the structural members including the skin panels share the load and affect one another to form a perfect body of light weight and high stillness.

  Motor vehicle body of normal control type has several front end panels welded or bolted together to provide shelter for the engine and front wheels. The upper panel of radiator support, left lamp support, right lamp support, left fender apron and right fender apron with their reinforcements are welded together to form a strong base of the front end. The bottom of the base is welded to the front cross member and the front side rails of the underbody and the rear of the base is welded to the dash board of the body shell. The left and right fenders are installed to the base through some screws and are easy to take off when they are damaged in the collision accident. The engine hood consists of the outer panel and the inner panel and is fixed to the dash board by two hinges. The front of the hood is locked to the upper panel of the radiator support through a safety latch.

1.2 Doors, windows, their accessories and sealing

Door is an important assembly of body. Fig. 3-2 shows types of doors sorted by their opening ways. The front-hinged door is safe and widely used because it can be closed by head-on air pressure as the motor vehicle is running. The rear-hinged door is quite rare because it is not safe and can be opened by head-on air pressure if it is not locked surely. The up-hinged door is widely used as the back door (also called "hatch back") of the car or the light bus, and sometimes it is used in low motor vehicles. The sliding door is widely used in the body sidewall. Its outstanding advantage is the possibility to open fully when the distance between the sidewall and the obstacle is rather small. The folding door and the outside swinging door are widely used in medium and large buses.

Fig. 3-2 Door Types

1-Rear-hinged door; 2-Front-Hinged door; 3-Up-hinged door; 4-Sliding door; 5-Folding door; 6-Outside swinging door

Door inside panel is the support base for all the components and parts including window glass, its guide channels and window regulator, door lock and its inside handle, door hinge, door check and door inside trim board. In new car models, there are some control buttons and mounted on the door inside panel, and the door lock outside handle is mounted on the door outside panel.

Curved glass is usually used to make the front and rear windshields of the motor vehicle because of beautiful shape and good visibility. The windshield of most modern cars is stuck on the window frame by special glue. For natural ventilation, the side window can be regulated up and down or fore and aft. There are sealing strips between the regulated window and its guide channels. Some of the side windows are smoked colored and have heat isolation layer to prevent the interior from hot sunshine and to make the interior atmosphere gentle and comfortable. In the bus of perfect ventilation heating and air-conditioning, the side windows cannot be opened to improve sealing performance.

In modern cars, sunroof becomes more and more popular. When the sunroof and other windows open, the body interior opens to the outside environment and is similar to a convertible body to let the passengers enjoy the warm sunshine and fresh air in wonderful seasons. The sunroof not only can increase interior illumination, but also is an effective structure of natural ventilation. According to different requirements, the sunroof can partially or fully open or close to provide an excellent function of all weather body structure.

1.3 Ventilation, heating and air-conditioning

Ventilation is necessary for taking in the fresh air to the interior and driving the air polluted by carbon dioxide and harmful emission from the engine outside. In cold weather, the fresh air should be heated to provide the interior with suitable temperature.

The operation principle of the heating system is to heat the air flowing through a radiator and to conduct it to the interior. The radiator is connected with the engine cooling system and heat comes from the engine cooling water.

The main principle of the refrigeration cycle goes like this: the first step, to lower the pressure so as to make the refrigerant change from liquid to gas, i. e. to evaporate and absorb heat; the second step, to increase pressure and to cool the refrigerant so as to make it reduce to the original liquid state, i. e. to condense and disperse heat.

Under the pressure of the compressor driven by the engine crankshaft through a V-belt, the circulation path of the refrigerant (expressed by thin arrows) is as follows: The first step, it flows from the storage tank through the expansion valve which lowers its pressure and increases its volume to become gas state, and then the refrigerant evaporates in the evaporator and absorbs heat, i. e. lowers the temperature of the surrounding air. The second step, the refrigerant from the evaporator flows through the compressor to increase pressure, goes through the condenser in front of the engine radiator to cool up, i. e. to reduce to liquid state, and returns to the storage tank. Under the action of the blower, fresh air comes from the air duct into the system, and then flows from the filter port through the evaporator and the radiator to the distribution box. In a cold season, cooling water of the engine can be conducted to the radiator to heat the air. The distribution box can lead the warm air through the outlet port to the windshield for defrosting or through the outlets to warm the interior. The blower can also let the interior air enter the system through the inlet port to form an interior circulation. When both the heating and the refrigerating systems stop working, the fan can also make the outside air flow through the interior and then conduct it outside to form compulsory ventilation.

Technical Words and Terms

1. shell	*n.* 车身壳体
2. front end panel	车前板制件
3. ventilation	*n.* 通风设备
4. way of load carrying	承载方式
5. separated body-frame structure	非承载式车身
6. combined body-frame structure	半承载式车身
7. integrated or monocoque body structure	承载式车身
8. convertible	*n.* 敞篷车身
9. structural section size	结构断面尺寸
10. normal control type	长头式
11. reinforcement	*n.* 加强件
12. engine hood	发动机罩
13. front-hinged door	顺开式车门
14. rear-hinged door	逆开式车门

15.	up-hinged door	上掀式车门
16.	sliding door	滑移式车门
17.	folding door	折叠式车门
18.	swinging door	外摆式车门
19.	guide channel	导轨,导槽
20.	window regulator	玻璃升降器
21.	door check	车门限位器
22.	door inside trim board	车门内护板或内饰板
23.	sunroof	*n.* 太阳车顶,天窗
24.	interior illumination	室内照明
25.	refrigeration cycle	制冷循环
26.	refrigerant	*n.* 制冷工质
27.	storage tank	贮液罐
28.	expansion valve	膨胀阀
29.	filter port	过滤口
30.	distribution box	分配箱
31.	outlet port	出口
32.	defrosting	*v.* 除霜
33.	compulsory ventilation	强制通风

Notes

1. The main feature of this kind of body structure is the connection of the body and the frame through flexible mountings such as rubber pads or springs.

这种车身结构的主要特点是车身与车架之间通过橡胶垫或弹簧等弹性件进行柔性连接。

2. In order to get rid of the rather heavy frame, almost all the cars and most of the buses choose the integrated body structure. Because the cab occupies only a small part of the whole length of the truck, it is impossible to use integrated body structure.

为了去掉沉重的车架,几乎所有的乘用车和大部分的公共汽车都选择了承载式车身结构。因为载货汽车的驾驶室仅仅占据了其整个车身长度的一小部分,所以它不能采用承载式车身结构。

3. For those motor vehicles without a complete body framework (such as convertibles) it is difficult to choose integrated body structure. Some of the local made buses always use the combined body-frame structure because the chassis (together with the frame) and the body are made by different manufacturers and it is easier to weld them together.

对于那些没有完整车身框架(例如敞篷车)的汽车,就很难选择承载式车身结构。一些国产客车经常用半承载式车身结构,这是因为底盘(与车架一起)和车身是由不同的汽车制造商生产的,采用半承载式结构可以很容易地将两者焊接在一起。

4. After careful consideration the structural parts are grouped together by flanged edge or lap welding in a particular order. At last the body shell is made up by rear floor assembly, left and

right side panel assembly, front floor and cowl assembly and roof assembly to form a perfect space structure.

仔细分析可以发现,这种结构件是通过螺纹或搭焊方式按照一个特别的顺序将其组合在一起的。这种车身壳体是由后地板总成、左右侧围总成、前地板和前围总成以及顶盖总成组成,最终形成了一个完美的空间结构。

5. The advantage of this kind of structure is the possibility of installing different bus bodies on a given chassis frame. Because the body is not used to share the loads of the frame, heavy weight must be the remarkable disadvantage.

这种车身结构的优势在于能够在给定的底盘架构上安装不同结构的客车车身。因为车身不再分担车架的负荷,车身质量偏大成为其最明显的缺点。

6. Many modern buses belong to the integrated body structure. The structure has a truss underbody instead of a thick and heavy frame. All the structural members including the skin panels share the load and affect one another to form a perfect body of light weight and high stillness.

许多现代公共汽车都采用承载式车身,这种结构具有一个桁架式底板,取代了粗大笨重的车架。包括围裙板在内的所有结构构件都将分担负载,各构件相互组合,形成了一个完美的轻质高强度的车身。

7. Curved glass is usually used to make the front and rear windshields of the motor vehicle because of beautiful shape and good visibility. The windshield of most modern cars is stuck on the window frame by special glue.

由于曲面玻璃具有漂亮的形状和良好的可视性,所以通常用来制作成汽车的前后挡风玻璃。现代汽车的挡风玻璃一般通过特制的胶水牢牢地粘在车窗框架上。

8. For natural ventilation, the side window can be regulated up and down or fore and aft. There are sealing strips between the regulated window and its guide channels.

为了实现自然通风,车辆侧窗能够控制升降,车窗与导槽间用密封条密封。

9. Some of the side windows are smoked colored and have heat isolation layer to prevent the interior from hot sunshine and to make the interior atmosphere gentle and comfortable. In the bus of perfect ventilation heating and air-conditioning, the side windows cannot be opened to improve sealing performance.

有些车辆的侧窗是茶色的,并且具有防止炽热阳光射入车内的隔热层,从而使车内的环境温和舒适。在装有良好的通风设备和空调的客车内,为了提高密封性能,车辆侧窗往往不能打开。

10. The operation principle of the heating system is to heat the air flowing through a radiator and to conduct it to the interior. The radiator is connected with the engine cooling system and heat comes from the engine cooling water.

车辆供暖系统的工作原理是加热流过散热器的空气并且将其导入驾驶室内。该散热器与发动机的冷却系统相连,其热量来自发动机的冷却液。

11. The main principle of the refrigeration cycle goes like this: the first step, to lower the pressure so as to make the refrigerant change from liquid to gas, i.e. to evaporate and absorb heat; the second step, to increase pressure and to cool the refrigerant so as to make it reduce to the original liquid state, i.e. to condense and disperse heat.

制冷循环的主要原理是:第一步,降低压力以便使制冷剂由液体转换为气体,也就是蒸发和吸收热量过程；第二步，提高压力并冷却制冷剂，使其还原为原始的液态，也就是凝结和散热过程。

12. Under the pressure of the compressor driven by the engine crankshaft through a V-belt, the circulation path of the refrigerant (expressed by thin arrows) is as follows: The first step, it flows from the storage tank through the expansion valve which lowers its pressure and increases its volume to become gas state, and then the refrigerant evaporates in the evaporator and absorbs heat, i.e. lowers the temperature of the surrounding air. The second step, the refrigerant from the evaporator flows through the compressor to increase pressure, goes through the condenser in front of the engine radiator to cool up, i.e. to reduce to liquid state, and returns to the storage tank.

在压缩机(由发动机曲轴通过 V 型带驱动)的压力下，制冷循环路径如下所示：第一步，制冷剂从储油罐流入安全阀，进行降压，同时体积变大，形成气态，然后在蒸发器里蒸发并吸收热量，即将周围的空气降温；第二步，制冷剂从蒸发器流到压缩机里，压力增大，经过发动机散热器前面的冷凝器降温，即还原为液态，并且回到储油罐中。

Exercises

Questions for discussion:

1. What is the use of a vehicle body?
2. How many kinds of body-frame structures?
3. What is the operation principle of the heating system?
4. What is the main principle of the refrigeration cycle?
5. Talk about some kinds of vehicle doors.

Fill in the blank according to the text

1. According to the way of load carrying, body shells can be classified into _____, _____, and _____ three kinds.
2. The engine hood consists of _____ and _____.
3. Types of doors sorted by their opening ways are _____, _____, _____, sliding door, _____ and swinging door.
4. Ventilation is necessary for taking in the _____ to the interior and driving the air polluted by _____ and _____ from the engine outside.
5. In a cold season, cooling water of the engine can be conducted to the _____ to heat the air.

Lesson 2
The Electrical System

Electricity is the flow of electrons. They are forced to move by electrical pressure, called voltage. The amount of electrons flowing through a circuit is called amperage. In an automobile, the electrical pressure is created by chemical action in the storage battery and by magnetic induction in the alternator.

An electric motor, called the starting motor, cranks the engine to enable it to draw in a combustible air-fuel mixture for starting. The ignition system furnishes the spark which ignites the compressed mixture. It increases the battery voltage to 20,000v which delivered to each spark plug in turn. The lighting system changes electron flow into light and the horn into sound. If the battery were the only supply of electrons necessary to operate all of the automotive electrical equipment, it would soon become discharged. To prevent this, an alternator, driven by the engine, produces enough electricity to operate the various electrical circuits. The excess is used to recharge the battery. To control the charging rate, according to the needs of the battery, a regulator is connected in the alternator circuit. It causes the charging rate to increase when the battery is low and to decrease when the battery becomes fully charged.

2.1 The Battery

The storage battery is often thought of as a storage tank for electricity. It does not, however, store electricity. The energy is stored in chemical form. When a connection is made from the battery to the starting motor, a chemical action takes place inside the battery, and a flow of electrons results.

2.2 The Alternator

Electricity can be produced by moving a conductor through a magnetic field. The opposite also holds true. By moving the magnetic field and holding the conductor, electricity can be generated in the conductor. This current is called an induced current. This is the basic principle of the alternator, an electromechanical device that changes mechanical energy into electrical energy.

The alternator has two main parts-a conductor and an electromagnet. The conductor is called the stator and the electromagnet, the rotor.

2.3 Starting System

The starting system of a car changes the battery's electrical energy into the mechanical energy needed to turn the crankshaft at about 2000 rpm. At that point, the engine can use the power of the burning air-fuel mixture to run by itself. Then the starter motor will disconnect from the crankshaft.

The basic parts of the starting system are the battery, starter motor, starter drive, starter solenoid or relay, and ignition switch.

2.4 Voltage Regulators

The voltage regulator of a car could be one of two types. The grounded voltage regulator regulates the amount of negative ground that goes into the rotor, while the grounded field voltage regulator controls the amount of positive ground that goes into the rotor. Both actions change the amount of direct current created by the alternator, which increases or decreases the amount of current provided to the battery as necessary to keep the amount of current within safe levels.

2.5 Electronic Ignition System

The ignition energy, high voltage and speed of operation of the traditional ignition system are limited mainly by the electrical and mechanical switching capacity of the contact breaker points. In electronic ignition system, however, the contact breaker points are replaced by non-contacting, non-wearing signal generators and electronic power switches, with most other parts of the traditional system retained. Typically, therefore, an electronic ignition system is made up of:

(1) An ignition coil.

(2) A distributor, in which the distributor cap, rotor, and advance/retard mechanism work exactly as in the conventional system.

(3) An electronic switch.

(4) Ignition cables and spark plugs.

Fig. 3-3 illustrates such a system. The ignition coil used in many electronic ignition systems has a low impedance primary winding, to reduce inductance and thus improve coil performance-this has been done simply by reducing the number of turns on the primary winding, which, in turn, increases the winding ratio to around 250:1 ~ 300:1. To limit the primary current a ballast resistor is added.

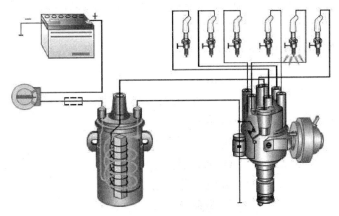

Fig. 3-3 Basic electronic ignition system

The ballast resistor (0.65ohm) also prevents overheating and provides thermal adjustment. From cold the resistance is low, therefore the primary current and secondary voltage is high. During idling the resistor heats up, resistance increases and the primary current is reduced. At high engine speeds, the time when the primary circuit closed is very short, so heating of the resistor is limited and the primary current remains high. When the starter motor is operated the ballast resistor is by-passed, in order to compensate for the voltage drop when the high starting current is drawn from the battery and thus provide the best conditions for starting.

From this basic electronic ignition system several others have evolved and are now in common use. All rely on the principle that the mechanical contact breaker points are replaced by a signal generator. The function of the signal generator is merely to generate signal corresponding to the positions of the pistons and feed them to a control unit. To this end, the signal generator may be housed in the distributor or any other place where information regarding piston position can be derived, e. g. directly from the flywheel or the camshaft. In the control unit the signals are conditioned to create a control waveform of sufficient magnitude to trigger the power switching transistor. This, in turn, triggers the ignition spark voltage in synchronism with the trigger signal pulses. The distributor assembly connects the coil's secondary voltage to the spark plugs in the correct timing sequence.

The control signal voltage can be generated in various ways, the most common being:

(1) Magnetic reluctance.

(2) Photo-electric effect.

(3) Hall effect.

Fig. 3-4 shows a block diagram of an electronic ignition system. Virtually all electronic ignition systems follow this simple format, in which a spark is created as the direct result of a signal from the signal generator. A signal conditioner shapes and amplifies the signal from the signal generator to a level where it is capable of driving a power switch (generally a transistor) which turns on and off current in the ignition coil's primary winding.

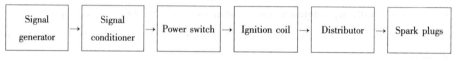

Fig. 3-4　Block diagram of a basic electronic ignition system

Technical Words and Terms

1. electron　　　　　　　　　　　n. 电子
2. amperage　　　　　　　　　　n. 电流强度,安培数
3. magnetic induction　　　　　　磁感应
4. electric motor　　　　　　　　电机
5. furnish　　　　　　　　　　　vt. 供给,保证,布置
6. spark　　　　　　　　　　　　n. 电火花
7. lighting system　　　　　　　　照明系统
8. discharge　　　　　　　　　　v. 放出,放电
9. recharge　　　　　　　　　　 v. 再充电
10. conductor　　　　　　　　　　n. 导体
11. induced current　　　　　　　感应电流
12. electromechanical　　　　　　adj. 机电的
13. run by itself　　　　　　　　　靠惯性
14. starter motor　　　　　　　　起动电机
15. starter drive　　　　　　　　　起动小齿轮
16. traditional　　　　　　　　　adj. 传统的,惯例的
17. capacity　　　　　　　　　　n. 性能
18. the contact breaker point　　　断电器触点
19. non-contacting　　　　　　　　非接触
20. non-wearing　　　　　　　　　不磨损

21. signal generator	信号发生器	
22. retain	*vt.* 保持,维持,保留	
23. electronic switch	电子开关	
24. cable	*n.* 电缆,索缆	
25. impedance	*n.* 阻抗,电阻	
26. performance	*n.* 性能	
27. ballast	*n.* 压载的,配重,镇流电阻	
28. thermal	*adj.* 热的,热力的	
29. primary current	初级电流	
30. circuit	*n.* 电路	
31. by-passed	旁路,迂回	
32. compensate	*v.* 补偿,补充,抵偿	
33. waveform	*n.* 波形	
34. magnitude	*n.* 大小,数量值,幅度	
35. transistor	*n.* 晶体管	
36. synchronism	*n.* 同步,同时	
37. in synchronism with	与……同步	
38. signal pulse	信号脉冲	
39. reluctance	*n.* 磁阻,阻抗,勉强	
40. photo-electric effect	光电效应	
41. Hall effect	霍尔效应	
42. format	*n.* 格式,规格,形式	
43. amplify	*v.* 放大,扩大,增强	

Notes

1. The lighting system changes electron flow into light and the horn into sound.
照明系统将电流变成光,喇叭将电流变为声音。

2. If the battery were the only supply of electrons necessary to operate all of the automotive electrical equipment, it would soon become discharged.
如果汽车上所有电器工作均由蓄电池供电,那么蓄电池很快就会把电能放完。

3. In electronic ignition system, however, the contact breaker points are replaced by non-contacting, non-wearing signal generators and electronic power switches, with most other parts of the traditional system retained.
在电子点火系统中,触点由非接触、无磨损的信号发生器和电子开关代替,但其他大多数元件与传统点火系统相同。

4. The ballast resistor (0.65ohm) also prevents overheating and provides thermal adjustment. From cold the resistance is low, therefore the primary current and secondary voltage is high.
附加电阻(0.65Ω)可防止初级线圈过热并能够进行热量调节。在温度低的情况下附加电阻阻值较低,因此,初级电流和次级电压较高。而在急速时附加电阻温度较高,阻值升高使得初级电流减小。

5. During idling the resistor heats up, resistance increases and the primary current is reduced. At high engine speeds, the amount of time when the primary circuit is closed is very short, so heating of the resistor is limited and the primary current remains high.

在发动机高速运转时,初级电路闭合的时间非常短,因此,限制了附加电阻的加热,从而可以保持较大的初级电流。

6. From this basic electronic ignition system several others have evolved and are now in common use.

以此基本电子点火系统为原型,目前已研制、改良出多种系统,并已广泛应用。

7. This, in turn, triggers the ignition spark voltage in synchronism with the trigger signal pulses.

按顺序依次触发信号脉冲,同时晶体管开关断开产生点火电压。

8. A signal conditioner shapes and amplifies the signal from the signal generator to a level where it is capable of driving a power switch (generally a transistor) which turns on and off current in the ignition coil's primary winding.

信号调节器从信号发生器里获取信号,并进行放大,使其能够打开断电开关(一般采用晶体管),此断电开关安装在点火线圈初级绕组中可以使初级电流导通或关断。

Exercises

Questions for discussion:

1. What does the electrical system include?
2. How does an alternator work?
3. How does starting system work?
4. How do voltage regulators work?
5. What is an electronic ignition system made up of?

Fill in the blank according to the text

1. In an automobile, the electrical pressure is created by chemical action in the _____ and by magnetic induction in the _____.

2. To control the charging rate, according to needs of the battery, a/an _____ is connected in the alternator circuit.

3. The basic parts of the starting system are the _____, _____, starter drive, starter solenoid or relay, and _____.

4. All rely on the principle that the mechanical contact breaker points are replaced by _____.

5. The control signal voltage can be generated in various ways, the most common being: Magnetic reluctance, _____ and _____.

Extension: Headlamp

A headlamp is a lamp attached to the front of a vehicle to light the road ahead. Headlamp performance has steadily improved throughout the automobile age, spurred by the great disparity between daytime and nighttime traffic fatalities: the U. S. National Highway Traffic Safety Administration states that nearly half of all traffic-related fatalities occur in the dark, despite only 25% of traffic travelling during darkness.

While it is common for the termheadlight to be used interchangeably in informal discussion, headlamp is the term for the device itself, while headlight properly refers to the beam of light produced and distributed by the device.

Other vehicles, such as trains and aircraft, are required to have headlamps. Bicycle headlamps are often used on bicycles, and are required in some jurisdictions. They can be powered by a battery or a small electrical generator on the wheel.

The earliest headlamps were fueled by acetylene or oil and were introduced in the late 1880s. Acetylene lamps were popular because the flame was resistant to wind and rain. The first electric headlamps were introduced in 1898 on the Columbia Electric Car from the Electric Vehicle Company ofHartford, Connecticut, and were optional. Two factors limited the widespread use of electric headlamps: the short life of filaments in the harsh automotive environment, and the difficulty of producing dynamos small enough, yet powerful enough to produce sufficient current.

"Prest-O-Lite" acetylene lights were offered by a number of manufacturers as standard equipment for 1904, and Peerless made electric headlamps standard in 1908. A Birmingham firm called Pockley Automobile Electric Lighting Syndicate marketed the world's first electric car lights as a complete set in 1908, which consisted of headlights, sidelights and tail lights and were powered by an 8 volt battery.

In 1912, Cadillac integrated their vehicle's Delco electrical ignition and lighting system, creating the modern vehicle electrical system.

"Dipping" (low beam) headlamps were introduced in 1915 by the Guide Lamp Company, but the 1917 Cadillac system allowed the light to be dipped with a lever inside the car rather than requiring the driver to stop and get out. The 1924 Bilux bulb was the first modern unit, having the light for both low (dipped) and high (main) beams of a headlamp emitting from a single bulb. A similar design was introduced in 1925 by Guide Lamp called the "Duplo". In 1927, the foot-operated dimmer switch or dip switch was introduced and became standard for much of the century. The last vehicle with a foot-operated dimmer switch was the 1991 Ford F-Series. Fog lamps were new for 1938 Cadillacs, and their 1954 "Autronic Eye" system automated the selection of high and low beams.

In 1935 Tatra T77a introduced light with cornering function - the front had three headlamps of which the central unit was linked to the steering, making it possible to turn this lamp with the steering wheel.

The standardized 7inch (178 mm) round sealed beam headlamp was introduced in 1940, and was soon required for all vehicles sold in the United States. Britain, Australia and other Commonwealth countries, as well as Japan, also made extensive use of 7inch sealed beams. With some exceptions from Volvo and Saab, this headlamp size format was never widely accepted in continental Europe, leading to different front-end designs for each side of the Atlantic for decades.

The first halogen lamp for vehicle headlamp use, the H1, was introduced in 1962 by a European consortium of bulb and headlamp makers. Shortly thereafter, headlamps using the new light source were introduced. These were prohibited in the U.S., where sealed beam headlamps were required. In 1978, sealed beam headlamps with internal halogen burners became available for use in the United States. Halogen sealed beams now dominate the sealed beam market, though it is considerably smaller than it was before replaceable-bulb composite headlamps returned to the U.S. in 1983.

High-intensity discharge (HID) systems were introduced in 1991s BMW;7-series. European and Japanese markets began to prefer HID headlamps, with as much as 50% market share in those markets, but they found slow adoption in North America. 1996's Lincoln Mark VIII was an early American effort at HIDs, and was the only car with DC HIDs.

Automotive headlamp applications using light-emitting diodes (LEDs) have been undergoing very active development since 2004. The first series-production LED headlamps were factory-installed on the Lexus LS 600h / LS 600h L presented in 2007 for 2008 models. Low beam, front position light and sidemarker functions are performed by LEDs; high beam and turn signal functions use filament bulbs. The headlamp is supplied by Koito. Full-LED headlamps supplied by AL-Automotive Lighting were fitted on the 2008 V10 Audi R8 sports car except in North America. The Hella headlamps on the 2009 Cadillac Escalade Platinum became the first U.S. market all-LED headlamps. Designs as of MY2010, such as those available as optional equipment on the 2010 Toyota Prius, give performance between halogen and HID headlamps, with system power consumption slightly lower than other headlamps, longer lifespans and more flexible design possibilities. As LED technology continues to evolve, the performance of LED headlamps is predicted to improve to approach, meet, and perhaps one day surpass that of HID headlamps.

The limiting factors with LED headlamps presently include high system expense, regulatory delays and uncertainty, and logistical issues created by LED operating characteristics. As a semiconductor, the performance of an LED is dependent on its temperature; a given diode will produce more light at a low temperature than at a high temperature. Thus, in order to maintain a constant light output, the temperature of an LED headlamp must be kept relatively stable. LEDs are commonly considered to be low-heat devices due to the public's familiarity with small, low-output LEDs used for electronic control panels and other applications requiring only small amounts of light; however, LEDs actually produce a significant amount of heat per unit of light output. Rather than being emitted together with the light as is the case with conventional light sources, an LED's heat is produced at the rear of the emitters. Unlike incandescent and HID bulbs, LEDs are damaged by high temperatures; prolonged operation above the maximum junction temperature will permanently degrade the LEDs and ultimately shorten the device's life. The need to keep LED junction temperatures low at high power levels requires thermal management measures such as heatsinks or cooling fans which are typically quite expensive.

Additional facets of the thermal issues with LED headlamps reveal themselves in cold ambient temperatures. Not only can excessively low temperatures lead to the LED's light output increasing beyond the regulated maximum, but heat must in addition be effectively applied to thaw snow and ice from the front lenses, which are not heated by the comparatively small amount of infrared radiation emitted forward with the light from LEDs.

LEDs are increasingly being adopted for signal functions such as parking lamps, brake lamps and turn signals as well as daytime running lamps, as in those applications they offer significant advantages over filament bulbs with fewer engineering challenges than headlamps pose.

Part II Introduction: Motor Vehicle and Society

If we review the history of human society, it is easy to find that the greatest contribution to the human civilization in the 20th century is the motor vehicle. Motor vehicle have changed the living style of our society, brought us a modern industry production mode, and pushed forward the transportation revolution, city planning and social progress.

The Most Important Transportation Tool

Motor vehicle is the most important transportation tool. In modern society, there is no transportation tool which can compare favorably with the motor vehicle. Although a railway train or a water ship may carry more passengers and goods than a motor vehicle, it is clear that they can only operate along particular routes (railways or water routes) and pick up or drop off passengers and goods at particular points (railway stations or wharfs). Although airplane is suitable for distant and fast transportation, it needs airports too. Evidently railway train, water ship and airplane are those kinds of transportation tools can only function along "lines and points" whereas motor vehicle is not. It is a kind of transportation tool functioning on "surface", that is, motor vehicles can go to almost everywhere in cities or country-sides. Moreover, they also have the advantage of "door to door" convenience, that is, to carry passengers and goods conveniently from one door to another door. Therefore, for the past several decades motor vehicle has become the most important and the most favorable transportation tool in the society.

Nowadays, motor vehicles have become necessities not only in public transportation, but also in people's daily life. Compared with the other transportation tools, the transportation quantity of motor vehicle is the most and compared with the other machine products, the number of motor vehicles is the most too. There are more than 900 million motor vehicles throughout the world. Among them 80% are passenger cars. Average rate of ownership, i.e. the population divided by the total number of motor vehicles, is about 7 persons per motor vehicle in the world. This rate is1.2 in U.S.A, about 2 in many developed countries such as Japan, west and north European countries and Australia, and 5 to 10 in South Korea, Russia and east European countries (Tab. 0-1). The reason why motor vehicles are so popular is that they can keep pace with people's daily activities. That is to say, motor vehicles can speed up work efficiency and living tempo. Once you own a car, you can go somewhere in your own way without constraint by the schedule and the route of public transportation tools. The motor vehicle has become such a satisfactory, efficient, convenient and comfortable tool in everyone's mind.

Average rate of motor vehicle ownership in some countries in 2011   Tab. 0-1

Country	Rate of ownership (persons/vehicle)	Country	Rate of ownership (persons/vehicle)
U.S.A	1.3	Japan	1.7
Italy	1.5	China	17.2
France	1.7	India	56

Pillar Industry of National Economy

Motor vehicle became a product in large quantities at the beginning of 20th century. Since then, human civilization developed with the motor vehicle industry progress. So far, motor vehicle has been a pillar industry of our society. The first "assembly line" appeared in Model T mass production by Henry Ford in 1913, who was the founder of Ford Motor Company. The new production method made the massive production of cars possible and high productivity resulted in low price and popularity. This new production technology was introduced to all the other industry processes and it led to a revolution of production method and a new era for the modern industry. But in the same time, increasing requirements and the automotive union make the automotive industry in the western shrink and face big challenge in surviving.

The annual production of motor vehicles in the world is nearly 70 million units (Tab. 0-2). A modern vehicle consists of more than 10 thousand parts which are made of various materials such as steel, alloys, plastics, rubber, glass, textures, wood and coatings, and by various manufacturing technologies such as smelting, casting, forging, cutting, welding, assembling and painting. Many kinds of industries are involved such as metallurgy, machine-building, chemical industry, electronic industry, electric power industry, petroleum industry and light industry. Many kinds of business are also involved such as banking, commerce, transportation, tourist trades and service trades (Fig. 0-2). It is for sure that none of the aspects of industry and businesses in the national economy does not concern automotive industry.

Top 10 Motor Vehicle Producing Countries in 2011   Tab. 0-2

Rank	Country	Passenger cars (1000 units)	Commercial vehicles (1000 units)	Total (1000 units)
1	China	14 485	3 934	18 419
2	U.S.A.	2 966	5 687	8 654
3	Japan	7 159	1 240	8 399
4	Germany	5 872	439	6 311
5	Korea	4 222	435	4 657
6	India	3 054	883	3 936
7	Brazil	2 535	872	3 406
8	Mexico	1 657	1 023	2 680
9	Spain	1 819	534	2 354
Total	Global Production	59 932	20 132	80 064

Another contribution of motor vehicle is its huge demand for labor force, from production line, marketing, after-sale service and car maintenance, to public transportation, highway con-

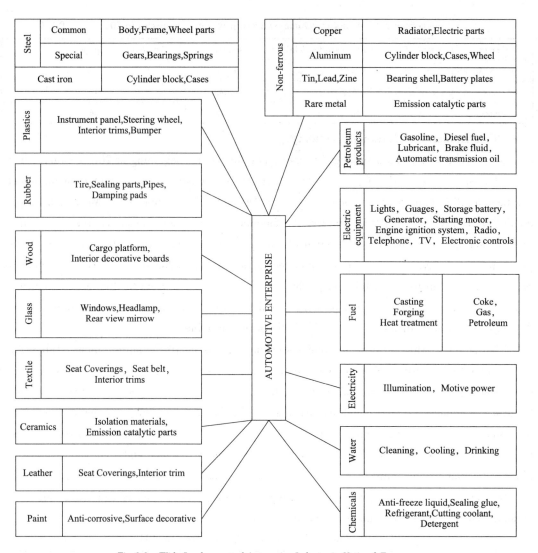

Fig. 0-2 Wide Involvement of Automotive Industry in National Economy

struction, 1/9 of the total laborers work in the automotive sectors in Japan now, and this ratio is even higher in the U.S. and Germany, which is 1/6. There are more than 3 million technical, management personnel and blue-collar workers in the manufacturing plants of motor vehicle in China now. Automotive sectors in China have created more than 30 million job positions which make up 1/7 of salary laborers in this country (Tab. 0-3). Undoubtedly, motor vehicles have brought a huge labor group and high rate of employment to the society.

Comparison of Laborers in Three Countries (1000 people)　　　Tab. 0-3

Item	U.S.	Japan	China
Number of laborers in automotive sectors	21000	7270	30000
Total number of laborers in the country	129520	64360	202000*
Comparison of the upper two items	1/6	1/9	1/7
*Laborers in cities and towns, total laborers in China are about 800 million.			

The automotive industry is also highly profitable. In the developed countries, lots of automotive firms such as GM, Daimler-Chrysler, Toyota, Ford and Volkswagen are powerful giants and rank top places among the list of "global top 500 companies" (Tab. 0-4). In these countries, the total production value of the automotive industry is 7% to 8% of GDP (Gross Domestic Product) and 30% of the production value of the machine-building industry. Therefore, all the developed countries in the world regard the automotive industry as "the pillar industry of national economy" without exception.

Rank of Powerful Automotive Firms among Global Top 500 Companies in 2012   Tab. 0-4

Global top 500 rank	Automotive firm	Revenues ($100 millions)
10	TOYOTA MOTOR	2 353.64
12	VOLKSWAGEN	2 215.51
19	GENERAL MOTORS	1 502.76
21	DAIMLER	1 481.39
27	FORD MOTOR	1 362.64
42	NISSAN MOTOR	1 191.66
45	EXOR GROUP	1 172.97
64	HONDA MOTOR	1 006.64
69	BMW	956.92
85	PEUGEOT	833.05
110	ROBERT BOSCH	716.00
117	HYUNDAI MOTOR	702.27
130	SAIC MOTOR	672.55
142	DONGFENG MOTOR GROUP	629.11
158	RENAULT	592.72
165	CHINA FAW GROUP	570.03
208	VOLVO	478.14
238	CHINA SOUTH INDUSTRIES GROUP	431.60
241	CONTINENTAL	424.16
251	JOHNSON CONTROLS	408.33
259	DENSO	399.54
266	KIA MOTORS	389.88
276	BRIDGESTONE	379.43
314	TATA MOTORS	345.75
350	SUZUKI MOTOR	318.17
379	AISIN SEIKI	291.83
382	MICHELIN	288.09
385	MAGNA INTERNATIONAL	287.48
428	MAZDA MOTOR	257.49
465	HYUNDAI MOBIS	237.36
475	ZHEJIANG GEELY HOLDING GROUP	233.56
482	MITSUBISHI MOTORS	228.90
487	GOODYEAR TIRE & RUBBER	227.67

Indicator of Latest Science and Technology

The modern automobile uses a lot of state-of-the-art science and technology, such as leading-edge materials and new structures in various components including improved electronics in its gauges and panel controls. These improvements have come as a result of many skilled and talented people performing constant research and development. This R & D (Research and Development) process is carried out through many means, for example, through thousands of scientific studies utilizing the latest theories, advanced methods of measuring, the latest in computer programming, computer design, and precision-controlled test environments. From there, the automotive industry has also seen improvements being made through advances in manufacturing processes, increases in the use of automation, and even through the introduction of newer management styles. Without doubt, the motor vehicle has become a product that displays the best that science and technology can offer. It is also an indicator and measure of greater capability for a nation that is on the rise. Ongoing development within the automotive industry will also result in helping to promote advances being made in the general science and technology fields.

As more and more people in China have purchased their family cars, the living style of the car owners have changed a lot. Because the highways have been greatly improve (it is possible driving 1000 km within one day), more and more people can enjoy their long travels by cars. For example, they can travel to their hometown during Spring Festival.

We can see roads divided by lanes, controlled traffic lights and signs, connected fly-over junctions, parking lots, city ring roads and highway networks between cities. Have you ever thought that all these facilities are built to meet the requirements of motor vehicles? Indeed, the motor vehicle has changed the city planning and our environment tremendously. Moreover, the effect of the motor vehicle on our society is not only substantial, but also spiritual. Motor vehicle brings us lots of cultural products and activities. Every day you can find the news related the motor vehicle from media such as TV programs, radios and newspapers. Not only lots of specialists work hard on their design, research, sales, service and advertisements, but also citizens take the motor vehicle as an interesting topic in their ordinary conversations. There are so many movies and magazines for enjoyment where the motor vehicles play important roles under the camera shots. Auto museums, auto shows and motor races have become the interesting activities around the world. They are usually most crowded places and attract so many auto fans, collectors and even fanatics in the society.

One of the famous books was titled as "The Machine That Changed the World". After long term investigation, James P. Womack, a professor of MIT (Massachusetts Institute of Technology) and his fellow researchers wrote this book. Here the machine means the motor vehicle. It might be proper to take the title of the book as conclusion of this section.

Unit 4 Vehicle Maintenance and Testing

Lesson 1
Vehicle Maintenance Inspection

After a long term operation, performances or technical conditions of a motor vehicle would not be as good as before. Parts would not fit each other very well because their shape has changed out of abrasion, heavy load and damage (Fig. 4-1). Accident might happen if not to take measure to solve such problems. The best way is to send the motor vehicle to the service shop.

Before repair, inspection and diagnosis are needed. Inspection is to examine the performances of the motor vehicle by the measurement of some particular parameters. Diagnosis is to analyze the inspection result and to find out the exact trouble cause.

The following describes basic maintenance tasks. These can be applied to almost any vehicle, past or present, which is driven on a regular or semi-regular basis. For vehicles that spend much of their time in storage, like sports cars in winter climes, a vastly different set of maintenance rules should be followed, and might even make a future. How To Do a Maintenance Inspection subject.

Fig. 4-1 Missing Friction Material and Exposed Rivets

1.1 Brakes

Brake adjustment should be checked during a driver's daily vehicle examination. When adjustment and maintenance is neglected, the results can be catastrophic, particularly on mountainous terrain.

Not all drivers are qualified to adjust brakes. Some drivers have caused accidents by unintentionally backing the brakes off when adjusting them. This can lead to runaway, increased stopping distances, jackknifing, trailer swing, or other control problems resulting from ineffective brakes or improper brake balance.

The compressor was not able to supply sufficient air to the system resulting in excessive air build-up times and low application pressures. It appeared that at some time in the vehicle's history the air line above was used as a handhold to gain access to the engine components and became kinked in the process. A driver can check air build-up times during the daily vehicle inspection.

1.2 Exhaust system

Carbon monoxide from diesel emissions can be dangerous. Prolonged exposure to concentrations of CO can lead to headaches, shortness of breath, nausea, dizziness or light-headedness.

These symptoms adversely affect a driver's ability to safely control a commercial motor vehicle.

In certain situations, exhaust system leaks can also lead to death. As an example, this can occur when a driver is resting inside the sleeper berth of an idling vehicle.

Proper vehicle inspections can address exhaust system issues before these problems occur. It is important to have the hood open when the engine is first started so that the initial smoke from start-up can be used to identify any system leaks. This can be accomplished by leaving the hood-open after the driver checks fluid levels in the engine compartment. Leaks may be more difficult to detect visually once the engine warms to operating temperature. While leaks may occur anywhere in the system, important areas to check include turbochargers, manifolds, flanges and couplers between exhaust system components, and clamps.

After a suspected CO poisoning incident has occurred, the use of a calibrated CO meter may be required to quantify CO levels within the occupant compartment. Additionally, it may be important to understand airflow from the engine compartment to the occupant compartment. Fatigue, drug and alcohol use, and other causes may have similar symptoms to CO poisoning.

1.3 Fuel system

Loss of fuel system integrity can result in vehicle fires (Fig. 4-2). The truck was part of a fleet that hauled and applied bulk fertilizer for agricultural uses. The fertilizers were highly corrosive to metallic parts and systems on the truck. A cause of the fire was determined to be a hole in the fuel supply line, resulting in a fuel leak. An inspection of other units in the fleet of trucks that hauled and applied the fertilizers revealed unusually excessive corrosion of many metallic parts including metal fuel lines and hydraulic brake lines. One of the other units in the fleet was found to have a small hole and corresponding leak in a metallic fuel line. For applications with highly corrosive materials, the level of detail and frequency of vehicle inspections should have increased vigilance.

Fig. 4-2 Fatal Truck Fire

1.4 Lighting Devices

Many post crash investigations include questions as to whether lights were illuminated at the time of an impact. Several post crash investigations have revealed light fixtures without light bulbs, and other investigations have revealed light bulbs that have been painted over when the vehicle was repainted. Proper vehicle inspections should have revealed many of these inadequate illumination issues.

1.5 Suspension

Failure of trunnion u-bolts (Fig. 4-3) on a loaded end-dump trailer led to a tip-over collision as the vehicle was in a low-speed turn. This particular problem would have been difficult for a driver to detect because the break occurred out of view between the upper and lower halves of the trunnion hub. Examination of recovered parts suggested that the failure sequence was progressive, initiating at the outside portion of the rear trunnion u-bolt. Because this member was in tension, a small gap opened at the fracture surface, allowing water and dirt to accumulate along with heavy oxidation. The ultimate separation of other u-bolt connections did not occur until sometime later. This was evidenced by cleaner fracture surfaces.

Fig. 4-3 Trunnion U-bolt Failure

Based upon an experience like this, a carrier may implement new procedures in an attempt to increase the safety of their operation and prevent future occurrences of the same type. A problematic component may need more careful monitoring than would be afforded by a routine daily vehicle inspection.

1.6 Frame

As part of their inspections, drivers should look for cracked, broken, loose or sagging frame members, adequate tire clearance, missing fasteners, and missing or disengaged locking pins on adjustable axle assemblies. Installation of a gasket material between the dissimilar metals at the time of manufacture or upon early detection of this problem could have prevented the total loss.

1.7 Tires

Among others, references such as the "Out of Service Tire Analysis Guide" and "Radial Tire Wear Conditions and Causes" published by The Maintenance Council of American Trucking Associations provide information and photographic depictions relevant to tire deficiencies. This type of information can help a driver or motor carrier to recognize developing conditions before they become a problem. Some tire deficiencies are rooted in tire-related causes and some are symptomatic of other root causes. These manuals help the reader discern deficiencies related to improper load and/or inflation, improper tire selection, misalignment, imbalance, run-out, poor suspension maintenance, poor driver practices, wheel and rim problems, and even the improper use of chains or other traction assists.

Conditions such as low air, damage, separations, and unusual or excessive tire wear can be easily detected through daily vehicle inspections. These deficiencies can then be corrected to prevent control problems and other hazards associated with tire disablements.

A semi-circular pattern of burnishing discovered on the frame of the converter dolly and elimination of other possible causes indicated that a run flat tire rubbed on the frame to cause the fire. This type of condition can also be a potential detriment to vehicle control and stability.

1.8 Wheels and Rims

The "Wheel and Rim out of Service Guide" published by The Maintenance Council of American Trucking Associations contains information and photographic depictions related to the causes of wheel and rim out of service conditions. As with tires, some causes are related to deficiencies in the wheels and rims themselves, and some deficiencies are rooted elsewhere. A driver should be able to identify common wheel and rim problems during the vehicle inspection. These include bolt hole cracks, hand hole cracks, rim cracks, wallowed or elongated bolt holes, distorted bolt hole chamfers, excessive wear or corrosion, bent flanges, burrs, and other damage that may cause tire damage, leaks, or the loss of a wheel assembly. As part of their daily vehicle inspection, drivers should look for any loose, missing, broken, cracked, stripped, or otherwise ineffective fasteners.

1.9 Windshield Glazing and Wipers

Visibility issues related to windshield glazing can be difficult to evaluate because windshields are often broken in accidents. Any vehicle that has a crack or discoloration in the windshield area within the sweep of the driver's side wiper should be placed in a restricted service condition according to CVSA O/OS criteria. The Minimum Periodic Inspection Standards also require that windshield wipers be operative at all times. The O/OS criteria require that the driver's side wiper must be inspected during inclement weather.

In a modern service shop there are quite a lot of advanced instruments and equipments for inspection and diagnosis. Being controlled by computers, they are intelligent, accurate, efficient and convenient. Many of them can examine the motor vehicle directly without disassembling any component off. The test results can be displayed, stored or printed. Some of the examples are engine universal inspector, engine leakage inspector, engine stethoscope, ignition timing gun, harmful emission analyzer, tester of braking performances, four wheel aligner, etc.

Technical Words and Terms

1. abrasion   n. 磨损
2. service shop   维修车间
3. inspection   n. 检查
4. diagnosis   n. 诊断
5. brake adjustment   制动碟
6. mountainous terrain   山区
7. runaway   n. 汽车失控
8. jackknifing   n. 折裂
9. trailer   n. 拖车
10. compressor   n. 压缩机
11. hood   n. 发动机罩
12. engine compartment   发动机室
13. manifolds   n. 阀组
14. coupler   n. 耦合器
15. hydraulic brake   液压制动器

16. trunnion	*n.* 轴颈
17. U-bolts	U 形螺栓
18. fracture surface	断裂面
19. monitor	*vt.* 监控
20. locking pin	插销
21. traction	*n.* 牵引
22. windshield	*n.* 挡风玻璃
23. periodic inspection	定期检修

Notes

1. After a long term operation, performances or technical conditions of a motor vehicle would not be as good as before. Parts would not fit each other very well because their shape has changed out of abrasion, heavy load and damage. Accident might happen if not to take measure to solve such problems. The best way is to send the motor vehicle to the service shop.

长时间使用后,车辆性能或技术状况将逐渐降低,一些零件由于磨损、承重和损坏而变形,相互之间间隙加大。如果不采取措施解决这些问题,容易发生事故,此时最好的方法就是将车辆送到修理厂进行维护。

2. It is important to have the hood open when the engine is first started so that the initial smoke from start-up can be used to identify any system leaks. This can be accomplished by leaving the hood-open after the driver checks fluid levels in the engine compartment.

在发动机第一次起动时,很重要的一点是将发动机罩打开,这样发动机起动时的初始烟雾能够用来检查是否有系统发生泄漏。驾驶员检查完发动机舱内的各个液面后即可关闭。

3. Examination of recovered parts suggested that the failure sequence was progressive, initiating at the outside portion of the rear trunnion u-bolt. Because this member was in tension, a small gap opened at the fracture surface, allowing water and dirt to accumulate along with heavy oxidation.

对于已修复零件的检查,建议检查顺序是从部分后轴颈 U 形螺栓开始,逐步向前。因为 U 形螺栓处于张力状态,断裂面上一个很小的裂缝就会使水和灰尘积累并导致发生严重的氧化反应。

4. A semi-circular pattern of burnishing discovered on the frame of the converter dolly and elimination of other possible causes indicated that a run flat tire rubbed on the frame to cause the fire. This type of condition can also be a potential detriment to vehicle control and stability.

在牵引车车架上可以看到一个抛光的半圆形图案,如果没有其他可能的原因,那就是轮胎摩擦车架造成的,这容易导致起火事故。这也是车辆操控性与稳定性的一个潜在危害。

5. These include bolt hole cracks, hand hole cracks, rim cracks, wallowed or elongated bolt holes, distorted bolt hole chamfers, excessive wear or corrosion, bent flanges, burrs, and other damage that may cause tire damage, leaks, or the loss of a wheel assembly.

这些现象包括螺栓孔裂纹、手孔裂纹、轮辋裂纹、浸泡或拉伸的螺栓孔、螺栓孔倒角弯曲、过度磨损或腐蚀、法兰盘弯曲、毛边以及其他形式的损坏,这些问题可能会导致轮胎损坏、漏气或者车轮组件丢失。

Exercises

Questions for discussion

1. What will occur if the brake is out of work?
2. How to inspect the exhaust system?
3. How to inspect the fuel system?
4. What will lead to if trunnion U-bolts failure?

Fill in the blank according to the text

1. When brake adjustment and maintenance is neglected, the results can be _____, particularly on mountainous terrain.

2. Prolonged exposure to concentrations of CO can lead to _____, shortness of breath, _____, _____, and light-headedness.

3. It is important to have the _____ open when the engine is first started so that the initial smoke from start-up can be used to identify any system leaks.

4. Conditions such as low air, _____, _____, and unusual or excessive tire wear can be easily detected through daily vehicle inspections.

Lesson 2
OBD Technology

2.1 Introduction

In the early 1980s, automobile manufacturers began using electronics and on-board computers to control many of the engine functions. The increasing complexity of vehicle technology led manufacturers to develop ways to effectively diagnose vehicle problems as a result of new electronic hardware. Thus, the earliest form of vehicle on-board diagnostics was developed by auto manufacturers to decrease the down-time spent diagnosing vehicles.

Due to these advances, it became more imperative to have equipment capable of communicating effectively with the vehicle OBD system and delivering this information to the technician. It was deemed necessary to standardize many aspects of the OBD system, including such things as the data link connector, communication protocol(s), and nomenclature. The Society of Automotive Engineers (SAE) developed these standardized methods or recommended practices to provide implementation guidance and design requirements for vehicle manufacturers complying with the OBD requirements and equipment and tool manufacturers developing service equipment, and to ensure vehicle and equipment compatibility. Some of these standards are referenced in the OBD Regulations making them a requirement for manufacturers to follow, such as the standards for scan tool operation.

2.2 Differences between On Board Diagnostic Systems (EOBD, OBDII, OBD-BR1 and OBD-BR2)

The Gasoline Engine Management Systems for passenger cars have the OBD-II (On Board

Diagnostic) for United States of America market, the EOBD (European On Board Diagnostic) for Europe and Brazil. This paper presents the differences between these OBD-BR1 and OBD-BR2 for four On Board Diagnostic Systems.

Emission related components are defined as a Power-train or Engine Management System input or output, which when it has failed, causes an Emission Impact or causes another On Board Diagnostic System to be disabled.

2.2.1 OBD-BR1

The Brazilian On Board Diagnostic System called OBD-BR1 was implemented in January 2007 for at least 40% of total vehicles commercialized by manufacturer. From January 2009 was increased for 100%.

The OBD-BR1 was a electric diagnostic for the following components: Manifold Absolute Pressure or Mass Air Flow Sensor, Throttle Position Sensor, Coolant Temperature Sensor, Intake Air Temperature Sensor, Oxygen Sensor, Vehicle Speed Sensor, Exhaust Gas Recirculation System, Camshaft Position Sensor, Crankshaft Position Sensor, Knock Sensor, Injector, Ignition Coil, Engine Control Module and other emission control component or system which should make diagnostic.

2.2.2 OBD-BR2

The OBD-BR2 was implemented in January 2010 for 60% of total vehicles commercialized by manufacturer. From January 2011 was increased for 100%. The OBD-BR2 is the OBD-BR1 plus the diagnostic of components that can contribute to an increase of pollutant emissions.

All On Board Diagnostic Systems should have a lamp to indicate an Emission Related Malfunction, see below:

(1) Malfunction Indication Lamp-MIL

The Diagnostic Malfunction Indication Lamp will turn ON according to the description below:

OBD-II - Since a Malfunction is detected, the Engine Management System can turn the MIL ON and record the failure up to two consecutive trips with the malfunction present. Once the MIL is ON, that diagnostic test shall pass for three consecutive trips without the same fault occurring to turn the MIL OFF.

EOBD - Since a Malfunction is detected, the Engine Management System can turn the MIL ON and record the failure up to ten consecutive trips with the malfunction present. Once the MIL is ON, that diagnostic test shall pass for three consecutive trips without the same fault occurring to turn the MIL OFF. After 40 key cycles of pass reports the malfunction will be eliminated from history memory.

OBD-BR1 - Since a Malfunction was detected, the Engine Management System should turn the MIL ON and record the failure. Once the MIL is ON, that diagnostic test must pass on three consecutive trips without the same fault occurring to turn the MIL OFF. After 40 key cycles of pass reports the malfunction will be eliminated from history memory.

(2) Catalytic Converter Degradation Diagnostic

The purpose of the catalytic converter degradation diagnostic is to determine the grade of the converter deterioration. The dual Oxygen Sensor method (one Oxygen Sensor before catalytic converter and another one after it) is used to relate the oxygen storage capacity of the converter. This method analyses the HC conversion efficiency.

OBD-II - The MIL will turn ON if the emissions exceed 1.75 times the applicable HC standard. The catalytic converter should maintain its characteristics at least 160,000km.

EOBD - The MIL will turn ON if the emissions exceed the absolute tailpipe HC standards. The catalytic converter should maintain its characteristics at least 100,000km.

OBD-BR1 - Not applied.

OBD-BR2 - The material available for OBD-BR2 Regulation is indicating that Brazil will follow EOBD standards.

(3) Oxygen Sensor Response Degradation Diagnostic

The purpose of the Oxygen Sensor response degradation diagnostic is to monitor the front Oxygen Sensor function. It is an indication of switching quality of the sensor.

OBD-II - The MIL will turn ON if that signal has deteriorated to a point where the emissions thresholds are reached 1.5 times the tailpipe standards.

EOBD - The MIL will turn ON if that signal has deteriorated to a point where the emissions thresholds exceed the absolute tailpipe standards.

OBD-BR1 - Not applied.

OBD-BR2 - The material available for OBD-BR2 Regulation is indicating that Brazil will follow EOBD standards.

(4) Misfire Diagnostic

The purpose of the Misfire Diagnostic is to continuously monitor for misfiring cylinders during the operation of engine. This misfire can occur due injector or ignition coil problems.

OBDII - The MIL will turn ON if the rate of misfire exceeds to a point where the emissions thresholds are reached 1.5 times the tailpipe standard. The diagnostic can be disabled below 15 percent of fuel tank level.

EOBD - The MIL will turn ON if the rate of misfire exceeds the absolute tailpipe standards. The misfire detection is below of 4500rpm engine speed and below of 2500m altitude. The diagnostic can be disabled below 20 percent of fuel tank level.

OBD-BR1 - Not applied.

OBD-BR2 - The material available for OBD-BR2 Regulation is indicating that Brazil will follow EOBD standards.

(5) Exhaust Gas Recirculation (EGR) System Degradation Diagnostic

The purpose of the exhaust gas recirculation system degradation diagnostic is to allow a precise control of the amount of exhaust gas directed from the exhaust manifold to the intake manifold.

OBD-II - The diagnostic is always performed and it is independent of pollutants caused in case of malfunction. For example: Feedback Sensor Signal malfunction, Valve Pintle Error and Excessive Flow.

EOBD - The diagnostic is required if a malfunction results in a pollutants higher than the absolute of tailpipe standards. For example: Feedback Sensor Signal malfunction, Valve Pintle Error and Insufficient or Excessive Flow.

OBD-BR1 and OBD-BR2 - This diagnostic is an Emission Related Component and the MIL will turn ON if the Engine Management System detects a malfunction.

(6) Fuel System or Fuel Trim Diagnostic

The purpose of the fuel system or fuel trim diagnostic is to monitor an average long term fuel multiplier value to determine how rich or lean the fuel system is running. The long term value is used by the engine control system to either add or subtract fuel to keep the fuel system at stoichiometry value.

OBD II - The MIL will turn ON if the system is running rich or lean enough where the emissions thresholds are reached 1.5 times the tailpipe standard.

EOBD - The MIL will turn ON if the emissions exceed the absolute tailpipe standards.

OBD-BR1 - Not applied.

OBD-BR2 - The material available for OBD-BR2 Regulation is indicating thatBrazil will follow EOBD standards.

(7) Vehicle Speed Sensor (VSS) Diagnostic

The purpose of the vehicle speed sensor diagnostic is to detect if the vehicle speed signal is missing.

OBD-II - The component input circuit tests is performed and it is informed as No VSS signal.

EOBD - The component input is tested and it is informed by Engine Management System that there is no VSS signal. The misfire detection may be disabled.

OBD-BR1 and OBD-BR2 - This diagnostic is an Emission Related Component and the MIL will turn ON if the Engine Management System detects a malfunction.

(8) Thermostat Monitoring

The purpose of the thermostat monitoring is to monitor and insure the engine reaches a temperature where all diagnostics will be enabled. The MIL will turn ON if the coolant temperature does not reach a temperature required for closed-loop operation within OBD-II specified time limits. This monitor can detect a skewed coolant sensor or a stuck problem in the thermostat.

This Diagnostic is applied only to OBD-II.

(9) Positive Crankcase Ventilation (PCV) System Monitoring

The purpose of the positive crankcase ventilation system monitoring is to monitor and insure the integrity of the connection between the crankcase and the PCV hose or valve.

(10) Idle System Monitoring

The purpose of the idle control system is to monitor when the actual idle speed is higher or lower than desired engine idle speed.

This Diagnostic is applied only to OBD-II.

(11) Evaporative Emissions System Monitoring

The purpose of the Evaporative Emissions System monitoring is to check any leaking in the evaporative system. The system requires two components: a canister vent shut-off solenoid and a fuel tank pressure sensor.

This Diagnostic is applied only to OBD-II.

Technical Words and Terms

1. down-time   故障时间
2. data link connector   数据传输连接器
3. power-train   动力系
4. Manifold Absolute Pressure   进气管绝对压力传感器
5. Mass Air Flow Sensor   空气质量流量传感器
6. Throttle Position Sensor   节气门位置传感器
7. Coolant Temperature Sensor   冷却液温度传感器
8. Intake Air Temperature Sensor   进入空气温度传感器
9. Oxygen Sensor   氧传感器
10. Vehicle Speed Sensor   速度传感器
11. Exhaust Gas Recirculation System   废气再循环系统
12. Camshaft Position Sensor   凸轮轴位置传感器
13. Crankshaft Position Sensor   曲轴位置传感器
14. Knock Sensor   爆震传感器
15. ignition coil   点火线圈
16. malfunction   *n.* 故障;失灵
17. Catalytic Converter   三元催化转化器
18. tailpipe   *n.* 排气管
19. misfire   *n.* 熄火
20. intake manifold   进气歧管
21. stoichiometry   *n.* 化学计量学
22. Positive Crankcase Ventilation   曲轴箱强制通风装置
23. idle speed   怠速
24. canister   *n.* 滤毒罐
25. vent   *n.* 通气孔
26. shut-off   节流阀

Notes

1. The increasing complexity of vehicle technology led manufacturers to develop ways to effectively diagnose vehicle problems as a result of new electronic hardware.

车辆技术的复杂性的不断增加使得汽车制造商不得不开发有效的诊断方法,由此产生了新的电子硬件产品。

2. Thus, the earliest form of vehicle on-board diagnostics was developed by auto manufacturers to decrease the down-time spent diagnosing vehicles.

因此,最早的车载诊断系统是由汽车制造商们研发出来,用以降低汽车诊断时的停机时间。

3. Emission related components are defined as a Power-train or Engine Management System input or output, which when it has failed, causes an Emission Impact or causes another On Board

Diagnostic System to be disabled.

排放组件是指动力系或发动机管理系统的输入或输出相关设备,当它失效时,会影响发动机排放或导致其他车载诊断系统的失效。

4. The purpose of the catalytic converter degradation diagnostic is to determine the grade of the converter deterioration. The dual Oxygen Sensor method (one Oxygen Sensor before catalytic converter and another one after it) is used to relate the oxygen storage capacity of the converter.

三元催化转化器退化诊断的目的是确定其退化程度。双氧传感器方法(一个氧传感器在三元催化转化器前面,另一个在后面)是用来测定转化器的氧含量。

5. The purpose of the exhaust gas recirculation system degradation diagnostic is to allow a precise control of the amount of exhaust gas directed from the exhaust manifold to the intake manifold.

废气再循环系统退化诊断的目的是对排气管中的废气循环到进气管进行精确地控制。

6. The purpose of the fuel system or fuel trim diagnostic is to monitor an average long term fuel multiplier value to determine how rich or lean the fuel system is running.

燃油系统或燃油调整诊断是监测很长一段时间平均燃油增长量,以决定燃油系统里的燃油量。

Exercises

Questions for discussion:

1. What the auto manufacturers develop OBD to do?
2. What the purpose of the Catalytic Converter Degradation Diagnostic?
3. What the purpose of the Misfire Diagnostic?

Fill in the blank according to the text

1. The purpose of the oxygen sensor response degradation diagnostic is to _____.
2. The purpose of the exhaust gas recirculation system degradation diagnostic is to allow a precise control of the amount of _____ directed from the exhaust manifold to the intake manifold.
3. The purpose of the _____ diagnostic is to monitor an average long term fuel multiplier value to determine how rich or lean the fuel system is running.
4. The purpose of the positive crankcase ventilation system monitoring is to monitor and insure the integrity of the connection between and _____.

Lesson 3
Vehicle Sensors

Performance of any control system is, first of all, related to the accuracy with which information about the operating variables or parameters is relayed to the controlling process. The sensors used to monitor the variables do so by converting the variables physical quantities into related electrical signals. Common measures in automobiles are temperature, pressure, flow, position, position/speed, knock and oxygen concentration.

3.1 Temperature Sensor

The ECM needs to adjust a variety of system based on temperatures. It is critical for proper operation of these systems that the engine reaching operating temperature and the temperature is accurately signed to the ECM. Temperature sensor measure Engine Coolant Temperature (ECT), Intake Air Temperature (IAT) and Exhaust Recirculation Gases (EGR), etc.

3.2 Manifold Absolute Pressure Sensor

The manifold absolute pressure sensor (MAP sensor) is one of the sensors used in an internal combustion engine's electronic control system.

Engines that use a MAP sensor are typically fuel injected. The manifold absolute pressure sensor provides instantaneous manifold pressure information to the engine's electronic control unit (ECU). The data is used to calculate air density and determine the engine's air mass flow rate, which in turn determines the required fuel metering for optimum combustion. A fuel-injected engine may alternately use a mass air flow sensor (MAF sensor is shown as Fig. 4-4) to detect the intake air flow. A typical configuration employs one or the other, but seldom both.

MAP sensor data can be converted to air mass data using the speed-density method. Engine speed (RPM) and air temperature are also necessary to complete the speed-density calculation. The MAP sensor can also be used in OBD II (on-board diagnostics) applications to test the EGR (exhaust gas recirculation) valve for functionality and is an application typical in OBD II equipped general motors' engines.

3.3 Mass air flow sensor

Fig. 4-4 Mass Air Flow Sensor

A mass air flow sensor is used to find out the mass flow rate of air entering a fuel-injected internal combustion engine. The air mass information is necessary for the engine's electronic control unit (ECU) to balance and deliver the correct fuel mass to the engine. Air changes its density as it expands and contracts with temperature and pressure. In automotive applications, air density varies with the ambient temperature, altitude and the use of forced induction, which means that mass flow sensors are more appropriate than volumetric flow sensors for determining the quantity of intake air in each piston stroke.

There are two common types of mass air flow sensors in use on automotive engines. These are the vane meter and the hot wire. Neither design employs technology that measures air mass directly. However, with additional sensors and inputs, an engine's electronic control unit can determine the mass flow rate of intake air.

Both approaches are used almost exclusively on electronic fuel injection (EFI) engines. Both sensor designs output a 0.0 ~ 5.0 volt or a pulse-width modulation (PWM) signal that is proportional to the air mass flow rate, and both sensors have an intake air temperature (IAT) sensor incorporated into their housings.

When a MAF is used in conjunction with an oxygen sensor, the engine's air/fuel ratio can be controlled very accurately. The MAF sensor provides the open-loop controller predicted air flow information (the measured air flow) to the ECU, and the oxygen sensor provides closed-loop feedback in order to make minor corrections to the predicted air mass.

3.4 Crankshaft Position Sensor

A crank position sensor is an electronic device used in an internal combustion engine to monitor the position or rotational speed of the crankshaft. This information is used by engine management systems to control ignition system timing and other engine parameters. Before electronic crank sensors were available, the distributor would have to be manually adjusted to a timing mark on the engine.

The crank sensor can be used in combination with a similar camshaft position sensor to monitor the relationship between the pistons and valves in the engine, which is particularly important in engines with variable valve timing. This method is also used to "synchronise" a four stroke engine upon starting, allowing the management system to know when to inject the fuel. It is also commonly used as the primary source for the measurement of engine speed in revolutions per minute.

3.5 Camshaft Position Sensor

This sensor is located near one of the camshafts. An AC signal is generated that is directly proportional to camshaft speed. That is, as the camshaft revolves faster the frequency increases. By knowing the position of the camshaft, the ECM determines when cylinder No. 1 is on the compression stroke.

3.6 Throttle Position Sensor

Throttle position sensor (TPS) is a sensor used to monitor the position of the throttle in an internal combustion engine. The sensor is usually located on the butterfly spindle so that it can directly monitor the position of the throttle. More advanced forms of the sensor are also used, for example an extra closed throttle position sensor (CTPS) may be employed to indicate that the throttle is completely closed. Some engine's electronic control units (ECUs) also control the throttle position and if that is done the position sensor is used in a feedback loop to enable that control.

3.7 Speed Sensor

As the term implies, the Speed Sensor (Fig. 4-5) measures how fast your car is travelling. It may be found in different locations depending on the vehicle, but in many models, it's positioned at the back of the differential. As mentioned, the sensor is crucial to the proper operation of various systems in your vehicle, so when it fails, related systems fail as well. For instance, if your sensor goes bad your odometer or speedometer will likely stop working. Since the sensor also regu-

Fig. 4-5 Speed Sensor

lates ignition timing and fuel flow, your horsepower will plummet. Your ride may also rumble abnormally and you'll encounter a lot of problems when shifting gears.

The Car Speed Sensor even plays a major role in your road safety. In many vehicles, the sensor is part of the Anti-Lock Braking System (ABS) that makes braking more precise. Through the signals sent by the sensor, the ABS is able to prevent the wheels from locking up and improve the vehicle's braking distance. This system is very important as the detection of minute speed variations actually reduces your risk of fishtailing on the highway. Another benefit of the sensor working with the ABS is that your tires last much longer as they don't skid as much because of precision braking.

3.8 Knock Sensor

The knock sensor detects engine knock and sends a voltage signal to the ECM. The ECM uses the knock sensor signal to control timing.

Engine knock occurs within a specific frequency range. The knock sensor, located in the engine block, cylinder head, or intake manifold is tuned to detect that frequency. Inside the block sensor is a piezoelectric element. Piezoelectric elements generate a voltage when pressure or a vibration is applied to them. The piezoelectric element in the knock sensor is tuned to the engine knock frequency. The vibrations from engine knocking vibrate piezoelectric element generating a voltage. The voltage output from the knock sensor is highest at this time.

3.9 Oxygen Sensor

Automotive oxygen sensors (Fig. 4-6), colloquially known as O_2 sensors, make modern electronic fuel injection and emission control possible. They help determine, in real time, if the air fuel ratio of a combustion engine is rich or lean. Since oxygen sensors are located in the exhaust stream, they do not directly

Fig. 4-6 Oxgen Sensor

measure the air or the fuel entering the engine. But when information from oxygen sensors is coupled with information from other sources, it can be used to indirectly determine the air-to-fuel ratio. Closed-loop feedback-controlled fuel injection varies the fuel injector output according to real-time sensor data rather than operating with a predetermined (open-loop) fuel map. In addition to enabling electronic fuel injection to work efficiently, this emissions control technique can reduce the amounts of both unburned fuel and oxides of nitrogen entering the atmosphere. Unburned fuel is pollution in the form of air-borne hydrocarbons, while oxides of nitrogen (NO_x gases) are a result of combustion chamber temperatures exceeding 1,300 K due to excess air in the fuel mixture and contribute to smog and acid rain.

The sensor does not actually measure oxygen concentration, but rather the difference between the amount of oxygen in the exhaust gas and the amount of oxygen in air. Rich mixture causes an oxygen demand. This demand causes a voltage to build up, due to transportation of oxygen ions through the sensor layer. Lean mixture causes low voltage, since there is an oxygen excess.

Technical Words and Terms

1. parameter   *n.* 参量
2. configuration   *n.* 结构
3. flowrate   *n.* 流量
4. ambient temperature   环境温度
5. vane meter   叶片式空气流量计
6. hot wire   (不用钥匙起动点火装置的)短路点火
7. Electronic Fuel Injection   电子控制燃油喷射系统
8. pulse-width modulation   脉冲宽度调制
9. proportional   *adj.* 成比例的
10. intake air temperature   进气温度
11. open-loop   开环的
12. closed-loop   闭环的
13. synchronise   *v.* 使同步
14. revolutions per minute   每分钟转速
15. odometer   *n.* 里程表
16. speedometer   *n.* 速度表
17. horsepower   *n.* 功率
18. plummet   *vi.* 骤然下跌
19. fishtailing   *vi.* 摆尾行驶
20. air-to-fuel ratio   空燃比

Notes

1. Performance of any control system is, first of all, related to the accuracy with which information about the operating variables or parameters is relayed to the controlling process.

首先，控制系统的性能与运行变量或参数被传递到控制程序的精确性息息相关。

2. In automotive applications, air density varies with the ambient temperature, altitude and the use of forced induction, which means that mass flow sensors are more appropriate than volumetric flow sensors for determining the quantity of intake air in each piston stroke.

在汽车使用过程中，空气密度随环境温度、海拔高度和压力而随时会发生变化，也就意味着在测定各个活塞行程的进气量时，空气流量传感器比体积流量传感器更准确。

3. The MAF sensor provides the open-loop controller predicted air flow information (the measured air flow) to the ECU, and the oxygen sensor provides closed-loop feedback in order to make minor corrections to the predicted air mass.

空气流量传感器为电子控制单元的开环控制器提供信号用来测试空气流量(流入的空气质量)，氧传感器为闭环反馈控制器提供反馈信息使其进行反馈式微量调节。

4. The crank sensor can be used in combination with a similar camshaft position sensor to monitor the relationship between the pistons and valves in the engine, which is particularly important in engines with variable valve timing.

曲轴位置传感器一般和凸轮位置传感器联合使用,用于监测发动机内活塞与气门之间的关系,它们在安装有可变气门正时装置的发动机中尤其重要。

5. As mentioned, the sensor is crucial to the proper operation of various systems in your vehicle, so when it fails, related systems fail as well.

综上可知,速度传感器在汽车控制过程中对正确操作各种系统起着决定性的作用,所以当它出现故障时,同时相关的多个系统也会发生故障。

6. For instance, your odometer or speedometer will likely stop working if your sensor goes bad. Since the sensor also regulates ignition timing and fuel flow, your horsepower will plummet. Your ride may also rumble abnormally and you'll encounter a lot of problems when shifting gears.

例如,如果速度传感器出现故障,里程表就会停止工作。另外,由于速度传感器的信号也用来控制点火正时和燃油喷射,所以将使得汽车功率急速下降,发动机会发出不正常的隆隆响声,变速器换挡时也会出现许多问题。

7. Through the signals sent by the sensor, the ABS is able to prevent the wheels from locking up and improve the vehicle's braking distance. This system is very important as the detection of minute speed variations actually reduces your risk of fishtailing on the highway.

通过获取速度传感器发出的信号,ABS 系统能够防止车轮抱死并且减小制动距离。另外,该系统可以检测车速每分钟的速度变化,降低车辆高速摆尾的危险,因此,该系统十分重要。

8. Since oxygen sensors are located in the exhaust stream, they do not directly measure the air or the fuel entering the engine. But when information from oxygen sensors is coupled with information from other sources, it can be used to indirectly determine the air-to-fuel ratio.

由于氧传感器安装在排气气流中,它们并不直接测量进入到发动机汽缸内的空气量或燃油量。但从氧传感器提供的信息与其他传感器信息综合分析后就可以间接地确定空燃比的大小。

9. Unburnt fuel is pollution in the form of air-borne hydrocarbons, while oxides of nitrogen (NOx gases) are a result of combustion chamber temperatures exceeding 1,300 kelvin due to excess air in the fuel mixture and contribute to smog and acid rain.

未燃尽的燃料是一种污染物,主要以碳氢化合物的形式在空气中传播。而氮氧化物是由于燃烧室的温度超过1300K 时,燃油混合物中空气过量而产生的,其扩散到大气中容易形成烟雾和酸雨。

Exercises

Questions for discussion

1. What did the vehicle sensors use to do?
2. Please list several common vehicle sensors.
3. Please introduce Oxygen Sensor briefly.

Fill in the blank according to the text

1. The _____ sensor provides instantaneous manifold pressure information to the engine's ECU.

2. A _____ sensor is used to find out the mass flowrate of air entering a fuel-injected internal combustion engine.

3. There are two common types of mass air flow sensors in use on automotive engines: these are the _____ and the _____.

4. A _____ sensor is an electronic device used in an internal combustion engine to monitor the position or rotational speed of the crankshaft.

5. A _____ sensor is a sensor used to monitor the position of the throttle in an internal combustion engine.

6. The _____ sensor measures how fast your car is travelling.

Extension 1: Road Test

High Speed Runway

High speed runway is a ring road, normally circular at both ends and straight at its central part, but some of the runways are elliptic. Most of the runways are 4 to 8 km long and have 3 lanes. Design speed of the runway is more than 200 km/h. It can provide long term continuous driving to examine the high speed performance and reliability of the motor vehicle, its components and parts.

Straight Dash

It is a straight runway for high speed dash (to develop the maximum speed). It is 2.5 to 4 km long and can be used to examine traction performance, braking performance, fuel economy, etc. In order to save construction investment, many proving grounds widen the central part of the ring runway and combine both functions together.

Roads for Reliability and Durability Test

During its whole life process, a motor vehicle may work on various road conditions. Therefore, roads of different pavement should be built on the proving ground to imitate the actual road conditions. Besides asphalt and concrete roads, other kinds of roads are needed, such as sandy, muddy, rocky, etc. The motor vehicle will make strengthened test on different road pavements so that the report of life evaluation can be obtained after a rather short period.

Body Twist

This kind of road pavement is made of trapezoid bumps arranged left and right alternatively and can imitate the crucial twisting situation of body, frame, front axle, rear axle, transmission system, etc.

Slopes

On the proving ground there should be some slopes of different gradients to examine the hill climbing performance of the motor vehicle. Other tests such as braking effectiveness and working condition of clutch can be examined on the slopes too.

Facility for Handling Stability Test

The most common facility is a circular field of cement concrete pavement with a diameter of 100 m. The test vehicle should make S-shape or 8-shape driving on the field to measure its deviation from the given direction. Water can be added to the field to make the pavement more slippery.

Slippery pavement is used to examine the operation performance or braking performance of a motor vehicle under low adhesive condition. Surface polish, water, ice or snow can be used to lower the adhesive coefficient of the pavement.

Lateral wind Installation can examine the aerodynamic stability of a motor vehicle. There are 15 big fans of diameter 2.7m arranged in a line beside the test road to develop strong wind perpendicular to the direction of the road. Lateral wind blowing onto the body makes the vehicle tend to deviate from its driving direction.

Pool Test

There are two kinds of pools on the proving ground, i.e. shallow pool (200 mm deep) and deep pool (1 ~ 2 m deep). The motor vehicle should go through the pool to examine the influence of water on its components such as electric equipment, brakes engine exhaust pipe, etc.

Facility for Collision Test

A facility for vehicle-barrier collision test includes a fixed barrier, four high speed cameras on the left, right, top and bottom of the car, illumination lights and ditch for installation of bottom camera. The above items are installed indoors. During the collision test, the test car driven by the motor and the winch through a wire cable goes down the slope and gradually accelerates. Then the speed of the car should be adjusted to a given constant speed. Being separated from the cable hook by the separating device, the car crashes to the barrier lastly.

Beside the above facility for head-on collision test, there are also facilities for lateral collision test, rear collision test, rollover test, etc.

Dummies are installed in the test car to imitate the motion of the occupants during the collision test.

Extension 2: Rig Test

Roller

Roller is an indoor test facility possible to make the motor vehicle run at a fixed location. The drive wheels of the test motor vehicle are placed on a roller and can rotate at different speeds.

Having the same axis with the roller, the dynamometer provides some resistant forces to the drive wheels of the motor vehicle. At the same time, it will measure the work done by the motor vehicle. Because the traction force acted on the drive wheels by the roller tends to push the motor vehicle forward, a cable is needed to balance this force and keep the motor vehicle standing at the location. The reading on the dial scale is the magnitude of the traction force. Readings of the platform scales under the front wheels of the motor vehicle may be different as it runs at different speed.

Hydraulic Servo Vibration Test

The test rig is an indoor test facility controlled by computer to imitate the forces caused by uneven road surfaces acting on four wheels of the motor vehicle. The test can be used for the study of vibration and life evaluation of the whole vehicle, its components and parts, which is a good way suitable for strengthened tests.

During the test, four road wheels are placed on four hydraulic actuators controlled by computer. According to a special computer program, the actuators reconstruct the uneven road condition and push the wheels of the motor vehicle up and down as if they are bumping on a real road. Moreover, the vibration amplitude can be enlarged easily for strengthened test.

In order to represent the real road condition, it is necessary to make a measuring apparatus rolling on typical roads to collect enough data, so called the "road pattern", which can be processed and compiled to become a special computer program.

Wind Tunnel

Wind tunnel is the facility to examine the aerodynamic performance of the motor vehicle. It can be used to measure six components (drag, side force, lift, pitching moment, yawing moment and rolling moment), to measure pressure distribution, and to display flow pattern. During the styling process, a special scale model should be made for a wind tunnel test to improve the body shape and its aerodynamic performance. It is impossible to measure six components at the same time by a road test. Therefore, the wind tunnel test has become an effective method for the study of aerodynamic performance of a motor vehicle.

According to the dimension, wind tunnel can be classified into two kinds, i.e. scale model wind tunnel and full size wind tunnel. According to the manner of the air flow, wind tunnel can be classified into two kinds, i.e. open circuit wind tunnel and closed circuit wind tunnel.

The tunnel consists of three sections, i.e. the contraction, the working section and the diffuser. Under the action of the fan, air enters the tunnel through the honeycomb, accelerates in the contraction, blows to the car/or car model in the working section and flows out through the diffuser. To install the car, a fixture connected by the six component balance is needed. Through the instruments in the working room, six components acting on the car can be measured.

Besides the measurement of force, the wind tunnel can also measure pressure distribution on the body surface of the car and display the flow pattern by the help of smoke, tuft, oil film, etc.

It is quite easy to know that air flowing out from the open circuit wind tunnel still has speed and kinetic energy. In other words, a considerable amount of energy wastes away. In order to save energy, a closed circuit to conduct the air flow from the diffuser back to the contraction is needed. That is the basic principle and basic structure of the closed circuit wind tunnel.

Engine Performance Test

The basic feature of an engine test rig is to connect the engine with a dynamometer. The dynamometer loads the engine and measures the torque and speed output by the engine. If electric dynamometer is used, it is essentially a generator to change the mechanical energy to electric energy which should be consumed by some electric equipment.

By means of the engine test rig, a number of engine performances can be measured such as the engine characteristics, emission analysis, comparison of different accessories, etc.

Transmission Performance Test

The main feature of a transmission performance test rig is to connect the input end of the test component to an electric motor and its output end to the dynamometer. The electric motor puts the component into action and the dynamometer absorbs the energy output by the component. Various components can be installed between the motor and the dynamometer to examine their performances, for example the torque and efficiency characteristics measurement of a torque converter, the gearbox performance test, etc.

Unit 5 Vehicle Modification and Recycling

Lesson 1
Car Tuning

Car tuning is a generalized term referring to the act of improving the performance or appearance of a vehicle. Most vehicles leave the factory set up for an average driver's expectations and conditions, tuning on the other hand, has become a way to personalize the characteristics of a vehicle to the owner's preference. Cars may be altered to provide better fuel economy, produce more power, or to provide better handling.

Car tuning is related to auto racing, although most performance cars never compete. Tuned cars are built for the pleasure of owning and driving. Exterior modifications include changing the aerodynamic characteristics of the vehicle via side skirts, front and rear bumpers, spoiler, splitters, air vents and light weight wheels.

1.1 Origin

In the 1970s and 80s, many Japanese performance cars were never exported outside the Japanese domestic market. In the late 1980s and early 1990s, grey imports of Japanese performance cars, such as the Nissan Skyline, began to be privately imported into Western Europe and North America. In the United States, this was in direct contrast to the domestic car production around the same time, where there was a very small performance aftermarket for domestic compact and economy cars; the focus was instead on sporty cars such as the Ford Mustang and Chevrolet Corvette, or on classic muscle cars.

Because of their light weight and the increasing availability of low-cost tuning equipment, economy and compact cars exhibit high performance at a low cost in comparison to dedicated sports cars. As professional sporting and racing with such vehicles increased, so did recreational use of these vehicles. Drivers with little or no automobile, mechanical, or racing experience would modify their vehicles to emulate the more impressive versions of racing vehicles, with mixed results.

1.2 Styles of modification

Modified cars can be significantly different from their stock counterparts. A common factor among owners/modifiers is to emulate the visual and/or performance characteristics of established styles and design principles. Sometimes these similarities are unintentional. Some of the many different styles and visual influences to car modification are following:

1.2.1 Rat styles
The characteristics of the rat rod style of hot rod and custom cars, imitating the "unfinished" appearance of some hot rods in the 40s, 50s and 60s.

1.2.2 Hot rod styles
The hot rod style largely consists of period specific vehicles, components and finishes to re-

produce characteristics of early hot rods from the 1930s and 1940s. This style may also include the associated styles of street rods and custom cars.

1.2.3 Modern styles

Modern styles include the recently established modification styles such as the Import scene, Lowriders, European (Euro-style), DUB, Cal Look, most of which are largely visually oriented.

1.2.4 Cultural/media styles

The characteristics are specific to cultures, stereotypes and media, such as boy racers and film specific cars. The Fast and the Furious (film series) provides an often emulated modification style.

1.2.5 Production car styles

Production car styles, in which the characteristics of current-model and luxury cars, sports cars, supercars and muscle cars are emulated, largely with the intent of improving or updating the vehicle appearance and/or technology to current market preferences.

1.2.6 Purpose built or racing car styles

Purpose built or racing car styles such as touring car racing, rallying, drifting and drag racing.

1.2.7 Sleepers

This is where a car owner will put every effort into performance and try to keep the car looking standard, usually in order to not raise suspicion.

1.3 Areas of modification

The essence of modification of a tuner car is an attempt to extract the greatest possible performance—or the appearance of high performance—from the base motor vehicle through the addition, alteration or outright replacement of parts. Although this largely involves modifying the engine and management systems of the vehicle to increase the power output, additional changes are often required to allow the vehicle to handle this power, including stiffened suspension, widened tires, better brakes, improved steering and transmission modifications and the installation of a short shifter. Although largely invisible from outside the vehicle, certain modifications such as low profile tires, altered suspension, and the addition of spoiler can change the overall appearance of the car.

1.3.1 Audio

Audio is a term used to describe the sound or video system fitted in vehicles. A stock audio system refers to one that was specified by the manufacturer when the vehicle was built in the factory. A custom audio installation can involve anything from the upgrade of the radio to a full-blown customization around the audio equipment. Events are held where entrants compete for the loudest, highest quality or most innovative sound systems.

1.3.2 Interior

All cars competing in each class must adhere to a strict set of regulations. As in some well known racing events, like NASCAR and NHRA, sanctioned events often require a minimum vehicle weight. In such cases the interior is stripped and lead weights or similar are added to meet that requirement.

Along with weight requirements, safety requirements are present. Requirements differ for different classes. Roll cages, fire extinguishers, reinforced bucket seats, seat harnesses, and the like are some of the required safety modifications. Roll cages may be difficult to install when the original equipment interior is present. Some tuners will have "gutted" interiors. Some even go as far as to not have a sound system or even an A/C.

1.3.3 Engine tuning

Engine tuning is the process of modifying the operating characteristics of an engine. In a typical engine set-up, there are various mechanical and electronic elements such as the intake manifold, spark plugs, mass air flow/volume air flow, etc. Modern engines employ the use of an ECM to provide the best balance between performance and emissions. Via the OBD communications protocol, the electronically controlled aspects of the engine can be modified in the process known as "mapping". Mapping can either be performed by changing the software within the ECU (chip tuning via firmware modification), or by provide false data via plug-in hardware (piggybacking). Mechanical components can also be replaced, such as turbochargers or superchargers.

Other standalone engine management systems are available. These systems replace the factory computer with one that is user programmable.

Poorly executed modifications can have a detrimental effect on performance as well as mechanical and electronic components. An example would be the use of an air compressor such as a turbocharger to increase the volume of air used in power stroke of the Otto cycle. In a typical chemical reaction, the air-fuel ratio must be a minimum of $14:1$. If higher ratios are used, higher pressures and temperatures are observed in the cylinders. Depending upon the build of the engine, such operating parameters can lead to premature failure such as warped cylinder heads and walls (temperature related), cracked connecting rods and crankshafts (excessive torque applied), engine seizing and blowouts.

1.3.4 Suspension tuning

Suspension tuning involves modifying the springs, shock absorbers, sway bars, and other related components of a vehicle. Shorter springs offer greater stiffness and a lower center of gravity at the cost of proper suspension geometry. Stiffer shock absorbers improve the dynamic weight shifting during cornering and normally have shorter internals to stop them from bottoming out when shorter springs are used. Stiffer sway bars reduce body roll during cornering, thus improving the grip that the tires have on the surface; this also improves handling response due to faster weight shifting (similar to stiffer springs). The danger with overly stiff sway bars is the lifting of the inner wheel, which reduces its traction. Other components that are sometimes added are strut bars, which improve the body stiffness and help better maintain the proper suspension geometry during cornering. On some cars, certain braces, anti-roll bars, etc., can be retrofitted from sports models.

For off road vehicles, the emphasis is on lengthening the suspension travel and installing larger tires to increase ground clearance.

These suspension modifications are in contrast to lowriders with hydraulic or pneumatic suspensions. Lowriders use another type of suspension tuning in which the height of each individual wheel can be rapidly adjusted by a system of rams, which, in some cases, makes it possible to "bounce" the wheels completely clear of the ground.

1.3.5 Body tuning

Body tuning involves adding or modifying spoiler and a body kit in order to improve the aerodynamic performance of a vehicle. Through the generation of down force, cornering speeds and tire adhesion can be improved, often at the expense of increased drag. To lighten the vehicle, bodywork components such as hoods and rear view mirrors may be replaced with lighter weight components.

Often, body modifications are done mainly to improve a vehicle's appearance, as in the case of non-functioning scoops, spoilers, wide arches or other aesthetic modification. Aftermarket spoilers or body kits rarely improve a car's performance. The majority, in fact, adds weight and increase the drag coefficient of the vehicle, thus reducing its overall performance.

Increasing the wheel track width through spacers and wide body kits enhance the cars cornering ability. Lowering the center of gravity via suspension modifications is another aim of body tuning. Often, suspension tuners unfamiliar with spring dynamics will cut stock springs, producing a harder, bouncy ride. It is also common to lower the car too far beyond the optimal center of gravity purely for appearance.

Competition cars may have light weight windows, or the windows may be completely removed, as auto glass adds significant weight. Plastic windows are much more vulnerable to scratches which reduce service life.

1.3.6 Tires

Tires have large effects on a car's behavior and are replaced periodically. Therefore tire selection is a very cost effective way to personalize an automobile. Choices include tires for various weather and road conditions, different sizes and various compromises between cost, grip, service life, rolling resistance, handling and ride comfort.

Technical Words and Terms

1. aerodynamic   *adj.* 空气动力(学)的
2. bumper   *n.* 保险杠
3. spoiler   *n.* 尾翼,扰流板
4. splitter   *n.* 副变速器
5. aftermarket   *n.* 后市场
6. stiffen   *v.* (使)变硬
7. suspension   *n.* 悬架
8. ECM   电子控制模组(电脑)
9. warped   *adj.* 反常的,乖戾的,(变)弯曲的,变形的
10. cracked   *adj.* 有裂缝的,声音沙哑的,精神失常的
11. side skirt   车侧裙
12. air vent   通风(系统)

13. car tuning 汽车改装
14. fuel economy 燃油经济性
15. low profile tire 低断面轮胎
16. roll cage 防滚架
17. intake manifold 进气歧管
18. spark plugs 火花塞
19. mass/volume air flow 空气流量计
20. air compressor 空气压缩机
21. Otto cycle 奥托循环
22. sway bar 稳定杆
23. anti-roll bar 防倾杆
24. off road vehicle 越野车
25. ground clearance 离地间隙
26. hydraulic suspension 液压悬架
27. pneumatic suspension 气动悬架
28. aerodynamic performance 空气动力学性能
29. tire adhesion 轮胎附着力
30. rear view mirror 后视镜
31. drag coefficient 阻力系数
32. rolling resistance 滚动阻力

Notes

1. Car tuning is a generalized term referring to the act of improving the performance or appearance of a vehicle.

汽车改装是一个广义的术语,包括改进汽车性能或外观的所有行为。

2. The essence of modification of a tuner car is an attempt to extract the greatest possible performance—or the appearance of high performance—from the base motor vehicle through the addition, alteration or outright replacement of parts.

汽车改装的本质是试图通过增加、改动或彻底更换原车部件以尽可能提高汽车性能或使其看起来具有更高的性能。

3. Stiffer shock absorbers improve the dynamic weight shifting during cornering and normally have shorter internals to stop them from bottoming out when shorter springs are used.

较硬的减振器可提高汽车转弯时重心变化的动态特性,它们一般情况下具有较短的减振腔,从而可防止使用短弹簧造成的触底反弹现象。

4. Through the generation of down force, cornering speeds and tire adhesion can be improved, often at the expense of increased drag.

通常可在牺牲动力性的代价下通过生成向下的作用力以提高汽车弯道行驶速度和轮胎附着力。

5. It is also common to lower the car too far beyond the optimal center of gravity purely for appearance.

单纯为了外观效果而较大地降低汽车重心的情况也很常见。

6. Choices include tires for various weather and road conditions, different sizes and various compromises between cost, grip, service life, rolling resistance, handling and ride comfort.

选择轮胎依据不同的天气和道路条件、不同的尺寸、价格、附着性能、使用寿命、滚动阻力、操纵性能以及乘坐舒适性，做出不同折中的方案。

Exercises

Questions for discussion

1. How many styles are there in modification?
2. What are the characteristics of the rat rod style?
3. What can be modified in car tuning?
4. What can be improved through the body modification?

Fill in the blank according to the text

1. Modified cars can be significantly different from their stock _____.
2. The characteristics specific to cultures, _____ and media, such as Boy racers and film specific cars.
3. The essence of _____ of a tuner car is an attempt to extract the greatest possible performance.
4. Body tuning _____ adding or modifying spoilers and a body kit in order to improve the _____ performance of a vehicle.

Lesson 2
National Code of Practice for Light Vehicle Construction and Modification (NCOP, Australia)

This subsection applies to all light vehicles and must be read and applied in conjunction with all the LA Codes applicable to the proposed modifications.

Modified vehicles must continue to comply with the Australian Design Rules (ADRs) to which they were originally constructed, except as allowed for in the Australian Vehicle Standards Rules (AVSR). These modified vehicles must also comply with the applicable in-service requirements of the AVSR.

Modified pre-ADR vehicles must continue to comply with the AVSR.

Compliance with the AVSR also means compliance with the equivalent regulations of a State or Territory of Australia.

2.1 Choice of Replacement Engine

A manufacturer's standard or optional engine should be selected and installed using all the standard components for that vehicle model. However, where this is not practicable, the following requirements should be met:

Any replacement engine should be of similar mass and power output to that of an engine fitted by the original vehicle manufacturer as standard or optional equipment;

When the replacement engine is larger in power output than an engine offered by the vehicle manufacturer as standard or optional equipment, the vehicle must be equipped with any necessary upgrading of equipment, e. g. brakes, front suspension, etc. ;

The power and/or torque of the replacement engine must not exceed the capacity of the vehicle driveline.

Using the engine manufacturer's published specifications, the dimensions of the selected engine should be checked against the vehicle to ensure that:

The engine, together with all of its components, fits into the available space without major frame, body or other modifications;

The engine mass and location of centre of mass must not result in excessive mass on the front or rear suspension;

The location of ancillary equipment, such as the cooling system, the intake and exhaust systems must be suitable for the vehicle layout;

The replacement engine must be installed in a position and on an angle that allows the driveline to operate correctly.

If the installation requires modifications to the vehicle structure, such as chassis rails and firewalls, the modification must be performed in accordance with the applicable LH Code(s).

2.2 Modification to Engine Components

Substitution or replacement of components such as camshafts, carburettors, engine management systems, exhaust systems, etc. must not be carried out unless it can be demonstrated that the vehicle will continue to meet the appropriate gaseous and noise emission standards (refer to Codes LT3 and LT4 in Section LT *Test Procedures*).

2.3 Engine Mounts

Providing detailed design guidelines for an engine/transmission support system is beyond the scope of this document. However, factors to be considered should include the following:

The engine mounts must provide for vibration isolation between the engine and the body;

The design and construction of the engine mounts must be adequate to withstand the torque output of the engine and the inertial forces from accelerating, braking and cornering; the installation of replacement engine mounting brackets does not require certification under the LH Codes provided that sub-frames, chassis members or body members are not altered.

2.4 Clearances

The engine must clear all surrounding components in the engine bay at maximum engine movement including under maximum torque in both forward and reverse gears. A clearance of at least 10mm must be provided beyond that required for maximum engine movement.

Additional clearance must be provided to components likely to deteriorate from the heat from nearby engine and exhaust components. In particular, flexible fuel pipes, power steering hose and steering column shaft couplings incorporating rubber or fabric components must be placed well clear of hot exhaust components and shielded if necessary.

When fitting a replacement engine to a vehicle with a beam type front axle, sufficient clearance must be provided between the top of the axle, steering linkages and drive shaft (on four wheel drive vehicles) and the engine (usually the sump) to allow the axle full bump movement.

2.5 Guarding

To minimize the danger to any person working on the vehicle with the engine running, any exposed rotating parts should be guarded.

Radiator cooling fans should be fitted with guards to restrict access to the top of the fan.

Where guards were originally fitted, the guards must be retained.

2.6 Brake Booster

The vacuum hose between the brake booster (where fitted) and the inlet manifold must be securely fastened at each end using hose clamps or similar. The vacuum connection on the inlet manifold must be located in a position that ensures sufficiently low pressure at the brake booster. This is usually downstream of the throttle body or inlet butterfly on petrol engines.

Some highly modified engines might not develop the required low pressure in the inlet manifold at idle for proper functioning of the brake booster. In such cases, the vehicle must be fitted with a vacuum reservoir or vacuum pump to meet the ADR braking requirements.

In the case of a diesel engine conversion on a vehicle with vacuum boosted brakes, it must be fitted with a vacuum pump of capacity adequate to meet the ADR braking requirements.

2.7 Exhaust System

Where possible, the muffler(s) and catalytic converter and/or particle trap from the exhaust system of the donor vehicle should be used.

Where alternative exhaust systems are fitted, the system must incorporate any engine emission control equipment, meeting the same standard, as that fitted in the exhaust system of the vehicle.

Where an exhaust system runs through an inner mudguard panel, the panel cutout must not weaken the inner guard and if necessary, the panel must be reinforced to compensate for the cutout. Exhaust systems passing through inner guard panels must clear the wheels, tires and suspension components over the full range of travel of the suspension and steering.

Exhaust systems must be provided with appropriate shielding, a minimum of 100mm ground clearance and also meet the ground clearance requirements of ADR.

The outlet of an exhaust system must be rearwards of any passenger side entry door or opening window. If any part of the exhaust system, including the outlet pipe, extends beyond the profile of the body (other than on the underside), it must be shielded. Exhaust outlets must also meet the requirements of ADR. Vehicles manufactured after June 1988 must not have the exhaust exiting to the left of the vehicle.

Modified exhaust systems must not unnecessarily restrict the flow of exhaust gases and must be free of tight bends and other restrictive components.

2.8 Fuel System

Only flexible hose specifically designed, manufactured and marked for use as a fuel hose, may be used for fuel supply or return in the fuel system. The pressure rating of the fuel hose must not be less than the operating pressure of the fuel system.

The ends of fuel hoses must be securely fastened with hose clamps or clips to prevent fuel leakage. In any event, the system used to secure the hoses or pipe joints must be suitable for the operating pressure of the fuel system.

Fuel lines must be positioned well clear of any component that can reach high temperatures and cause the fuel to vaporize or damage flexible fuel hoses. These components can include parts of the engine and accessories such as the exhaust system, turbocharger and air-conditioning compressor.

Fuel lines must be adequately supported and shielded where necessary to prevent damage from hot components and road debris.

Fuel lines must be adequately protected from chafing or damage where they pass through panels, bulkheads or chassis members.

Fuel vapor hoses or pipes associated with the evaporative emission system (charcoal canister) must be connected and the system must continue to operate as designed.

2.9 Engine Cooling System

Hoses between the radiator and the engine should allow for any movement between them. The hoses should be positioned and supported (if necessary) to avoid excessive force on their connections. Hoses must not be kinked.

The engine thermostat must not be removed. It is designed to enable the engine to quickly reach and remain at its normal operating temperature, which in turn reduces exhaust emissions.

The system should be designed to prevent cavitations at the coolant pump. This may be achieved by avoiding any restriction on the pump suction inlet and ensuring that the coolant level in the reservoir is higher than the highest point in the engine galleries and the coolant pump.

A close-fitting shroud should be mounted between the extremities of the radiator and the cooling fan to ensure efficient cooling (and to minimize danger from exposed rotating fan blades).

2.10 Windscreen Demister

Heater hoses that supply the windscreen demister system must be re-connected to ensure that it functions correctly.

2.11 Electrical System

Electrical wires in wiring looms must be protected from mechanical damage by wrapping with tape or enclosing them in conduit, or other covering. Looms must be supported on the vehicle at positions no more than 600mm apart with allowance being made for the relative movement that can occur between the engine/transmission and the body/chassis.

The replacement engine's alternator output rating and the battery capacity should be compatible with the vehicle's electrical systems and the replacement engine.

Adequate protection from excessive heat should be provided for all electrical harnesses (and other hose, rubber and plastic components). All heat and noise insulation material as originally fitted should be retained.

With some engine substitutions the battery has to be relocated to the passenger or luggage compartment. Unless a special kind of battery (e. g., a sealed gel cell) is used in these locations, the battery must be fully enclosed with the enclosure vented to outside the vehicle. Electrically insulated enclosures such as sealed marine battery boxes should be used. The battery must be securely fastened to the vehicle. Battery cables must be shielded where necessary to prevent damage from road debris and be secured to the body at a maximum spacing of 600mm. Rubber grommets must be fitted where cables pass through holes in body panels and chassis sections.

2.12 Fabrication

All work must be performed in accordance with recognized engineering standards. Cutting, heating, welding or bending of components should be avoided by choosing unmodified production components wherever possible.

2.12.1 Welding, Fasteners and Electroplating

Mandatory requirements and guidance on the above items are contained in Section LZ *Appendices*.

For the use of fasteners refer to Appendix A *Fasteners*;

For welding techniques and procedures refer to Appendix C *Heating and Welding of Steering Components*;

For electroplating refer to Appendix D *Electroplating*.

2.12.2 Mating Parts

Standard features such as splines, tapers and keyways must conform to published standards and their mating parts must conform to matching standards.

2.13 Engine Capacity

For certification purposes under Codes LA1, LA2, LA3 and LA4, the recommended maximum capacity (swept volume) of engines for passenger cars and passenger car derivatives is outlined in Tab. 5-1 below. An engine may not be a suitable replacement even if its capacity falls within the limits specified in Tab. 5-1. Owners are therefore advised to check details of a proposed engine conversion with an engineering signatory prior to commencing any work.

Recommended Maximum Engine Capacity   Tab. 5-1

MASS OF VEHICLE	Maximum Engine Capacity (refer to notes below)	
	Naturally Aspirated	Turbo/Supercharged
All vehicles originally weighing less than 800 kg.	Original mass (kg) × 3.0 = max. capacity in cc's	Original mass (kg) × 2.5 = max. capacity in cc's
All vehicles originally weighing between 800 kg and 1100 kg.	Original mass (kg) × 4.0 = max. capacity in cc's	Original mass (kg) × 2.75 = max. capacity in cc's
All vehicles originally weighing more than 1100 kg.	Original mass (kg) × 5.0 = max. capacity in cc's	Original mass (kg) × 3.0 = max. capacity in cc's

Tab. 5-2 provides examples as to how the maximum engine capacity is determined.

Examples of Maximum Recommended Engine Capacity   Tab. 5-2

Vehicle	Naturally Aspirated	Forced Induction
1970 Corolla (4 cyl 746 kg)	2238 cc (746 × 3)	1865 cc (746 × 2.5)
1977 Celica (4 cyl 1067 kg)	4268 cc (1067 × 4)	2934 cc (1067 × 2.75)
1973 Falcon XBGT (1557 kg)	7785 cc (1557 × 5)	4671 cc (1557 × 3)

The maximum engine capacity for rotary engines is calculated by multiplying the swept volume of all rotors by two (e.g. a 13B rotary engine has a swept volume of 1308 cc resulting in a calculated maximum capacity of 2616 cc). Tab. 5-3 provides examples of how the engine capacity of rotary engines is determined.

Examples of Maximum Recommended Engine Capacity for Rotary Engines   Tab. 5-3

Rotary engines	Displacement	Sweep Volume	Maximum Capacity
10A	491 cc × 2	982 cc	1964 cc
12A	573 cc × 2	1146 cc	2292 cc
13B	654 cc × 2	1308 cc	2616 cc
20B	654 cc × 3	1962 cc	3924 cc

Tab. 5-1 does not apply to commercial (ADR Category NA and NB1) or four-wheel drive off-road (ADR category MC) type vehicles such as commercial vans, light trucks, small buses, etc. for which there are no set recommended limits.

Technical Words and Terms

1. driveline   n. 动力传动系统
2. shield   n. 盾,护罩,盾形奖牌,保护人;vt. 保护,掩护,庇护,给……加防护罩
3. butterfly   n. 节气门蝶形阀体
4. muffler   n. 消声器,消音器
5. mudguard   n. 挡泥板
6. bulkhead   n. 舱壁,隔板
7. cavitation   n. 气蚀现象,孔蚀现象
8. shroud   n. 护罩

9. demister		n. 除雾器,去雾器
10. conduit		n. 导管,水道,沟渠
11. alternator		n. 交流发电机
12. compatible		adj. 兼容的,相容的,可以并存的,能共处的
13. mandatory		adj. 强制的,命令的,受委托的
14. derivative		n. 导数,微商,衍生物,派生物,派生词
15. front suspension		前悬架
16. vibration isolation		隔振
17. torque output		转矩输出
18. inertial force		惯性力
19. engine bay		发动机舱
20. fuel pipe		燃料管
21. power steering hose		动力转向软管
22. steering column shaft		转向柱
23. front axle		前桥
24. steering linkage		转向联动装置
25. drive shaft		传动轴
26. radiator cooling fan		散热器冷却风扇
27. brake booster		制动助力器
28. vacuum hose		真空软管
29. vacuum reservoir		真空罐,真空储存器
30. vacuum pump		真空泵,真空机
31. catalytic converter		催化转化器
32. particle trap		颗粒捕集器
33. air-conditioning compressor		空调压缩机
34. charcoal canister		炭罐
35. rubber grommet		橡胶密封圈
36. mating part		配偶件
37. swept volume		工作容积,体积排量,活塞排量

Notes

1. Any replacement engine should be of similar mass and power output to that of an engine fitted by the original vehicle manufacturer as standard or optional equipment.

用于替换的发动机应该是与原装发动机具有相近质量和功率输出的标准设备或通用设备。

2. The engine must clear all surrounding components in the engine bay at maximum engine movement including under maximum torque in both forward and reverse gears.

不管车辆前进或倒退,当发动机输出转矩最大时,发动机的最大前后移动量必须保证其与舱内周边零件保持一定的距离。

3. Some highly modified engines might not develop the required low pressure in the inlet

manifold at idle for proper functioning of the brake booster.

一些高度改装的发动机可能不会出现制动助力器正常工作所需的进气歧管低压状态（车辆怠速时）。

Exercises

Questions for discussion

1. How many aspects are regulated in this code?
2. Which standards must be followed in engine components modification?
3. What should be guarded to minimize the danger to any person working on the vehicle with the engine running?
4. What is the fuel hose pressure rating regulation in fuel system modification?

Fill in the blank according to the text

1. A manufacturer's standard or optional engine should be selected and installed using all the _____ components for that vehicle model.
2. The design and construction of the engine _____ must be adequate to withstand the torque output of the engine and the inertial forces from _____, braking and cornering.
3. The vacuum _____ between the brake booster (where fitted) and the inlet manifold must be securely fastened at each end using hose clamps or similar.
4. Electrical wires in _____ looms must be protected from mechanical damage by wrapping with tape or enclosing them in conduit, or other covering.

Lesson 3
Vehicle Recycling

Vehicle recycling is the dismantling of vehicles for spare parts. At the end of their useful life, vehicles have value as a source of spare parts and this has created a vehicle dismantling industry. The industry has various names for its business outlets including wrecking yard, auto dismantling yard, car spare parts supplier, and recently, auto or vehicle recycling. Vehicle recycling has always occurred to some degree but in recent years manufacturers have become involved in the process. A car crusher is often used to reduce the size of the scrapped vehicle for transportation to a steel mill.

Approximately;12-15 million vehicles reach the end of their use each year in just the United States alone. These automobiles, although out of commission, can still have a purpose by giving back the metal that is contained in them. The vehicles are shredded and the metal content is recovered for recycling, while the rest is put into a landfill. The shredder residue of the vehicles that is not recovered for metal contains many other recyclable materials including 30% of it as polymers, and;5% ~ 10% of it as residual metals. Modern vehicle recycling attempts to be as cost-effective as possible. Currently, 75% of the materials are able to be recycled. As the most recycled consumer product, end-of-life vehicles provide the steel industry with more than 14 million tons of steel.

3.1 Process

The process of recycling a vehicle (Fig. 5-1) is extremely complicated as there are many parts to be recycled and many hazardous materials to remove. Briefly, the process begins with incoming vehicles being inventoried for parts. Then, recyclers start the engine in order to inspect for leaks. After inventory, fluids are drained and removed. After the fluids are removed, the final remaining hazardous materials such as battery, mercury, and sodium azide (the propellant used in air bags) are removed. After all of the parts and products inside are removed, the remaining shell of the vehicle is crushed and recycled.

Fig. 5-1 Vehicle Recycling Process

3.2 Benefits

Recycling steel saves energy and natural resources. The steel industry saves enough energy to power about 18 million households for a year, on a yearly basis. Recycling metal also uses about 74 percent less energy than making metal. Thus, recyclers of end-of-life vehicles save an estimated 85 million barrels of oil annually that would have been used in the manufacturing of other parts. Likewise, recycling keeps 11 million tons of steel and 800,000 non-ferrous metals out of landfills and back in consumer use. Before the 2003 model year, some vehicles that were manufactured were found to contain mercury auto switches, historically used in convenience lighting and antilock braking systems. Recyclers remove and recycle this mercury before the vehicles are shredded to prevent it from escaping into the environment. In 2007, over 2100 pounds of mercury were collected by 6265 recyclers.

3.3 Policies

If a vehicle is abandoned on the roadside or in empty lots, licensed dismantlers in the United States can legally obtain them so that they are safely converted into reusable or recycled commodities. In 1997, the European Commission adopted a Proposal for a Directive which aims at making vehicle dismantling and recycling more environmentally friendly by setting clear targets for the recycling of vehicles. This proposal encouraged many in Europe to consider the environmental impact of end-of-life vehicles. In response, there are companies that will provide services including: the pick-up of end-of-life vehicles from anywhere in North America, the assurance that the vehicle is handled appropriately, the de-pollution of the vehicle in an authorized treatment facility, and the recycling of the vehicle at shredding operations. In September 2000, this legislation was officially adopted by the EP and Council. On July 1, 2009 and the next 55 days, the Car Allowance Rebate System, or "Cash for Clunkers", started as an attempt at a green initiative by the United States Government in order to stimulate automobile sales and improve the average fuel economy of the United States. Many cars ended up being destroyed and recycled in order to fulfill the program, and even some exotic cars were crushed. Ultimately, as carbon footprints are of concern, some will argue that the "Cash for Clunkers" did not reduce many owners' carbon footprints. A lot of carbon dioxide is added into the atmosphere to make new cars. It is calculated that if someone traded in an 18 mpg clunker for a 22 mpg new car, it would take five and a half years of typical driving to offset the new car's carbon footprint. That same number increases to eight or nine years for those who bought trucks.

Technical Words and Terms

1. dismantling   *n.* 解散,(枪支)分解
2. polymer   *n.* [高分子]聚合物
3. hazardous   *adj.* 有危险的,冒险的,碰运气的
4. clarify   *v.* 得到澄清,变得明晰,得到净化
5. initiative   *n.* 主动权,首创精神; *adj.* 主动的,自发的,起始的
6. clunker   *n.* 年久失修的旧机器
7. mercury   *n.* 水银,水银柱,精神
8. approximately   *adv.* 大约,近似地,近于
9. landfill   *n.* 垃圾填埋地,垃圾堆
10. attempt   *n.* 企图,试图,攻击; *v.* 企图,试图,尝试
11. wrecking yard   废料场
12. auto dismantling yard   汽车拆除场
13. shredded   *adj.* 切碎的
14. non-ferrous metal   有色金属
15. treatment facility   处理设施
16. shredding operation   分解操作
17. carbon footprint   碳排放量
18. residual metal   残留金属

Notes

1. The shredder residue of the vehicles that is not recovered for metal contains many other recyclable materials including 30% of it as polymers, and 5% ~ 10% of it as residual metals.

汽车的非金属部分通常含有很多其他可回收材料,其中包括30%的高分子材料和5% ~ 10%的金属残留物。

2. Thus, recyclers of end-of-life vehicles save an estimated 85 million barrels of oil annually that would have been used in the manufacturing of other parts.

因而,回收报废汽车每年约节省85万桶石油,这些石油可被用于制造业的其他领域。

3. If a vehicle is abandoned on the roadside or in empty lots, licensed dismantlers in the United States can legally obtain them so that they are safely converted into reusable or recycled commodities.

如果在美国车辆被遗弃在路边或空地,一些经过授权的拆解者可依法取得它们的所有权,从而使那些汽车被安全地转换成可重复使用或回收的商品。

Exercises

Questions for discussion

1. Why does the industry have vehicle recycling process?
2. How many steps of the process of recycling a vehicle?
3. What are the policies of vehicle recycling around the world?

Fill in the blank according to the text

1. The process of recycling a vehicle is extremely complicated as there are many parts to be recycled and many _____ materials to remove.

2. Before the 2003 model year, some vehicles that were _____ were found to contain mercury auto _____, historically used in convenience lighting and antilock braking systems.

3. If a vehicle is _____ on the roadside or in empty lots, licensed dismantlers in the United States can legally obtain them so that they are safely converted into reusable or recycled _____.

Extension: Adapting Motor Vehicles for People with Disabilities

Introduction

A Proven Process for Gaining Freedom on the Road

The introduction of new technology continues to broaden opportunities for people with disabilities to drive vehicles with adaptive devices. Taking advantage of these opportunities, however, can be time consuming and, sometimes, frustrating.

The information in this lesson is based on the experience of driver rehabilitation specialists and other professionals who work with individuals who require adaptive devices for their motor vehicles. It is centered around a proven process-evaluating your needs, selecting the right vehicle, choosing a qualified dealer to modify your vehicle, being trained, maintaining your vehicle-that can help you avoid costly mistakes when purchasing and modifying a vehicle with adaptive equipment.

Also included is general information on cost savings, licensing requirements, and organizations to contact for help. Although the brochure focuses on drivers of modified vehicles, each section contains important information for people who drive passengers with disabilities.

Investigate Cost Saving Opportunities & Licensing Requirements

Cost Saving Opportunities

The costs associated with modifying a vehicle vary greatly. A new vehicle modified with adaptive equipment can cost from $20,000 to $80,000. Therefore, whether you are modifying a vehicle you own or purchasing a new vehicle with adaptive equipment, it pays to investigate public and private opportunities for financial assistance.

There are programs that help pay part or all of the cost of vehicle modification, depending on the cause and nature of the disability. For information, contact your state's Department of Vocational Rehabilitation or another agency that provides vocational services, and, if appropriate, the Department of Veterans Affairs. You can find phone numbers for these state and federal agencies in a local phone book. Also, consider the following.

(1) Many nonprofit associations that advocate for individuals with disabilities have grant programs that help pay for adaptive devices.

(2) If you have private health insurance or workers' compensation, you may be covered for adaptive devices and vehicle modification. Check with your insurance carrier.

(3) Many manufacturers have rebate or reimbursement plans for modified vehicles. When you are ready to make a purchase, find out if there is such a dealer in your area.

(4) Some states waive the sales tax for adaptive devices if you have a doctor's prescription for their use.

You may be eligible for savings when submitting your federal income tax return. Check with a qualified tax consultant to find out if the cost of your adaptive devices will help you qualify for a medical deduction.

Licensing Requirements

All states require a valid learner's permit or driver's license to receive an on‐the‐road evaluation. You cannot be denied the opportunity to apply for a permit or license because you have a disability. However, you may receive a restricted license, based on your use of adaptive devices.

Evaluate Your Needs

Driver rehabilitation specialists perform comprehensive evaluations to identify the adaptive equipment most suited to your needs. A complete evaluation includes vision screening and, in general, assesses:

(1) Muscle strength, flexibility, and range of motion.

(2) Coordination and reaction time.

(3) Judgment and decision making abilities.

(4) Ability to drive with adaptive equipment.

Upon completion of an evaluation, you should receive a report containing specific recommendations on driving requirements or restrictions, and a complete list of recommended vehicle modifications.

Finding a Qualified Evaluator

To find a qualified evaluator in your area, contact a local rehabilitation center or call the Association for Driver Rehabilitation Specialists (ADED). The association maintains a data base of certified driver rehabilitation specialists throughout the country. Your insurance company may pay for the evaluation. Find out if you need a physician's prescription or other documentation to receive benefits.

Being Prepared for an Evaluation

Consult with your physician to make sure you are physically and psychologically prepared to drive. Being evaluated too soon after an injury or other trauma may indicate the need for adaptive equipment you will not need in the future. When going for an evaluation, bring any equipment you normally use, e.g., a walker or neck brace. Tell the evaluator if you are planning to modify your wheelchair or obtain a new one.

Evaluating Passengers with Disabilities

Evaluators also consult on compatibility and transportation safety issues for passengers with disabilities. They assess the type of seating needed and the person's ability to exit and enter the vehicle. They provide advice on the purchase of modified vehicles and recommend appropriate wheelchair lifts or other equipment for a vehicle you own. If you have a child who requires a special type of safety seat, evaluators make sure the seat fits your child properly. They also make sure you can properly install the seat in your vehicle.

Select the Right Vehicle

Selecting a vehicle for modification requires collaboration among you, your evaluator, and a qualified vehicle modification dealer. Although the purchase or lease of a vehicle is your responsibility, making sure the vehicle can be properly modified is the responsibility of the vehicle modification dealer. Therefore, taking the time to consult with a qualified dealer and your evaluator before making your final purchase will save you time and money. Be aware that you will need insurance while your vehicle is being modified, even though it is off the road.

The following questions can help with vehicle selection. They can also help determine if you can modify a vehicle you own.

(1) Does the necessary adaptive equipment require a van, or will another passenger vehicle suffice?

(2) Can the vehicle accommodate the equipment that needs to be installed?

(3) Will there be enough space to accommodate your family or other passengers once the vehicle is modified?

(4) Is there adequate parking space at home and at work for the vehicle and for loading/unloading a wheelchair?

(5) Is there adequate parking space to maneuver if you use a walker?

(6) What additional options are necessary for the safe operation of the vehicle?

If a third party is paying for the vehicle, adaptive devices, or modification costs, find out if there are any limitations or restrictions on what is covered. Always get a written statement on what a funding agency will pay before making your purchase.

Choose a Qualified Dealer to Modify Your Vehicle

Even a half inch change in the lowering of a van floor can affect a driver's ability to use equipment or to have an unobstructed view of the road; so, take time to find a qualified dealer to modify your vehicle. Begin with a phone inquiry to find out about credentials, experience, and references. Ask questions about how they operate. Do they work with evaluators? Will they look at your vehicle before you purchase it? Do they require a prescription from a physician or other driver evaluation specialist? How long will it take before they can start work on your vehicle? Do they provide training on how to use the adaptive equipment?

If you are satisfied with the answers you receive, check references; then arrange to visit the dealer's facility. Additional information to consider is listed below.

(1) Are they members of the National Mobility Equipment Dealers Association (NMEDA) or another organization that has vehicle conversion standards?

(2) What type of training has the staff received?

(3) What type of warranty do they provide on their work?

(4) Do they provide ongoing service and maintenance?

(5) Do they stock replacement parts?

Once you are comfortable with the dealer's qualifications, you will want to ask specific questions, such as:

(1) How much will the modification cost? Will they accept third party payment? How long will it take to modify the vehicle?

(2) Can the equipment be transferred to a new vehicle in the future?

(3) Will they need to modify existing safety features to install the adaptive equipment?

While your vehicle is being modified, you will, most likely, need to be available for fittings. This avoids additional waiting time for adjustments once the equipment is fully installed. Without proper fittings you may have problems with the safe operation of the vehicle and have to go back for adjustments.

Some State Agencies specify the dealer you must use if you want reimbursement.

Obtain Training on the Use of New Equipment

Both new and experienced drivers need training on how to safely use new adaptive equipment. Your equipment dealer and evaluator should provide information and off-road instruction. You will also need to practice driving under the instruction of a qualified driving instructor until you both feel comfortable with your skills. Bring a family member or other significant person who drives to all your training sessions. It's important to have someone else who can drive your vehicle in case of an emergency.

Some state vocational rehabilitation departments pay for driver training under specified circumstances. At a minimum, their staff can help you locate a qualified instructor. If your evaluator does not provide on-the-road instruction, ask him or her for a recommendation. You can also inquire at your local motor vehicle administration office.

Maintain Your Vehicle

Regular maintenance is important for keeping your vehicle and adaptive equipment safe and reliable. It may also be mandatory for compliance with the terms of your warranty. Some warranties specify a time period during which adaptive equipment must be inspected. These "checkups" for equipment may differ from those for your vehicle. Make sure you or your modifier submits all warranty cards for all equipment to ensure coverage and so manufacturers can contact you in case of a recall.

Unit 6 Automobile Financial Service

Lesson 1
Car Leasing

As a sunrise industry, car rental industry is exerting more influences on the modern world. The health of the car rental industry partially determines whether the whole car industry can maximize its profits.

China's car rental industry started after the 1989 Beijing Asian Games, since then it has developed like bamboo shooting after a spring shower. With years of development, car rental has expanded itself to small and medium sized cities other than many capital cities. According to incomplete statistics, there are about 2,000 car rental companies with about 60,000 registered cars.

The world financial crisis not long before has a big effect on both individuals and companies. They all tighten their "purses" to purchase new cars. However, their needs of cars are not reduced. Thus, it is golden time to strive to develop our car rental industry. However, compared with foreign ones, China's car rental industry still faces many problems that need to be dealt with in order to let it develop healthily.

Major problems of car rental industry in China:

1.1 Lacking of Related Laws and Regulations

Up till now, although Chinese government has promulgated a few laws and regulations about car rental, the total legal system is far from sound and complete. Besides, as an infant industry, car rental industry is facing many new problems in new situations which cannot be solved with the former laws at the same time of developing itself. As a result, it develops with great restrictions lacking of enough related laws and regulations to support.

Take three major problems as examples:

(1) Based on a depth interview with a manger of Shouqi Car Rental Company, the authors found the fact that operating cars cannot be operated cross different regions, due to no support of the related laws which make it difficult to implement an extranet network cross regional borders.

(2) There is no clear definition that which party should bear the burden of car accidents as well as the responsibility. Although the Law of the People's Republic of China on Road Traffic Safety does not clearly state that the car rental company should bear the joint and several responsibilities, many courts still let the lessor share some responsibilities which leads to a loss to the lessor.

(3) Some lawbreakers make use of the leaks of the car rental contract to entice away the car. Thus, the car rental company has to pay their own money in exchange of the cars according to a deputy to the National People's Congress in 2010.

1.2 Lacking of Domestic Sound Credit Evaluation and Counseling System

According to a new report, in March 2010, the police in Guilin province arrested a suspect who rented 32 cars fraudulently during 6 months and received unlawfully money counting more than 1 million. This young man told the policemen that the reason that he cheated in the rent was that he wanted to pay off the loan sharks. From this case, it is manifest that social credibility is low and personal credit identification system of internal car rental companies is not perfect, which causes serious impacts such as rental arrears and cheated cars. Totally, low social credibility covers two aspects. One of them comes from problematic customers. Because of unclear credit information, it is risky for the car rental companies to rent the cars. Some criminals pay painstaking effort on cheating and delaying, which restricts the development of car rental industry. It is reported that cheated rental rate in domestic market is above 6%. On the other hand, a few rental companies are itching to make money at any cost. For example, they provide cars with potential safety hazard. When problematic cars need to be maintained or identified, they will charge compensation fee as much as possible. As a result, imperfect credit system causes company loss as well as indirectly creating opportunities to lawbreakers to take the advantage of the loopholes.

1.3 Lacking of Enough Publicity and Advertising

By using group discussion consisting of people from various working areas, the authors surprisingly found that there were still many people do not notice the car rental industry and from those who were aware of it still did not realize the real benefits of it. In fact, the authors themselves have to admit that it is hard to find some advertisements about the car rental companies. Besides, although some car rental companies have built up its own websites, the information is outdated which is not attractive to customers. Overall, the customer awareness of this industry is low and media and publicity coverage need to be expanded in the future.

1.4 Consumptive Psychologies—People Would Rather Buy a Car Instead of Renting

Having interviewed with a group of people, the authors found almost 80% people said that they would rather buy a car compared with renting a car. The reason is simple, the feeling of own and rent a car is totally different. It also slows down the pace of the car rental industry.

1.5 Heavy Taxes for Car Rental Company

For car rental companies, different kinds of taxes are a big burden. In the year of 1995, State Taxation Administration announced that car rental business tax should be collected as high as 5% of its turnover. So far, the tax fee for car rental companies consists of three links-purchasing, owning and using cars. In the first phase, added value tax, sales tax and license fee cannot be ignored. Insurance fee, management fee for cars and road toll should be paid when cars are owned. Housing tax, annual examine fee are also covered during the using process. As domestic high tax restriction policy is placed on car purchasing, car rental companies faced with frequent updating period of cars cannot bear such high taxes and fees. In return, to cover these high cost the car rental companies have to raise the price of their cars. Different from China, many developed countries have issued policies like soft loan and lower tax fee, which fasten the progress of car rental industry. Compared with them, China seems to have a relatively strict tax policy on the car rental industry.

1.6 Problems of Car Licenses Management

After several field interviews with many car rental companies, the authors found that another problem that many managers worried about is the management of car licenses. The scale of the car rental is almost determined by the number of cars allowed to rent, consequently, car licenses are vital to the car rental companies. Lacking of clear and standardized management and regulations on car licenses leads to various requirement of car licenses base on different regions, which result in many potential problems such as the ease of copying the real car licenses and the difficulty to recall cars.

Technical Words and Terms

1. leasing		*n.* 租赁,谎言;*v.* 出租
2. rental		*adj.* 租赁的;*n.* 租金收入,租金
3. bamboo		*n.* 竹,柱子
4. statistics		*n.* 统计,统计学
5. strive to		努力
6. promulgate		*vt.* 公布,转播,发表
7. infant industry		新生的工业
8. joint and several		连带的,共同的和个别的
9. entice		*vt.* 诱使,怂恿
10. deputy		*n.* 代理人,代表;*adj.* 副的,代理的
11. fraudulently		*adv.* 欺骗性的
12. loan shark		放高利贷者
13. arrears		*n.* 拖欠,待完成的事
14. be itching to		渴望
15. hazard		*n.* 危险,冒险;*vt.* 赌运气,冒……的风险
16. turnover		*n.* 营业额,流通量;*adj.* 翻过来的,可翻转的

Notes

1. China's car rental industry started after the 1990 Beijing Asian Games, since then it has developed like bamboo shooting after a spring shower.
中国的汽车租赁业始于1990年北京亚运会后,自那时起,它就像雨后春笋般快速发展起来。

2. Some lawbreakers make use of the leaks of the car rental contract to entice away the car.
一些不法分子利用汽车租赁合同中的漏洞骗走汽车。

3. Overall, the customer awareness of this industry is low and media and publicity coverage need to be expanded in the future.
总之,顾客对汽车租赁业认识不多,将来应扩大媒体及宣传报道。

Exercises

Questions for discussion

1. Please list the main problems of the car rental industry in China.
2. What the consequence of the lacking of domestic sound credit evaluation and counseling system?
3. What's the consumptive psychology of the consumers? Why?
4. What does the low social credibility include?
5. What does the tax fee for car rental companies consist?

Fill in the blank according to the text

1. Car rental industry is facing many new problems such as _____, lacking of _____, and lacking of _____ in new situations.
2. For car rental companies, _____ are a big burden.
3. Because of _____, it is risky for the car rental companies to rent the cars.
4. The scale of the car rental is almost determined by _____, consequently, _____ are vital to the car rental companies.

Lesson 2
Car Loan

2.1 Introduction of Loan

Like all debt instruments, a loan entails the redistribution of financial assets over time, between the lender and the borrower.

In a loan, the borrower initially receives or borrows an amount of money, called the principal, from the lender, and is obligated to pay back or repay an equal amount of money to the lender at a later time. Typically, the money is paid back in regular installments, or partial repayments; in an annuity, each installment is the same amount.

The loan is generally provided at a cost, referred to as interest on the debt, which provides an incentive for the lender to engage in the loan. In a legal loan, each of these obligations and restrictions is enforced by contract, which can also place the borrower under additional restrictions known as loan covenants. Although this article focuses on monetary loans, in practice any material object might be lent.

Acting as a provider of loans is one of the principal tasks for financial institutions. For other institutions, issuing of debt contracts such as bonds is a typical source of funding.

The most typical loan payment type is the fully amortizing payment in which each monthly rate has the same value over time.

The fixed monthly payment P for a loan of L for n months and a monthly interest rate c is:

$$P = L \cdot \frac{c(1+c)^n}{(1+c)^n - 1}$$

A Car Loan is a type of debt, a personal finance product where the financier lends the customer funds for the purchase of a vehicle, and secures the loan against that vehicle. A Car Loan can also be known as a Consumer Loan or a Secured Car Loan. We will organize the amount you require which is repaid over a period of up to 7 years. A deposit is not required on most cases, but may assist in your approval chances. The loan has a fixed interest rate and the interest is calculated on the unpaid balance daily, just like a home loan. Extra or additional payments will obviously reduce the outstanding balance and therefore reduce the interest charges. This can have the effect of shortening the term and reduce the overall cost of the loan.

Although it is a personal use loan, depreciation and interest charges could be tax effective claims if the car is for business or work related usage.

2.2　The Market for Auto Loans

According to Aizcorbe, Kennickell, and Moore (2003), automobiles are the most commonly held non-financial asset. For example, in 2001, over 84% of American households owned an automobile. In contrast, approximately 68% of American households owned their primary residence. Furthermore, loans related to automobile purchases are one of the most common forms of household borrowing (Aizcorbe and Starr-McCluer 1997 and Aizcorbe, Starr, and Hickman, 2003). Consistent with the high penetration of automobile ownership among households and the average automobile purchase price, Dasgupta, Siddarth, and Silva-Risso (2003) note that the vast majority of auto purchases are financed. In fact, Aizcorbe, Starr, and Hickman (2003) report that in 2001 over 80% of new vehicle transactions were financed or leased. As a result, given the size of the U.S. automotive market, it is not surprising that automobile credit represents a sizeable portion of the fixed-income market. For example, in 2002, debt outstanding on automobile loans was over $700 billion, and a growing percentage of this debt is held in "asset backed securities".

Financing for automobile purchases comes from three primary sources: dealer financing, leasing, and third party loans. Based on a sample of auto sales in Southern California between September 1999 and October 2000, Dasgupta, Siddarth, and Silva-Risso (2003) report that 24% of the transactions were leased, 35% of the sales were dealer-financed, and the remaining 40% of the cash transactions were most likely financed from third-party lenders (credit unions or banks). Furthermore, using a national sample of 654 households that purchased new vehicles, Mannering, Winston, and Starkey (2002) find that 51.6% financed, 28.1% paid cash, and 20.3% leased. Based on these surveys, clearly third-party financing represents a sizable portion of the automobile credit market.

One of the key features of the third-party auto loan market is the standard practice of using a "house rate" for pricing loans, such that all qualified borrowers with similar risk characteristics pay the same rate at any given point in time. In other words, prospective borrowers secure a loan before they contract to buy. The lender simply underwrites the loan based on the borrower's credit score and required down payment. With the loan commitment in hand, the borrower then shops for a particular vehicle. As a result, these lenders do not incorporate information about the purchase decision into the loan pricing.

In contrast, before lenders originate a mortgage, typically they have information on the underlying asset as well as the borrower's personal characteristics. Thus, information about the underlying asset often plays a role in determining the mortgage contract rate. For example, lenders know that a borrower who seeks a loan above the government-sponsored enterprise "conforming loan limit" is almost certainly purchasing a high-valued asset, while a borrower who requests an FHA-insured mortgage is likely purchasing a lower-valued home. Since standard mortgage-pricing models show that the volatility of the underlying property value is important in determining the probability of mortgage termination, borrowers originating mortgages on properties with higher volatilities pay higher contract rates.

Extending this analogy to the auto-loan market, if third-party lenders required information about the car being purchased prior to approving the loan, then they could price that into the loan. Currently, this is not the practice. Thus, our study suggests an avenue for lenders to potentially increase auto-loan profitability by utilizing the information about the car being purchased when they set their loan terms.

Loan characteristics include automobile value, automobile age, loan amount, loan-to-value (LTV), monthly payments, contract rate, time of origination (year and month), as well as payoff year and month in the cases of prepayment and default. We also have access to the automobile model, make, and year. Borrower characteristics include credit score (FICO score), monthly disposable income, and borrower age. The majority of the loans originated in eight northeast states.

Technical Words and Terms

1. redistribution   n. 重新分配
2. be obligated to   对……负责任
3. installment   n. 安装,分期付款,部分
4. incentive   n. 动机,刺激;adj. 激励的,刺激的
5. covenant   n. 契约,盟约,盖因合同;vt. 立约承诺;vi. 订立盟约、契约
6. amortize   v. 分期偿还
7. deposit   n. 存款,保证金;vt. 使沉淀,存放;vi. 沉淀
8. depreciation   n. 折旧,贬值
9. mortgage   n. 抵押;vt. 抵押
10. disposable income   可支配收入

Notes

1. For other institutions, issuing of debt contracts such as bonds is a typical source of funding.

其他机构发行的债务,例如债券,是一种典型的资金来源。

2. Although it is a personal use loan, depreciation and interest charges could be tax effective

claims if the car is for business or work related usage.

尽管汽车租赁是一种个人使用的贷款,但如果租赁的汽车是用于商业或工业活动,则车辆折旧费及利息就可以成为一种有效的税收手段。

Exercises

Questions for discussion

1. How to repay a car loan?
2. Where does the financing for automobile purchases come from?
3. What's the most typically loan payment type?
4. What does the loan characteristics?
5. What does the borrower characters contain?

Fill in the blank according to the text

1. In a loan, the borrower initially receives or borrows an amount of money, called _____.

2. The loan has a _____, the interest is calculated on the _____, just like a home loan.

3. The most typical loan payment type is _____ in which each monthly rate has _____ over time.

4. One of the key features of the third-party auto loan market is _____ for pricing loans.

5. In contrast, before lenders originate a mortgage, typically they have information on the _____ as well as the borrower's personal characteristics.

Extension: Proposed Suggestion about Car Rental Industry

Enacting and Improving Rules and Regulations and Introducing Related Measures

Building a strong and prefect legal system and intensifying law enforcement including clearly define the extent to which the car rental company should be responsible for and give the lessor the right to recall their cars freely based on the improved contract law.

Building a Sound Credit System

Constructing a sound credit system is vital. In western countries, almost all the problems can be solved by using the identity card and driver license. Chinese government can follow this model by adding more domestic requirement. Social credit organizations should be also involved in order to build an internal customer credit information service flat. Besides, credit price and punishment system can be taken into consideration to regulate people's behaviors in national networking system. At the same time, customers should build personal credit account so that their credit situations can be searched conveniently by the bank, the car rental companies and the insurance company. Moreover, it is advisable to educate the public on the importance of having great credit.

Promoting Publicity and Advertising

It is suggested to use various multimedia tools to launch advertising campaigns in order to raise customer awareness and then turn them to the final consumers. Branding plays a key role here since it is easier for people to remember a brand name compared with functional features. Moreover, it is important to create positive word of mouth to let the public advertise the companies in a good way without cost. In addition, in modern China, the car rental companies should also combine its physical shop with the Internet shop together as a click-and-mortar business to exert more influences.

One of the best ways is to link this industry to the weekends and holidays to achieve Holiday Economy effect.

Furthermore, another innovative way to advertise is using affinity marketing. For instance, the car rental company can cooperate with a hotel to serve the hotel's existing customers by offering the car rental services to them.

Sale by Lease

To cater for consumers' psychological mentality, car rental companies are encouraged to sell their cars by leasing at the same time. This can be accompanied by delivering the concept that sale by lease can bring great benefits to consumers.

Government Formulates a Favorable Tax Policy

The authors think that one of the best solutions to solve tax problem is offering a favorable financial tax policy. Since car rental industry in China still at the initial stage, strong support should be provided by government to reach rapid growth. We can learn from other countries' measures of supporting the car rental industry, such as lowering rate of the additional tax on purchasing cars, policy banks offering low rate loans and reducing their turnover taxes.

Unified Management of Car Licenses

It is suggested that the relevant departments should introduce a set of unified management standards of the rental car licenses as soon as possible. Standardized color, font size, steel sealing, specific code should be all incorporated. For example, it may be useful to require the rental car licenses in a same pattern like CR × × × × × ×, such as CR111665 or CR873390, with the same beginning CR which stands for Car Rental. At the same time, the relevant departments should also pledge the suitable number of cars in such an infant industry.

Glossary

A

abrasion	*n.* 磨损
accommodate	*vt.* 供给,容纳
adaptability	*n.* 适应性,改编
adjoining	*adj.* 邻接的,相邻的;*v.* 邻接
aerodynamic	*adj.* 空气动力(学)的
aerodynamic performance	空气动力学性能
aftermarket	*n.* 后市场
agent	*n.* 剂,介质
air compressor	空气压缩机
air control ring	空气量调节圈
air filter	空气滤清器
air vent	通风(系统)
air-conditioning compressor	空调压缩机
air-to-fuel ratio	空燃比
align	*vi.* 排列,排成一行,定位;*vt.* 使结盟
alloy	*n.* 合金;*vt.* 使成合金
alternator	*n.* 交流发电机,振荡器
aluminum	*n.* [化]铝
ambient temperature	环境温度
amperage	*n.* 电流强度,安培数
amplify	*v.* 放大,扩大,增强
anchor	*vi.* 抛锚;*vt.* 抛锚,使固定;*n.* 锚
antifreeze	*n.* 防冻液,防冻剂
anti-freezing coolant	防冻液,防冻冷却液
anti-roll bar	防倾杆
approximately	*adv.* 大约,近似地;近于
arcing	*n.* 电压
armature	*n.* 电枢
arrears	*n.* 拖欠,待完成的事
as per	按照,依据;如同
astute	*adj.* 机敏的,狡猾的,诡计多端的
at required intervals	在规定时间
atomize	*v.* 把……喷成雾状,使雾化
attach	*vt.* 系上,贴上,使依附
attempt	*n.* 企图,试图,攻击;*v.* 企图,试图,尝试

auto dismantling yard	汽车拆除场
automatic transmission	自动变速器
axle beam	前桥梁
axle housing	桥壳
axle shaft	半轴；

B

baffle plate	隔板,折流板
ballast	*n.* 压载的,配重,镇流电阻
bamboo	*n.* 竹,柱子
band	*n.* 带,乐队,松紧带镶边
be fed to	向……提供……
be itching to	渴望
be obligated to	对……负责任
be prone to	易于……
bellows	*n.* 波纹管,真空膜盒
bending moment	弯矩
bevel gear	锥齿轮
bias	*adj.* 偏斜的；*adv.* 偏斜地；*n.* 偏见,偏爱,斜纹
bleed	*vt.* 使出血,榨取；*vi.* 渗出,流血
bleed valve	放气阀,排气门
blowby	*n.* 窜气
bolt	*n.* 螺栓；*v.* 用螺栓紧固
bond	*n.* 结合,债券；*vt.* 使结合
boost pressure	增压压力
booster	*n.* 助力器,支持者
bore	*n.* 枪膛,孔；*v.* 钻孔
brake adjustment	制动碟
brake booster	制动助力器
brake shoe	制动蹄
breaker point	断电器触点
build up	增大,集结
bulkhead	*n.* 舱壁,隔板
bumper	*n.* 保险杠
butterfly	*n.* 节气门蝶形阀体
bypass valve	分流阀,旁通阀
by-passed	旁路,迂回

C

cable	*n.* 电缆,索缆

caliper	n. 制动钳,卡钳;vt. 用卡钳测量
cam	n. 凸轮
camber	n. 车轮外倾,弧形;vt. 外倾角,使拱起
camshaft	n. 凸轮轴
Camshaft Position Sensor	凸轮轴位置传感器
canister	n. 滤毒罐
capacity	n. 性能
car tuning	汽车改装
carbon footprint	碳排放量
carburetor	n. 化油器
carcass	n. 尸体,残骸
cast	n. 铸件;v. 浇铸
caster	n. 转向轴线后倾,后倾角
Catalytic Converter	三元催化转化器
cavitation	n. 气蚀现象,孔蚀现象
cellular	adj. 多孔的,蜂窝状的
centrifugal	adj. 离心的
centrifugal fan	离心式风扇
chain	n. 链(条)
charcoal canister	炭罐
circuit	n. 电路
circulatory	adj. 循环的
circumference	n. 圆周,周围
clamp	n. 夹子,夹具,夹钳;vt. 夹住
clarify	v. 得到澄清,变得明晰,得到净化
closed-loop	闭环的
clunker	n. 年久失修的旧机器
clutch	n. 离合器,控制;vi. 攫,企图抓住;vt. 抓住
coil spring	螺旋弹簧
combined body-frame structure	半承载式车身
common bias ply tire	普通斜交轮胎
compatible	adj. 兼容的,相容的,可以并存的,能共处的
compensate	v. 补偿,补充,抵偿
compressor	n. 压缩机
comprise	vt. 包含,包括,由……组成
compulsory ventilation	强制通风
condenser	n. 电容器
conductor	n. 导体
conduit	n. 导管,水道,沟渠
configuration	n. 结构

connecting rod	n. 连杆
considerable concentration	一定浓度的可燃混合气
continuously variable mechanical transmission	机械式无级变速器
control module (CM)	(电子)控制组件,控制模块
convertible	n. 敞篷车身
coolant	n. 冷冻剂,冷却液,散热剂
Coolant Temperature Sensor	冷却液温度传感器
cooling agent	冷却介质
cord	n. 帘布层,绳索;vt. 用绳子捆绑
coupler	n. 耦合器
covenant	n. 契约,盟约,盖因合同;vt. 立约承诺;vi. 订立盟约、契约
cracked	adj. 有裂缝的,声音沙哑的,精神失常的
crankcase	n. 曲轴箱
crankpin	n. 曲柄销
crankshaft	n. 曲轴
Crankshaft Position Sensor	曲轴位置传感器
cushion	n. 垫子;vt. 给……安上垫子
cushion layer	缓冲层
cylinder	n. 汽缸
cylinder head	n. 汽缸盖

D

damping resistance	阻尼力
data link connector	数据传输连接器
deflect	vt. 使偏转,偏斜,使转向;vi. 转向,偏斜
deflection	n. 偏转,变形,变位,弯曲
defrosting	v. 除霜
demister	n. 除雾器,去雾器
deposit	n. 存款,保证金;vt. 使沉淀,存放;vi. 沉淀
depreciation	n. 折旧,贬值
deputy	n. 代理人,代表;adj. 副的,代理的
derivative	n. 导数,微商,衍生物,派生物,派生词
destruction	n. 毁坏,破坏
diagnosis	n. 诊断
diagnostic	adj. 诊断的,特征的;n. 诊断法
diaphragm	n. 膜片,薄膜,振动膜
differential	adj. 微分的,差别的;n. 微分,差别,差速器
disc brake	盘式制动器
discharge	v. 放出,放电

dismantling	n. 解散,(枪支)分解
disposable income	可支配收入
disposal	n. 处理,处置,清除
dissipate	vt. 浪费,使消散;vi. 驱散,放荡
dissipation	n. 分散,消散
distribution box	分配箱
distributor cap	分电器盖
door check	车门限位器
door inside trim board	车门内护板或内饰板
double wishbone type	双横臂式
doughnut	n. 油炸圈饼,环状物,【美俚】汽车轮胎
down-time	故障时间
drag coefficient	阻力系数
drag link	直拉杆
drain cock	放水龙头
drive axle	驱动桥,传动轴
drive shaft	传动轴
driveline	n. 动力传动系统
drivetrain	n. 动力传动系
driving member	主动件
driven member	从动件
drum brake	鼓式制动器
dwell time (DT)	延迟时间,延长时间,停歇时间
down-shift	换入低挡

E

eccentric	adj. 离心的
ECM	电子控制模组(电脑)
elastic	adj. 有弹性的,灵活的,易伸缩的;n. 松紧带,橡皮圈
electric motor	电机
electromagnet	n. 电磁体(铁)
electromechanical	adj. 机电的
electron	n. 电子
electronic	adj. 电子的
Electronic Fuel Injection	电子控制燃油喷射系统
electronic switch	电子开关
enclose	v. 封入,装入
engage	vi. 从事,啮合;vt. 吸引,占据,预定
engine bay	发动机舱

engine compartment	发动机室
engine hood	发动机罩
entice	vt. 诱使,怂恿
equalize	vt. 使相等,平衡,补偿；vi. 成为相等
ethylene glycol	乙二醇
even	adj. 偶数的,平坦的,相等的；adv. 甚至；vt. 使平坦,使相等；vi. 变平
evolve	vt. (使)发展,(使)进化
Exhaust Gas Recirculation System	废气再循环系统
expansion valve	膨胀阀

F

fan drive belt	风扇皮带
filter	n. 滤清器
filter port	过滤口
fin	n. 鳍,翅片
final drive	主减速器
final drive unit	最终传动装置,主(轮边)减速器
fishtailing	vi. 摆尾行驶
flange	n. 边缘,轮缘,凸缘
flowrate	n. 流量
flywheel	n. 飞轮
folding door	折叠式车门
foreign matter	杂质,异物
format	n. 格式,规格,形式
foundation	n. 基础,根本
fracture surface	断裂面
framework	n. 架构,框架,结构
fraudulently	adv. 欺骗性的
friction	n. 摩擦,摩擦力
front axle	前桥
front end panel	车前钣制件
front suspension	前悬架
front-hinged door	顺开式车门
fuel economy	燃油经济性
fuel pipe	燃料管
fuel rail	燃油分配管
full-flow type	全流式
furnish	vt. 供给,保证,布置

G

gear ratio	速比
gear set	齿轮组
grate	*vi.* 发出摩擦声；*vt.* 磨擦
groove	*n.* 凹槽，槽；*vt.* 开槽于
ground	*n.* 接地，搭铁，路面
ground clearance	离地间隙
guide channel	导轨，导槽

H

Hall effect	霍尔效应
handbrake	*n.* 驻车制动
harmony	*n.* 协调，和谐，融洽
hazard	*n.* 危险，冒险；*vt.* 赌运气，冒……的风险
hazardous	*adj.* 有危险的，冒险的，碰运气的
heater core	加热器芯子
high tension wiring	高压电线，高压电路
honeycomb	*n.* 蜂房，蜂窝结构
hood	*n.* 发动机罩
horsepower	*n.* 功率
hose	*n.* 软管
hot wire	（不用钥匙起动点火装置的）短路点火
housing	*n.* 外壳，外罩
hub	*n.* 中心，轮毂
hydraulic brake	液压制动器
hydraulic suspension	液压悬架
hydraulic system	液压系统

I

idle speed	怠速
ignition coil	点火线圈
ignition timing	点火正时
impede	*v.* 阻碍，妨碍，阻止
impedence	*n.* 阻抗，电阻
impeller	*n.* （驱动）叶轮，驱动涡轮
imperceptible	*adj.* 感觉不到的，极细微的
impulse-reaction centrifugal filter	冲击-反击式离心过滤器
in conjunction with	连同，共同；与……协力；
in contact with	和……接触，和……保持联系

in series	串联,连续的,逐次的
in synchronism with	与……同步
incentive	n. 动机,刺激;adj. 激励的,刺激的
incipient	adj. 起初的,初始的
incline	vt. 使倾向于,使倾斜;n. 倾斜,斜面
inconstant angular velocity	等角速度
incorporate	vt. 把……合并,列入,包含;vi. 合并,混合
induce	v. 引起,诱发,感应
induced current	感应电流
inertia	n. 惯性,惯量
inertial force	惯性力
infant industry	新生的工业
initiative	n. 主动权,首创精神;adj. 主动的,自发的,起始的
injector	n. 喷油器
inspection	n. 检查
installment	n. 安装,分期付款,部分
intake	v. 进气,空气摄入
intake air temperature	进气温度
Intake Air Temperature Sensor	进入空气温度传感器
intake manifold	进气歧管
integral	adj. 整体的,完整的;n. 部分,积分,完整
integrated or monocoque body structure	承载式车身
interior illumination	室内照明
intermediate	adj. 中间的;vi. 起媒介作用

J

jackknifing	n. 折裂
jet nozzle	喷油嘴
joint and several	连带的,共同的和个别的
jounce	n. 震动,颠簸;vt. 使震动,使颠簸;vi. 震动

K

kickback	n. 转向盘反冲,怠速回摆,逆转,回跳
king pin	主销
Knock Sensor	爆震传感器
knuckle	n. 关节;vi. 开始认真工作

L

landfill	n. 垃圾填埋地,垃圾堆

latch	n. 挂钩,止动销;vi. 占有,抓住
leaf spring	钢板弹簧
lean mixture	稀混合气
leasing	n. 租赁,谎言;v. 出租
lengthwise	adv. 纵向地;adj. 纵向的
lighting system	照明系统
lining	n. 衬套,衬垫(带)
linkage	n. 联动装置,连接,结合
loan shark	放高利贷者
lobe	n. 凸轮凸台,凸角
locking pin	插销
longitudinal swing arm type	纵摆臂式
low profile tire	低断面轮胎
lubricate	v. 润滑,加润滑油
lubricating oil	润滑油
luxury	n. 奢侈(品),享受;adj. 奢侈的

M

magnetic induction	磁感应
magnitude	n. 大小,数量值,幅度
main bearing cap	主轴承盖
malfunction	n. 故障失灵
mandatory	adj. 强制的,命令的,受委托的
maneuver	n. 调动,演习;vt. 演习,调遣
manifold	n. 歧管
Manifold Absolute Pressure	进气管绝对压力传感器
manifolds	n. 阀组
Mass Air Flow Sensor	空气质量流量传感器
mass flow sensor	质量流量传感器
mass/volume air flow	空气流量计
master cylinder	主缸,制动主缸
mating part	配偶件
maze	n. 迷宫,迷惑;vt. 迷失,使混乱
McPherson type	麦弗逊式悬架
mercury	n. 水银,水银柱,精神
metal belt	金属带
misfire	n. 熄火
modulator	n. 调节器
module	n. 组件,模块,电子控制总成
moment	n. 力矩,时刻

momentarily	*adj.* 随时的,立刻的
monitor	*vt.* 监控
mortgage	*n.* 抵押;*vt.* 抵押
mountainous terrain	山区
mounting lug	安装用吊耳
mudguard	*n.* 挡泥板
muffler	*n.* 消声器,消音器
multi-plate clutch	多盘离合器

N

nickel	*n.* [化]镍
nominal height-width ratio of tire profile	轮胎断面名义高宽比
nominal profile width (in.) of tire	轮胎名义断面宽度
non-contacting	非接触
non-ferrous metal	有色金属
non-wearing	不磨损
normal control type	长头式

O

odometer	*n.* 里程表
off road vehicle	越野车
oil control ring	*n.* 油环
oil cooler	润滑油冷却器
oil filter	机油滤清器
oil pressure relief valve	机油减压阀
oil pump	油泵
on-board computer	车载电脑
open-loop	开环的
operating temperature	工作温度,运转温度
optional	*adj.* 随意的,任选的,可选择的
Otto cycle	奥托循环
outlet pipe	排气管
outlet port	出口
overlap	*n.* 重叠,重复;*vt.* 与……重叠
Oxygen Sensor	氧传感器

P

pack	*n.* 包装,组合件;*vt.* 包装,压紧
pad	*n.* 衬垫,垫片,基座;*vi.* 填补,走
pan	*n.* 盘,槽

parallelogram	n. 平行四边形
parameter	n. 参量
particle	n. 微粒
particle trap	颗粒捕集器
partition	n. 隔板,隔开
passage	n. 通路,走廊,一段(文章)
pattern	n. 模式,图案,样品;vt. 模仿,以图案装饰;vi. 形成图案
performance	n. 性能
periodic inspection	定期检修
perpendicular	adj. 垂直的,正交的;n. 垂线,垂直位置
photo-electric effect	光电效应
pickup coil	传感线圈
pick-up screen	集滤器
pinion	n. 小齿轮;翅膀,鸟翼;vt. 绑住,束缚
pinpoint	vt. 查明,确认;adj. 详尽的,精确的;n. 针尖,精确位置
piston	n. 活塞
piston clearance	n. 活塞间隙
pitman arm	摇臂
planet gear	行星齿轮
planetary	adj. 行星的
plug	vt. 插入,塞住;n. 插头,塞子
plummet	vi. 骤然下跌
ply	n. 厚度,板层,褶;vt. 使用,不住地使用,折,弯;vi. 辛勤工作
pneumatic suspension	气动悬架
polymer	n. [高分子]聚合物
Positive Crankcase Ventilation	曲轴箱强制通风装置
positive displacement type	容积式
positive displacement type	变容式,容积式
power steering hose	动力转向软管
power-train	动力系
precarious	adj. 危险的,不确定的
predicament	n. 窘况,困境,状态
pressure plate	压盘
pressure regulator	燃油压力调节器
primary current	初级电流
primary winding	初级线圈,初级绕组
promulgate	vt. 公布,转播,发表

prone	adj. 易于……的,倾斜的,有……倾向的
propeller shaft	传动轴
proportional	adj. 成比例的
pulley	n. 滑轮,滑车,带轮
pulse	n. 脉冲,脉搏,电流突然增加或减弱
pulse-width modulation	脉冲宽度调制

Q

quart	n. 夸脱(容量单位)

R

rack and pinion type	齿轮齿条式
radial tubeless tire	子午线无内胎轮胎
radiator cooling fan	散热器冷却风扇
radiator core	散热器芯
rate of wear	磨损率,磨损度
reaction-type centrifugal filter	反馈式离心过滤器
rear view mirror	后视镜
rear-hinged door	逆开式车门
rebound	n. 回弹,篮板球;vt. 使回弹;vi. 回升
recharge	v. 再充电
reciprocating	adj. 往复的
re-circulating ball type	循环球式
redistribution	n. 重新分配
refrigerant	n. 制冷工质
refrigeration cycle	制冷循环
regulate	vt. 调节,调整,校准,控制,管理
regulator	n. 调节器
reinforcement	n. 加强件
reluctance	n. 磁阻,阻抗,勉强
reluctor	n. 磁阻轮,变磁阻转子
rental	adj. 租赁的;n. 租金收入,租金
residual metal	残留金属
resistor	n. 电阻器
resume	v. 恢复,重新开始,再继续
retain	vt. 保持,维持,保留
retract	vt. 缩回,缩进
return moment	回正力矩
revolutions per minute	每分钟转速
ribbon	n. 带状物,带子

rim	n. 边,边缘,轮辋;v. 作……的边
ring gear	齿圈
road crown	道路(横断面)的鼓形
roll cage	防滚架
rolling resistance	滚动阻力
rotor	n. 轮子,涡轮
rubber grommet	橡胶密封圈
rubber tube	橡胶内胎
run by itself	靠惯性
runaway	n. 汽车失控
runout	n. 径向振摆,偏转

S

sandwich	vt. 夹入,挤进;n. 三明治
scenario	n. 方案,情况,场景
screen	n. 滤网
scuffing	n. 变形,刮痕,擦伤;v. 使磨损
sector shaft	齿扇轴
seizure	n. 卡死,卡住,咬住
semicircular	adj. 半圆的
sensor	n. 传感器
separated body-frame structure	非承载式车身
service shop	维修车间
servo	n. 伺服,伺服机构
shell	n. 车身壳体
shield	n. 盾,护罩,保护人;vt. 保护,掩护,庇护,给……加防护罩
shock absorber	减振器
shoe	n. 制动片,闸瓦;vi. 给……穿上鞋
shredded	adj. 切碎的
shredding operation	分解操作
shroud	n. 护罩
shut-off	节流阀
shutter	n. 百叶窗
side skirt	车侧裙
side wall	胎侧
signal generator	信号发生器
signal pulse	信号脉冲
single control arm type	单摆臂式
situate	vt. 设置,定位,使位于;adj. 位于……的

slap	vt. 拍, 拍击; n. 拍
slave cylinder	辅助(汽、油)缸, 制动轮缸
sleeve	n. 套管, 轴套, 衬套, 缸套
sliding door	滑移式车门
slipping	n. 滑动; adj. 逐渐松弛的; v. 滑动
spark	n. 电火花
spark plugs	火花塞
speedometer	n. 速度表
spin	vi. 旋转; vt. 使旋转; n. 旋转, 疾驰
splash	v. 溅, 泼, 使飞溅
spline	n. 花键, 齿条; vt. 开键槽, 用花键连接
splitter	n. 副变速器
spoiler	n. 尾翼, 扰流板
spoke	n. 轮辐, 刹车
spring eye	弹簧孔
sprocket	n. 链轮齿
spur gear	圆柱齿轮
squeeze	vi. 压榨; vt. 挤, 握紧 挤榨; n. 压榨
starter drive	起动小齿轮
starter motor	起动电机
statistics	n. 统计, 统计学
stator	n. 固定片, 定子
steering axis inclination	转向轴线内倾
steering column shaft	转向柱
steering linkage	转向联动装置
steering nut	转向螺母
steering screw	转向螺杆
stiffen	v. (使)变硬
stiffness	n. 刚度, 僵硬, 坚硬, 顽固
stoichiometry	n. 化学计量学
storage tank	贮液罐
strive to	努力
structural section size	结构断面尺寸
strut type	滑柱式
submerge	vi. 淹没, 潜入水中; vt. 淹没, 沉浸
sump	n. 油底壳, 贮槽
sun gear	太阳轮
sunroof	n. 太阳车顶, 天窗
supercharger	n. 增压器
surging	v. 浪涌, 冲击, 波动

suspension	n. 悬架
sway bar	稳定杆
swept volume	工作容积,体积排量,活塞排量
swinging door	外摆式车门
symmetry	n. 对称(性),匀称
symphony	n. 交响乐,谐声,和声
synchronise	v. 使同步
synchronism	n. 同步,同时
synchronize	vt. (使)同步,(使)同时发生,(使)同速
synthetic	adj. 合成的,人造的

T

tailpipe	n. 排气管
terminal	n. 接线头,接线柱
the contact breaker point	断电器触点
thermal	adj. 热的,热力的
thermostat	n. 节温器
thread	n. 螺纹,线;vt. 穿过;vi. 通过,穿透过
throttle	n. 节气阀,风门;vt. 压制,使……节流; vi. 节流
throttle body	节气门体
Throttle Position Sensor	节气门位置传感器
tie rod	横拉杆
tighten	vt. 变紧,使变紧;vi. 绷紧,拉紧
tilt	v. (使)倾斜,翘起
tire adhesion	轮胎附着力
tire carcass	外胎
toe [to]	n. 前束
toe-in	正前束
toe-out	负前束
torque	n. 转矩,[力]扭矩,项圈,金属领圈
torque converter	变矩器
torque output	扭矩输出
torsion bar	扭杆
tracking	n. 随辙,追踪;v. 跟踪
traction	n. 牵引
traditional	adj. 传统的,惯例的
trailer	n. 拖车
transfer	n./v. 传到,传递
transformer	n. 变压器

transistor	n. 晶体管
trap	n. 圈套,(对付人的)计谋,(练习射击用的)抛靶器,(捕捉动物的)夹子
trapezoid	n. 梯形,不规则四边形;adj. 四边形的
tread of crown	胎冠(胎面)
treatment facility	处理设施
trigger	v. 触发
trunnion	n. 轴颈
TSI (Turbo FSI)	双增压-燃油分层直喷
tubing	n. 管道,导管;v. 使成管状
turbine	n. 涡轮(机)
turbocharger	n. 涡轮增压器
turbulence	n. 扰流,湍流
turn	n. 一圈,(线圈的)匝数
turnover	n. 营业额,流通量;adj. 翻过来的,可翻转的
twist	n. 扭曲,拧,扭伤;vt. 捻,扭伤;vi. 扭动

U

U-bolts	U 形螺栓
universal joint	万向节
unplug	vt. 拔去(塞子,插头等)
untwist	n. 拆开,解开
up-hinged door	上掀式车门
up-shift	换入高挡

V

vacuum advance	真空式点火提前
vacuum hose	真空软管
vacuum pump	真空泵,真空机
vacuum reservoir	真空罐,真空储存器
valve	n. 气门,阀;[解剖]瓣膜,真空管,活门
vane	n. 叶片,叶轮
vane meter	叶片式空气流量计
vaporize	vt./vi. (使)蒸发,(使)汽化
V-belt	V 形传送带
Vehicle Speed Sensor	速度传感器
velocity ratio	传动比
vent	n. 通气孔
ventilation	n. 通风设备
vibration isolation	隔振

viscosity	*n.* 黏度
volatile property	挥发性
voltage	*n.* 电压

W

warm up	预热
warped	*adj.* 反常的,乖戾的,(变)弯曲的,变形的
water cooling system	水冷系统
water jacket	水套
waveform	*n.* 波形
way of load carrying	承载方式
weiss type U-joint	球叉式万向节
weld	*v.* 焊接,熔接
wheel alignment	车轮定位
window regulator	玻璃升降器
windshield	*n.* 挡风玻璃
with the advent of	随着……的出现
wrecking yard	废料场

Abbreviations

Abbreviation	English	Chinese
ABS	anti-lock brake system	防抱死制动系统
A/C	air conditioning	空调
AC	air cooling	风冷
ACL	air cleaner	空气滤清器
ACT	air charge temperature	进气温度
A/F 或 AF	air fuel (ratio)	空燃比
AFC	air flow control	空气流量控制
AFS	air flow sensor	空气流量传感器
AI	air injection	空气喷射
ALB	anti-lock brake	防抱死制动器
ALD	auto-locking differential	自锁式差速器
ATS	air temperature sensor	绝对压力传感器
AWD	all wheel drive	全轮驱动
BA	brake assist	辅助制动装置
BAS	brake assisted system	制动助力系统
BAT	battery	蓄电池
BDC	bottom dead center	下止点
BMC	brake master cylinder	制动主缸

续上表

Abbreviation	English	Chinese
BP	back pressure	背压
BPM	brake pressure modulator	制动压力调节器
BPS	barometric pressure sensor	大气压力传感器
BTE	brake thermal efficiency	制动热效率
BTR	brake transmission ratio	制动传动比
C (cap.)	capacity	容量
CAC	charge air cooler	进气冷却器
CAD	computer aided design	计算机辅助设计
CF	cooling fan	冷却风扇
CFI	central fuel injection	中央燃油喷射
CL	clutch	离合器
CLSW	clutch switch	离合器开关
CIS	computer ignition system	计算机控制点火系统
CNG	compressed natural gas	压缩天然气
CO	carbon monoxide	一氧化碳
CPC	clutch pressure control	离合器压力控制
CPU	central processing unit	中央处理器
CPS	crankshaft position sensor	曲轴位置传感器
CTE	coefficient of thermal expansion	热膨胀系数
CVRT	continuously variable ratio transmission	无级调速变速器
CVT	continuously variable transmission	无级变速器
DFI	direct fuel injection	直接燃油喷射
DI	distributor ignition	分电器点火
DIFF	differential	差速器
DS	detonation sensor	爆燃传感器
DSL	diesel	柴油发动机
EA	electric automobile	电动汽车
EC	engine control	发动机控制
ECA	electronic control assembly	电子控制总成
ECI	electronically controlled injection	电子控制燃油喷射
ECU	Electronic Control Unit	电子控制单元
ECV	electrically controlled vehicle	电控汽车
EFI	electronic fuel injection	电子燃油喷射
EGR	exhaust gas recirculation	废气再循环
EM	engine maintenance	发动机维护
EP	exhaust pipe	排气管
EV	electronic vehicle	电动车辆

续上表

Abbreviation	English	Chinese
FI	fuel injection	燃油喷射
FDI	fuel direct injection	燃油直接喷射
F/R	front engine/rear wheel drive	前置发动机/后轮驱动
FS	factor of safety	安全系数
FWB	front wheel brake	前轮制动器
FWD	front-wheel Drive	前轮驱动
FWD	four-wheel-drive	四轮驱动
GAS	gasoline	汽油
GPS	global positioning system	全球定位系统
GR	gear ratio	齿轮传动比
GVW	gross vehicle weight	全车总重
HTC	hydraulic torque converter	液力变矩器
IA	intake air	进气
IA	input axis	输入轴
IAC	idle air control	怠速控制
IFI	indirect fuel injection	间接燃油喷射
IFS	independent front suspension	前独立悬架
IRS	independent rear suspension	后独立悬架
IT	ignition timing	点火正时
L/C	lock-up clutch	锁定离合器
LO	lubricating oil	润滑油
LS	leaf spring	钢板弹簧
LSD	limited slip differential	防滑差速器
MAP	manifold absolute pressure	歧管绝对压力
MCU	microprocessor control solenoid	微处理控制单元
MFI	mechanical fuel injection	机械燃油喷射
MFI-C	multi port fuel injection continuous	连续多点燃油喷射
MON	motor octane number	马达法辛烷值
MPFI	multipoint fuel injection	多点燃油喷射
NGL	natural gas liquefied	液化天然气
NPS	neutral position switch	空挡开关
NOX	nitrogen oxides	氮氧化物
OCV	oil control valve	机油控制阀
OFL	oil filter	机油滤清器
OPS	oil pressure sensor	油压传感器
PCV	positive crankcase ventilation	曲轴箱强制通风
PKB	parking brake	驻车制动器

续上表

Abbreviation	English	Chinese
PSC	power steering control	动力转向控制
PSP	power steering pressure	动力转向压力
rpm	revolutions per minute	每分钟转数
RWD	rear wheel drive	后轮驱动
SFI	sequential fuel injection	顺序燃油喷射
SPI	single point injection	单点燃油喷射
TBI	throttle body fuel injection	节气门体燃油喷射
TCC	torque converter clutch	变矩器锁止离合器
TCS	traction control system	驱动力控制系统
TDC	top dead center	上止点
TPS	throttle position sensor	节气门位置传感器
TWC	three way catalytic converter	三元催化转化器
VIN	vehicle identification number	车辆识别号
VR	voltage regulator	电压调节器
VSS	vehicle speed sensor	车速传感器
VSV	vacuum solenoid valve	真空电磁阀
4WS	four wheel steering	四轮转向

References

[1] 陈家瑞. 汽车构造[M]. 3 版. 北京:机械工业出版社,2009.

[2] 刘璇,于秀敏. 实用汽车英语[M]. 2 版. 北京:北京理工大学出版社,2012.

[3] 王怡民. 汽车专业英语 [M]. 北京:人民交通出版社,2007.

[4] 李卓森. Automotive Fundamentals [M]. 北京:人民交通出版社,2009.

[5] 陈焕江,徐双应. 交通运输专业英语[M]. 2 版. 北京:机械工业出版社,2008.

[6] 郭玲. 汽车英语 [M]. 北京:北京大学出版社,2005.

[7] John Scott, Norris Hoover, Richard Fay and Ric Robinette. Daily Vehicle Inspection and Vehicle Maintenance Issues in Accident Reconstruction [M]. Detroit: World Congress,2007.

[8] Volkswagen Group of America. Self-Study Program 824803 The Volkswagen 2.0 Liter Chain-Driven TSI Engine[M]. U.S.A. 2008.

[9] Arvon L. Mitcham. On-Board Diagnostic Hand-Held Scan Tool Technology:Adherence to the Society of Automotive Engineers Requirements for Scan Tools and an Evaluation of Overall Scan Tool Capability[M]. U.S.A. 2000.

[10] LUAN Zhi-Qiang,etc. Automobile Finance Service Management—Major Problems and Suggestions for Car Rental Industry in China's Mainland[C]. Wuhan, China. 2010.